AN ESSAY ON HARDY

AN ESSAY ON
HARDY

JOHN BAYLEY

CAMBRIDGE UNIVERSITY PRESS

CAMBRIDGE

LONDON NEW YORK MELBOURNE

Published by the Syndics of the Cambridge University Press
The Pitt Building, Trumpington Street, Cambridge CB2 1RP
Bentley House, 200 Euston Road, London NW1 2DB
32 East 57th Street, New York, NY 10022, USA
296 Beaconsfield Parade, Middle Park, Melbourne 3206, Australia

First published 1978

Printed in Great Britain
at the Alden Press, Oxford

Library of Congress Cataloguing in Publication Data
Bayley, John, 1925–
An essay on Hardy.
1. Hardy, Thomas, 1840–1928 – Criticism
and interpretation. I. Title.
PR4754.b38   823'.8   77-80826
ISBN 0 521 21814 4

I

HARDY SEEMS NATURALLY AND CONTINUOUSLY PRESENT IN his poetry, even when it is in the form of a tale or spoken in an invented voice. It seems his normal mode of expression. In the novels, too, the voice could only be his own; yet there he gives the impression of a man who would rather be silent than speak. The man who watches and reflects does not seem quite the same man as the one who talks to us, but neither can he evade him. Often he seems to want to, and to want to disown the novels as products of a trade undertaken to earn a living; yet he is pinned down in them against his will.

He never got over his surprise, sometimes outrage, at what other people thought and said about them. A ruminative man might force himself into garrulity, when writing for a living, by assuming a *persona* outside himself, which he could leave in the grasp of the public, as a lizard leaves its tail. A Shakespeare, or a Dickens, could both do that in their own way; but Hardy's selfhood, like that of Keats, seems helplessly all of a piece. When George Moore mocked his style, in *Conversations in Ebury Street*, Hardy's resentment was fierce. He scribbled, but of course never published, an epitaph for Moore:

> Heap dustbins on him:
> They'll not meet
> The apex of his self-conceit.

Hardy was then an old man of almost legendary fame, his gentleness and serenity a byword. But his instinctive reaction was that of the young Keats to Byron's reported sneers. Deep down he can have been no more modest than any other great writer, but his knowledge of his own genius never assumed, even in his maturity, the usual form of confident indifference, or detachment.

This relation to his work and audience is unique to Hardy, and to our present relation with him. It means we may still respond today to the real pleasures of his text in ways quite different to those in which we are usually taken on by a novelist. For one thing his words may make us feel that the words of other novelists are much more settled in place, have the air of being dealt out for good. Hardy's words and sentences give the impression of continuing instability: while reading we are waiting for something unexpected, good or bad, to happen to them, and this kind of expectation is a characteristic part of the pleasure.

It is an attention that grows with re-reading. Going back to the Victorian novelists always brings rewards more or less complex. Thackeray almost alone, perhaps, never equals again the degree of pleasure the first reading gives us: he lacks further resources to follow up with. George Eliot and Dickens – Trollope too – have plenty; and they derive for the most part from our increased perception of the geometry of the work, and the way idiosyncrasy and subtlety contribute to the general perspective of meaning. Perceptions with Hardy are of a rather different sort. His text may come increasingly to strike us as an affair of collaterals, effects not isolated from but independent of each other, with a purpose and intentness of their own. The feel of its continuity may none the less seem to increase, as its larger issues and claims diminish, and as other kinds of satisfaction reveal themselves. This may sound like a description of weakness rather than strength; I shall try to show it is not.

Hardy observed once, interrogatively, that there was no technique – was there? – for writing prose. Like many of his remarks it is hard to know in what spirit to take this, but it seems likely he did feel it to be too ordinary a medium to be crafted like verses. He professed to be 'much struck' by Coventry Patmore's opinion that the beauties of *A Pair of Blue Eyes* could not have 'the immortality which would have been impressed upon them by the form of verse'. At the same time he was studying style, as he also tells us, from re-reading 'Addison, Macaulay, Newman, Sterne, Defoe, Lamb, Gibbon, Burke, *Times* Leaders, etc.', and concluding that 'the whole secret of a living style and the difference between it and a dead style, lies in not having too much style'. 'Being a little careless, or rather seeming to be . . . brings wonderful life in to the writing'. 'This', he goes on, 'is of course simply a carrying into prose the knowledge I have learnt in poetry'.

The comments on style are extremely shrewd, but how the knowledge acquired in writing poetry could be carried into prose is not quite so simple a question as Hardy is inclined to make out. The characteristics of his poetry depend on formal patterns and frames of versification. The syntax and paragraphing in the novels, particularly the early ones, give the impression of missing these things, and unwillingly possessing, in consequence, a freedom in which they are far from easy. He can find no safety in style: exposition is also a kind of exposure. And yet his prose words do none the less seem to have a space round them, like the words in poetry, though in the prose medium it makes them often seem awkward and vulnerable in their arrangement. It is hard to believe this is really intentional, even though Hardy may deliberately have let himself be 'remiss' at times, as Burton in *The Anatomy of Melancholy* tells us he found it convenient to be. But though his verses may be flat with equanimity, they are never remiss in this sense – they are always taut and exact. In their freedom from this kind of poetic concentration his words in prose seem quite unregarding of themselves, and unchosen, even as they appear to retain the separateness and distinction of language in poetry.

This remains so no matter how many facts and details they may be conveying – for Charles Reade's example led the aspiring author to copy Defoe also in providing factual information – and in the midst of all their labours of observation or sententiousness the sentences remain plain and open. Meredith's prose is much more obviously that of a poet than Hardy's, which is what makes it so difficult to read. Its energy of insight and self-enjoyment, its profusion of 'good things', is decidedly fatiguing; even though it is only fair to say such a late novel as *One of Our Conquerors* is easier as well as more rewarding on second or subsequent occasions, when we have learnt to keep out some of its glitter with mental dark glasses.

Although every Hardy text is far more effectually *aesthetic* than anything of theirs – he is in a sense the most aesthetic of all

English novelists – it is none the less instructive to compare him with other novelists who write with their own kinds of clumsiness or carelessness, real or assumed – novelists such as Dreiser, Faulkner, or John Cowper Powys. Faulkner, in particular, seems held by the way he writes, enclosed in it like a refuge, as if the blankness and size and dilution of America called for such a style in order to preserve the novelist against them. Powys is often said to have affinities with Hardy, in scope and 'power' being a sort of cosmic optimist to Hardy's pessimist: those different pretensions to scope and power do not make him at all resemble Hardy, except in one respect. He too disconcerts judicious criticism, irritates its purists, and threatens their criteria. With his boisterous, cliché-ridden style, his seemingly naïve and facile absorptions, he *ought* to be bad – but is he? However different Hardy's case may be, he was certainly treated, by James and Stevenson and others, with the same sort of dismissal or reservation which those who are quite out of sympathy with his world apply to Powys. Nor, in the case of Hardy's novels, is such a dismissal itself unheard of, even today.

In reading Hardy, as in reading Powys, there are kinds of disappointment which do not seem to matter. But not for the same reasons. With Powys, as with Faulkner, or with Lawrence himself, *totality* of style soon declares itself. The positiveness of the text soon takes on predictability, becoming a completely homogeneous and recognisable medium into which we slip, so that as we attend to what they are saying and narrating we cease to notice the medium and its emphases. Such a habituation on the reader's part shows there is nothing unstable in the text, as there is in Hardy's. Disappointment, if it comes, is thus a complete thing: a boredom with, or alienation from, the text. In Hardy, disappointment is a reaction much more intimate and intermingled, which may turn out to present itself as an actual asset, a greater clarity in the experience of the pleasure. This relates to Hardy's seeming lack of desire to speak. Sometimes his voice appears to trail away; sometimes to reproduce small talk mechanically, like a shy man at a dinner-table. There is then a kind of lukewarmness in the text itself, which is very typical: one can become addicted to it.

This hesitancy, passivity, a lack of rigour behind the

maintaining of literary appearances, must have been detected by
Henry James and contributed to his irritation. Compare his own
masterly handling of the father's reactions to an unsuitable
suitor in *Washington Square* with the similar situation in *A Pair of
Blue Eyes*. Hardy seems to get no grip on the dramatic point of
the thing. When the rector, Elfride's father, discovers her lover's
identity, he seems – like his author – uncertain how the part
should be played. His previous jokes and anecdotes, and now his
indignation, appear perfunctory and random: the plot is left
waiting for relevance to put its shoulder to the wheel. Hardy is
apparently not interested in hitting off the *idea* of a disapproving
parent, but only in noting the inadequate reactions of a
specimen he has observed and imagined. His lack of drive puts a
space of inept actuality round the incident, and in that space the
reader is left both flat and attentive, much more involved in
what is going on, and in the atmosphere of the text, than it seems
at the time concerned to justify.

James's Dr Sloper consummately realises his author's conception, and plays the part for which he is planned. James cannot
afford to let him keep any of the uncertainties of the anecdote,
recorded in his *Notebooks*, on which he is based. And in omitting
it from the revised edition of his works, nearly thirty years after
it was written, James may have been acknowledging the
preponderance of the theatrical in this superb *nouvelle,* at a time
when he had become concerned with more ingenious techniques of naturalism, with finding the 'key that fits the compli-
cated chambers of *both* the narrative and the dramatic lock'. The
way they treat a similar theme, at this early stage of their
development, is the more significant in that both Hardy and
James are aiming at something popular, at a story of love and
suspense. Certainly the first requirement of *Washington Square,*
from which all its other rigidities proceed, is that Catherine
Sloper must 'love' her suitor in a conveniently absolute sense:
and this correlates exactly to the rigour with which James
handles the story. Elfride in *A Pair of Blue Eyes* has, conversely,
no proper sense of 'love', even though her situation demands it;
and this, like the inconsequentiality of her father, seems the
natural ally of Hardy's own lack of grip.

His is a vulnerability which makes us engrossed at the same

time that we feel the sense of disappointment; or the two reactions can succeed one another. Our satisfaction in the text can increase as we read, to the point that we know we are in a master's hands; then, quite abruptly, it may fall off and subside. This disappointment is not like feeling – as we might in a novel of Dickens, or with a Browning monologue – that the narrative has gone off the boil, and is reproducing itself for a slack time with mechanical facility. Hardy never falls back on being Hardy, as Dickens does on the Dickensian manner, or Thackeray on being Thackerayan. He has nothing in this sense to fall back on. Nor is there any question of a cover-up, such as even the unpretending skill of Jane Austen resorts to – still less the rare signs in George Eliot of a failure in her intention, showing themselves through a methodical accumulation of analysis.

No; Hardy's vulnerability within his own novel, is that of a private man in a public place, a shy man in a salon, anxious to learn how it goes, and conform to its manners while taking his own observations. His conformities are themselves an aspect of his literary solitude, and they make him appear, at unguarded moments, more peculiarly himself. For in and before Hardy's time the novelist was expected to be very much a man in society, able to say what he wanted, and in the way he wanted, provided he kept up appearances. Hardy kept them; whatever his protests to the contrary the conventions of the time suited him very well. They gave him his chance to be private, even when he seems most concerned to play his part, as it were, in the animation of the salon.

Hardy's position here, its air at once awkward and natural, as if the text really were a man in a formal social situation, marks him off from any novelist today. From contemporaries and predecessors too, no doubt, but the contrast with our time has the more revealing emphasis. It looks almost preposterous, indeed, if we take the hint offered to us in a well-known contemporary novel*, ingeniously constructed to hold the reader's interest, deliberately taking a Hardy-style plot, set in his country, and in the year 1867, when Hardy returned to Dorset, and to some conjectured amorous complication, after his formative five

* John Fowles: *The French Lieutenant's Woman.*

years in London. The novel refers to him frequently, and Mr Fowles is even franker about Hardy's influence in an essay he has given us on the way his own novels are composed. He feared this novel might be labelled as 'a clumsy pastiche of Hardy':

The shadow of Thomas Hardy, the heart of whose 'country' I can see in the distance from my workroom window, I cannot avoid . . . I don't mind the shadow . . . It is somehow encouraging that while my fictitious characters weave their own story in their 1867, only thirty miles away in the real 1867 the pale young architect was entering his own fatal life-incident.*

The central episode of his novel is clearly inspired by what he calls Hardy's 'own mysterious personal life'. He identifies himself with the earlier writer by imagining a woman, as Hardy so often does. A woman stands gazing out to sea, as in a Hardy poem. Who is she? What does she want? Yet it is not event and narration that Mr Fowles's novel offers us, but a shadow image of the author's own vision. His woman is an 'idea' to herself, as she is to him. And a passage early on in the novel explains why:

The story I am telling is all imagination. These characters I create never existed outside my own mind. If I have pretended until now to know my characters' minds and innermost thoughts it is because I am writing in (just as I have assumed some of the vocabulary and voice of) a convention universally accepted at the time of my story: that the novelist stands next to God. He may not know all, yet he tries to pretend that he does. But I live in the world of Alain Robbe-Grillet and Roland Barthes.

We . . . know that a genuinely created world must be independent of its creator; a planned world (a world that fully reveals its planning) is a dead world. It is only when our characters and events begin to disobey us that they begin to live.

The novelist is still a God . . . What has changed is that we are no longer the Gods of the Victorian image, omniscient and decreeing; but in the new theological image, with freedom our first principle, not authority.

I have disgracefully broken the illusion? No. My characters still exist, and in a reality no less, or no more real than the one I have just broken . . . I find this new reality (or unreality) more valid.

* 'Notes on an Unfinished Novel', from *Afterwards*, New York, 1969.

Some readers will accept these comments merely as their
author's affidavit that he is abreast of the changing fashions of his
craft; whole others, fresher to the business, may feel stimulated
by what seems incisive proof of our superior modern awareness
in these matters. Like the Victorians we want to be pleased with
our progressive selves, and the novelist who tells us he has
assumed the 'vocabulary and voice' of 1867 cleverly combines
these with the enlightenment of the modern novel to show just
how pleased with ourselves we are, as it may be he is too.

This novelist is very sure of himself, where Hardy is not, and
this sets a very wide space between them. He is as far from
Hardy as Meredith was in Hardy's own time, or as Fielding and
Sterne and Diderot were a hundred years earlier. All, in their
fashion, made a point of abdicating from the conventional
responsibilities of the writer in the salon, into the freedom of
being their own confident and enterprising selves. Hardy does
the opposite. He takes refuge in the divison of roles the age
offered – the private, the literary, the social – like a deer in the
thickets. Of all novelists he owes most to a society which,
whatever it exacted in the way of conformity, licensed its
members to protect and compartmentalise their lives; while at
the same time it extended the maximum credulity to the
authenticity of their creations.

The two are certainly connected; and that is why Hardy can
use the structure of Victorian society itself as a kind of inner
support for his imagination: when he is saying the Emperor has
no clothes he is also clinging to the Imperial coat-tails.By using
every amenity which a rigid society mutely offers, even as its
precepts loudly admonish, he becomes more subtle in his
openness than the novelist who can claim to throw all that sort
of thing away when he begins to talk to us: much more so than
the novelist of today who can fashion every hypothesis and
indulge every fantasy, unhampered by the need to sustain
illusion. Aided by his native literalness Hardy takes up the cause
of illusion far more seriously than do Thackeray or Trollope.
Illusion is sustained most potently in his novels by his apparent
reluctance to speak – the crafty story-teller knows that such a
reticent sobriety is the best index of the truth he is telling – while they scatter it to the winds by their fluency.

Hardy's attitude to *consciousness* is totally, even disconcertingly, *modern*. Only his attitude to society is of its time. This fact alone makes nonsense of most of Mr Fowles's assumptions. And I bring up his novel because its merits serve to show with singular clarity why the air of freedom in a Hardy story is so much stronger than in his own, despite the new kind of claims that he makes. That freedom in Hardy depends on a relation to society which is intimately connected with the illusion he is creating as a novelist. As a writer Mr Fowles has no relation to society at all: he merely gives it his views, which include an assurance that the stories he tells it are untrue. The conventions of the Victorian novel may have been as untenable as its society's conception of God, but its illusory characters appear more solid than those who are programmed by the modern novelist to run free and to 'disobey' him. The freedom which Mr Fowles announces as his first principle may seem to resemble that of a man on a desert island, for whom everything perceived returns only the echo of his own consciousness. His audience, as well as his characters, find themselves marooned with him. And however free and alone, he is far less interesting than Hardy in company.

Since ambiguity depends upon illusion, the alternatives that Mr Fowles offers his characters suggest less to the reader's imagination than the determined fates which Hardy and his contemporaries contrive for theirs. Hardy's relation to God or to gods was certainly idiosyncratic, but less than any novelist, past or present, did he desire to make his own rules and announce his own tables of the Law. Like his Giles Winterborne, he is by nature, as a novelist, 'one of those silent unobtrusive beings' who 'scrutinise others' behaviour' the more closely in consequence, but whose independence makes no claim to being a law unto itself. It is significant that Winterborne is deeply disturbed, shocked almost, at the idea that Grace's marriage might be dissolved, although this means he may yet win her hand:

Surely the adamantine barrier of marriage could not be pierced like this! It did violence to custom.

Winterborne, like his creator, has a sound idea of what barriers are best decreed in the novel; and for his art to seem real Hardy needed their adamantine reassurance, alike in his writing and his plotting, invention and imagination.

Hardy's vulnerability, and the measures he takes against it, prevent him from ever seeming facile. They impede fluency, as they do any other open indulgence, like that easy relation with their readers, over the head of the novel as it were, which is claimed by Dickens and Thackeray and George Eliot, and which Mr Fowles has sought to imitate for his own purposes and as a foil for the new conventions he employs. A sufficiently hearty fluency is of course the natural enemy of illusion, patronising as it does the novel's need for it. 'What I object to about the mid-Victorians', observed Virginia Woolf in a letter, 'is their instinctive fluency'. She wanted to restore illusion to the novel, illusion of her own kind, that of the feel of life itself.

In this she saw Hardy as a shadowy kind of ally, or at least precursor. She understood and felt at home with him – one of his poems is quoted in her first novel, *The Voyage Out* – and she cultivated intensively the kind of helplessness which is immanent in his style. Fluency, the sign of the power and confidence of the Victorians, their ability to take artifice in their stride, oppressed her; she had to escape from it. Hardy had also escaped, in his novels, by his own more private and unobtrusive methods. The library audience that first responded to him must have felt this as some sort of relief, after the extrovert power of the big novelists. T. S. Eliot thought that the modern poet must 'dislocate language', if necessary, into his meaning. And this development, which Yvor Winters chided Eliot for advocating, calling it 'the fallacy of expressive or imitative form', was pursued by Virginia Woolf, by Joyce, by Hemingway, until it became a commonplace of the modern manner.

In Hardy's text it is already implicit, as we shall see, though it does not seem conscious, and it is certainly not pursued with method and concentration. But when his characters bumble, his text bumbles too; he does not in the least mind falling flat, if there is no occasion for rising, and in life as he saw it there seldom is. The quality of disappointment we taste in our experience of his text may seem to be a formalisation of disappointment as a bulky ingredient in life – certainly in life as he presents it. And in the art of his prose this negative deprivation becomes a positive quality and a positive pleasure. Its lapses resemble those in daily consciousness, but transposed into art, the resultant natural instability registering (as Virginia Woolf assiduously sought to do) the turnings on and off of the mind, the dullness or keenness with which impressions are recorded. There is something unperturbed in this fluctuation as if the writer accepted it as a necessary condition, for him, of the business. Though Hardy is so sensitive he is never in the least apologetic: an aspect of the *privacy* which seems like intimacy by other means, and gives us an elusive sense of him instead of his continued presence as a personality and a will.

Instability grows less marked as the list of Hardy's novels grew longer. In the last three, from *Tess of the D'Urbervilles* onward, it is hardly in evidence at all. What suggests itself instead is a greater rigidity, a methodical build-up instead of deflations and relaxations. There is an air of concentration at the outset of *Tess,* a bent to get everything possible out of the scenic atmosphere of the rural drama; and there is a deliberation which seems to stabilise a method throughout both *Jude the Obscure* and *The Well-Beloved.* Hardy has become much more concerned with the completed achievement in a more ambitious sense, as is implied by his comment that had he known *Tess* would do so well he would have tried to make it a 'really good' novel, and the remark that *Jude* was 'a miserable accomplishment' compared with 'what I meant to make it'.

These three novels have in consequence less of Hardy's poetry in them than the earlier ones. In his poems Hardy is never seen striving to rise to the height of an ideal conception, nor failing to bring such a thing off. And this too, in its way, could have a bearing on what in them seems imitative form, naturally produced. 'World' suggests as much, when it talks to Hardy in one of his latest poems:

> 'I do not promise overmuch,
>   Child; overmuch;
> Just neutral-tinted haps and such',
>   You said to minds like mine.

The poems do not promise much to us either, nor the earlier

novels; and yet in them – the novels that is – the poetry of the text becomes as it goes on a continuous pleasure, leisurely and low-keyed: so that one may want to read them again and again for the sake of their flavour and texture, when more obvious masterpieces of fiction have expended themselves. However sensational their contrivances, and their vocabulary, we can feel beneath the text the philosophy of *He Never Expected Much*. Nor should the reader expect too much, for what is true of life must also be true of art. Wiser not to make too great demands on either. Enough 'the homeliest of heart-stirrings'.

What follows from this is more radical, more innovatory even, than might at first sight appear. We think of art as accepting no average, and recognising, ideally, no limitations other than those its form imposes. Of its kind the work must have perfection; and yet it is this presumption to which something in Hardy remains indifferent. If he achieves greatness it is without its outward and visible signs, the absoluteness of achievement which is as evident in *Middlemarch* as in *Madame Bovary*, in *The Portrait of A Lady* as in *Women in Love*. Of course, as Lawrence pointed out, it is the special function of the novel to be 'incapable of the absolute'; it is in the nature of its achievement to be more relative than in other arts.

But, that said, the relation between Hardy's feel for life's indifference, his 'meditative sense of the unfitness of things', like that of the railway porter in *Jude*, and those imperfections that are native to his art, is peculiarly close and personal. In the epoch in which Marx and Engels were proclaiming the contradictions in the individual situation, and assuming their removal in a just society, Hardy's art quietly presents such contradictions as being what life is all about. Who wants to live without contradictions in their situation? All good novels are apt to ask that question in some form: certainly Hardy's novels cannot help themselves asking it.

In his diary for the year 1887 he refers to his politics as those of an 'Intrinsicalist', indicating that he did not care for standardisation and the mass grouping of ideologies. 'I am equally opposed to aristocratic privilege and to democratic privilege. By the latter I mean the arrogant assumption that the only labour is hand-labour – a worse arrogance than that of the aristocrat.' A phrase used by a public figure today* – *'literacy is divisive'* – would, once he had grasped what it meant, seem to him to be saying something eminently right and proper. The social comment most frequently made in the novels is that there is no such thing as class solidarity; the work-folk of a country place resolve themselves when closely observed into individuals just as different from each other as those in London drawing-rooms (one of his favourite spots to exercise Intrinsicalism). He was on the side of any improvement – bicycles outside the doors of farm-workers and carpets on the stairs inside – but living was something for each individual to do in his own way, and his own suggestions here are negative ones, concerned with the small sequential aspects of living and perceiving. All his texts might say with Laforgue: *'Que la vie est quotidienne . . .'* And it is this above all which gives them more in common with Virginia Woolf, or the *nouveau roman,* than with any of his Victorian contemporaries. The most Victorian thing about his novels is their plot: the least, their sense of time, place, and event.

This indeed may be what misled Mr Fowles. His own novel dangles multiple alternative endings before the reader, echelonned in pairs to make a lively termination, and it is more than possible that he had in mind Hardy's own retrospective comments on the endings of *The Return of the Native* and *The Woodlanders,* in which he suggests that readers with an 'austere artistic code' may prefer a conclusion without a marriage and without a reconciliation. No such endings exist, however, and it seems clear that Hardy never wrote them. More important, the possibility of them is not even mentioned until years after the novel has come out, and when we have read the novels it is hardly possible to imagine them ending in any other way than they do. We do not feel, as we may do with Dickens' *Great Expectations,* that either ending will do equally well: on the contrary, the weight of Hardy's plot insists in the most literal way possible on its own completion.

And all the more strongly because the plot is not associated with meaning. It happens as it does happen, like the mummers' play. Nothing could be more different than the possible endings devised by Mr Fowles, or left open in a *nouveau roman.* In this

* Sir Edmund Leach, Provost of King's College, Cambridge.

respect Hardy is the least modern, the most traditional of novelists. But though he does not invite us to choose our ending, or decide for ourselves what has occurred, he does slide out of omniscience. He makes use of his creations for the overwhelming need of what happened in the tale, but he does not make them clear; nor does he encourage them to get things clear, for our benefit, about themselves. At least two of his heroes – Clym Yeobright in *The Return of the Native* and Angel Clare in *Tess* – are apparently treated somewhat in the way that George Eliot would have done it: they are displayed, and even analysed, in terms of their background and environment, and the temperament that has grown out of these. Sue Bridehead, in *Jude the Obscure,* is put on the spot a great deal more, studied as an individual case in terms of modernity and sex, and the nervous strains that interrelate them.

But these observations and analyses, so important in other novelists, do not in a Hardyan context bulk very large. The ending of *Great Expectations* is not important because Pip himself is very much so: he has been finally established, in his own eyes and for us, before the final page. But in Hardy event itself is what matters; explanations are relevant but not significant. As he uses fictional solutions he does not endorse them, or make us feel that they are in relevant and significant correspondence with society, its problems and development, as are most of the stories fashioned by his contemporaries. When he tells us, in *The Mayor of Casterbridge,* that 'character is destiny', the world he has created, and the events that have occurred in it, remain silent.

But this famous phrase of Novalis is quite at home in the novel from which Hardy almost certainly borrowed it – George Eliot's *The Mill on the Floss.* It belongs to a different order of things from the story of Henchard. It has to do with explanation and retrospection, not with the indeterminate road and country – 'one that might have been matched at almost any spot in any county in England at this time of the year' – which Henchard and his wife walked 'in ignoring silence . . . as a natural thing', before the rum and furmity at the fair and the drunken impulse that followed. That impulse belongs to what it is the fashion to call the existential world, the world of

Meursault and Lord Jim, rather than that of nineteenth-century determinism.

The road and the hot afternoon have their own irreducible atmosphere: stuffy, stifling, and opaque. Cutting through all such atmospheres in George Eliot are the incisive, vigorous metaphors that generalise and control them, but when Hardy uses these they stand off from the text without it seeming to become aware of them. In the affectionate nature of Angel Clare 'there lay hidden a hard logical deposit, like a vein of metal in a soft loam, which turned the edge of everything that attempted to traverse it'. Such an image in George Eliot would not only tell us much, but also in what terminological mode we were to take in the nature of Clare. Hardy seems to use it with the good will of one who has discovered that it pays to be able to write like that, but without very much inner conviction.

Such an absence of conviction in his vocabulary of comment and comparison seems in Hardy an earnest of involuntary sincerity. Analysing it, though, a critic might come to feel just the opposite: that the parade of intellectualism argued weakness and evasion. Something resembling weakness is indeed a key factor in Hardy's text; its manifestations baffling but also, deep down, reassuring. It seems part of an admission that for a dealer in words life must be talked about, but that talking about it won't do much good. Art demands – and with emphasis in Hardy's time – appearances of greatness where the nature of things in life is smallness, and the relation of the two in Hardy is never anything else than equivocal. His humour, emphatic or obscure, depends on this. His honesty is all the more characteristic for the ways in which it compromises itself with pretension:

The mill still worked on, food being a perennial necessity; the abbey had perished, creeds being transient. One continually sees the ministrations of the temporary outlasting the ministration of the eternal.

Clearly Hardy is proud of that, but the pride is not naïve: it is aware of what has been scored and aware, too, that this is not very considerable. The reason why his essays are so lifeless is the complete absence in them of such undertones; they seem totally *bien pensant,* handed out from the Hardy office as it were, with none of this concealed play of intercourse within them between novelist and reader, novelist and private man. In *The Profitable Reading of Fiction,* or *British Authors on French Literature,* Hardy puts his point of view with such flat-footed sincerity that one can hardly believe that he means no more than he says. No wonder he felt when young and in search of employment that doing reviews would be the last thing he would be good at.

On the other hand how much he must have enjoyed writing his own life, and all the possibilities of subterranean comedy it afforded. A record of cathedral visiting with his brother in 1911 is followed, without further comment, by a short paragraph:

He makes only one note this spring: 'View the matrices rather than the moulds.'

It is certainly worth our while to do so. The matrix is Hardy's temperament, with its strange blend of transparency and guile. If we felt he was trying to have us on we would not respond. It is as if his gift for literalness surprised itself in the utterance, or just after, by an apprehension of its comic side. But the literalness could startle or repel an audience as well as charm them. In some matrix of Hardy's experience, for instance, was formed the conviction at the heart of *Jude the Obscure*: that there is something repellent, an aspect of general unfitness, about marriage being licensed for habitual and lawful sex as a pub is licensed for drinking. Invited to behold the most common human experience in this way the audience did not like it at all, whereas for Hardy it was the most obvious and natural of conclusions. In the impact of such literalness Hardy involuntarily got something of the shock effect that Swift obtained with all forethought and calculation in the satire of *A Modest Proposal*.

But though Hardy's effects can be so absolute – moving us, shocking us, delighting us – they still remain at the side of his text, and its peculiar effects and pleasures. Literalness proceeds out of a hidden source, or rather a blankness, an endowment of not seeing himself. Novelists are usually the most self-conscious of men, for it is their acute sense of themselves (Tolstoy is the most obvious example) which affords their powers of explanation. Even Dickens, a somnambulist in many respects, is intensely desirous of understanding what has made himself and his characters – Pip, Miss Wade, George Silverman, David Copperfield – into the persons they are. And this process defines not only his activity but the novelist himself, in a way in which Hardy never is quite defined.

There is a parallel here which is not wholly fanciful. Hardy's is in its way an English, or Wessex, version of the Gogol 'secret', about which Russian critics discourse. What exactly is Gogol 'like'? From what proceeds his effect on the reader? The author Andrei Bely commented: 'We still do not know what Gogol *Is*'. It is the sort of slightly pretentious comment, in a sense self-evident, which does none the less express what we feel about a particular kind of writer. It would not occur to anyone to make it about Tolstoy or Dostoevsky, Dickens or George Eliot or Meredith. We know who they are as they knew themselves, and – as writers – came to know themselves. Encompassed by isolation and vertigo in the act of creation, Gogol despaired of finding out what it meant for him to *be* a writer. From Belinsky onwards criticism has variously pronounced him a writer of social protest, or a comedian and aesthete whose achievement is to have secured the most memorable and comical artistic equivalent of contingency itself of the 'nothing in particular'.

All this, it must be admitted, has little to do with the indefinabilities of Hardy, who despite his reticence is never consciously evasive, and who is besides totally lacking in Gogol's extreme theatricality. Yet he had something of the same uncertainty in relation to the culture and intellectual fashions of the time, the same uncertainty – in the context of that culture – about where he was and what doing. His autodidacticism, his acquired learning, helped to disorientate him, as it helps to give that characteristic instability to his prose. There is a sharp contrast in it between the physical perceptions, which are always his own, and the opinions and ideas which seldom are: it is indeed a part of his honesty to advertise their coming from somewhere else, again in a way that no other novelist does. He appeals to poets and sages, scientists, philosophers and painters, as if without the support of Aeschylus or Van der Weyden he could never be quite sure of himself. This is very different alike from the confident philistinism of Dickens, which carries him along with absolute certainty, and the intellectual confidence of George Eliot, which placed itself among its peers, speaking in the same accents as them but with her own voice and her own convictions.

In the vertigo of his uncertainties Gogol clung to words, to the 'grainy' quality of the Russian language. The words are what matter to him, for the objects they describe are 'nothing in particular' – indeed they are made nothing in particular by the words themselves, with all their agile evasive scurrying freedom. The same cause in Hardy has the opposite effect. Things matter to him more than the words which describe them, the latter being treated absent-mindedly, especially when Hardy is refreshed in his prose progress, with all its deference to contemporary culture and idea, by the arrival of some object which he can look at and note in all the vigour of itself. In *The Romantic Adventures of a Milkmaid*, the Baron takes Margery's jacket, which she has entrusted to him for the measuring of a ball-dress, and 'rolled and compressed it with all his force till it was about as large as an apple-dumpling, and put it in his pocket'. In *Desperate Remedies*, Manston indicates to his companion a raindrop which is the precursor of a violent storm:

He pointed to a round wet spot as large as a nasturtium leaf, which had suddenly appeared upon the white surface of the step.

Hardy is engrossed, in writing, by exactly what happened where, who was walking along what road at what time. It would not be an exaggeration to say that the intersection of Prince, the Durbeyfields' horse, and the horse drawing the rubber-tyred mail-cart, at four or so in the morning, at a point between Marlott and Casterbridge, is more prominent in our process of absorbing and enjoying Hardy than is the significance of the episode in the chain of events which is to lead Tess to the scaffold, and to the triumph of the President of the Immortals. Such a meeting is in the grain of Hardy's texture, whereas the significance of Tess is lifted above it on to a more theoretical plane.

The small things are more important in Hardy than the big things, but in so being they also become the big things – Margery's jacket wadded into a compact shape like an apple-dumpling is the most important thing in that tale, and a reason why the tale is by no means slight. Hardy seems grudging with it – that is part of the secret – as if when writing in prose he produced such information with a curious reluctance, into a medium that might not care about it. The reluctance of course makes the information seem all the more precious. But it also gives it a homeless quality, and memorable because homeless, situated at some meeting-point of space and time with consciousness, like a cross-roads in solitary country. There are no homes in Hardy, as Dickens has them, just as there are no norms, no steady pressure of belief or philosophy or message, such as all other novels of his time are conditioned to give us, and which we take for granted as much in Dickens as in E. M. Forster. Irresponsibility is like an object seen at dusk, out of the corner of the eye and at a distance, in the middleground of his pronouncements, a hidden and steadfast equivalent of the unstable surface of his prose. Sometimes he confronts it directly, when it becomes something plain and quaint –

'I would give a great deal to possess real logical dogmatism.'
'So would I.'

Thus Paula and Somerset in *A Laodicean*. Hardy's passion for the past is for a homeless place, where nothing has happened but the invisible certainties of event. Few people in whom he is interested in the novels possess a proper home. Tess's sleep at Stonehenge is a vast blown-up equivalent, on the coarse scale he took pleasure in increasingly in the later novels, of those earlier, clear-toned, undomestic pictures which are more inconspicuously but penetratingly memorable.

We shall be returning to the novels concerned. But even Stonehenge, we might note here, is really the climax of a more characteristic sequence: the strange idyll which Clare and Tess have lived for a few days together in a shut-up country house in the New Forest. Its atmosphere recalls the unused mansion in which Lady Constantine entertains her lover in *Two on a Tower*.

The tower itself is a fairy-tale of the domestic; like the occluded houses it has the atmosphere and details of a home transposed into unhomely oddities. They are the kind that appear, in a comedy context, at the unfortunate evening party given by Giles Winterborne to Grace and her father, which shows his paternal home in the same light as the hut in the woods Grace will occupy later, and outside which he will die of fever. Venn's caravan, lurking in the nettle-grown hollow among the furze, is the most congenial domicile on Egdon; the least, the love-nest of the just married Clym and Eustacia, silent in the brooding August of the heath, with the figure on the hill watching two others enter, and itself being watched on approach by another figure at the window. But the most subtly unhomely of Hardy's big houses is the one he knew best, Kingston Maurward manor house at Stinsford, the model for Knapwater House in the first published novel, *Desperate Remedies*. It is equalled in this by the neighbouring abode of the steward, on the step of which fell the great rain-drop, heralding the storm that gives him an opportunity to show the heroine round. The desolation of Dickens's Dedlock Park seems merely cinematic by comparison.

Perhaps when Hardy left the paternal cottage at Upper Bockhampton, where he had been so happy as a child, he never found another home. Stinsford church and churchyard, which he continued to haunt till the end of his life, were in a sense no doubt substitutes, of a peculiarly Hardyan sort. Still, it is easy to falsify the perspective by psychologising; in fact, like so many great artists, Hardy combines his own idiosyncrasies with the most ordinary human feelings and needs, and his chief idiosyncrasy is probably his emperor-has-no clothes insistence on what others who have felt much the same way come to take for granted. It is, for example, a very normal human experience to find that marriage and the home have not much to do with the imagination of romance and passion, but Hardy dwells on this with all the unexpected kinds of literalness his art deals in. The conventions of the novel that use marriage as a terminal device, though not necessarily to conclude the book, are used by him with disconcerting thoroughness to suggest that there is nothing much worth having in life except the kinds of experience the novel conventionally offers – passion, misfortune, or happy endings that are really unhappy ones. It is a view of life that seems on occasion to parody literary artifice, and this is what happens, it seems to me, in the notorious story called 'Barbara of the House of Grebe', one of *A Group of Noble Dames*.

Barbara falls in love with a young man called Willowes, handsome and virtuous but in a humble way of life, and her family becomes reconciled to her elopement. Her husband is sent off to Italy for a year, to acquire polish, and there his heroic conduct in a fire results in ghastly facial disfigurement. He returns; Barbara shudders away from him, and then has a change of heart only to find he has renounced her and gone away. Nothing more is heard; it is assumed he is dead, and she marries Lord Uplandtowers, a frigid but persistent suitor. She now dotes on the memory of her old love, and cherishes by night a lifesize marble statue of him. Her new husband finds this out and gets a craftsman to alter the head of the statue so that it resembles the disfigured man. He then torments his wife with this apparition, keeping it in a cupboard at the foot of their bed, from which it can be revealed by a pulley, until she clings to him in a passion of servile dependence, hating and recoiling from the memory of her handsome lover. She cannot bear to let her lord out of her sight, and bears him many children, only one of whom survives her own early death.

Burton and Jacobean drama one might say, together with Hardy's countryman's relish for the quaintly gruesome? The piece is notably lacking in any of the real pleasures of his text. But it was singled out by reviewers as a very characteristic example, and one of Hardy's morbidity; George Moore derided it, and in *After Strange Gods*, T. S. Eliot castigated it as an instance of the evils of mere 'self-expression' in literature, the self expressed being no very 'wholesome' affair. An essay by J. I. M. Stewart* ably defends Hardy from this charge, but there seems to me no doubt that Eliot was right in perceiving something intimate in the tale, for all its impersonal status in a series as a quaint anecdote told by an elderly surgeon. (There is Hardy's usual literalness in finding what he conceives as a suitable subject for a Chaucerian 'Surgeon's Table'.) But in fact he is

* 'The Integrity of Hardy', *Essays & Studies*, 1948.

carrying to the limit of fantasy the theme of marriage and the
home, the theme personified in *The Well-Beloved* and in Sue
Bridehead of *Jude the Obscure*. The Hardyan claim from which
fantasy commences is conveyed in a characteristic metaphor
early on, after the lovers have eloped and their ardour begun to
cool:

> . . . a lover's heart after possession being comparable to the earth in its
> geologic stages . . . first a hot coal, then a warm one, then a cooling
> cinder, then chilly – the simile shall be pursued no further.

Willowes as husband is no longer handsome but repellent; as a
statue he can be passionately loved once more, until the statue
too is deformed, the deformer then being clung to like a lover
for protection, instead of appearing as a normal husband.

It is the kind of high-life tale which Hardy might have
exchanged with a rural audience appreciating it without any
notion of morbidity. As usual he was hurt by the reviewers,
because they attached to him personally the repulsion they felt,
whereas for him it was no more than an ingenious and
externalised anecdote. This is just why it is worth noticing at
some length. It *is* a repellent story, because it uses and parodies a
deep theme of Hardy's imagination without the author himself
being present within it. It shows how he informs literary matter
in his texts – his novels – by preserving in it his own unstable
and homeless being, the being which lends all its own literalness
to a convention and a plot. It is the very stability of 'Barbara of
the House of Grebe' which isolates it from Hardy's work and
gives it in detachment that slightly odious quality which –
ironically – is detected by Eliot and the other critics, and
imputed in isolation to the author himself.

The fantasy of the tale is certainly Hardy's own, but when we
meet it elsewhere in his novels it may remind us of the freedom
they possess– freedom from any weighing-down responsibility
to their own preoccupations. Self-expression is not in this sense a
kind of duty for Hardy as it appears to be for so many recent
novelists, in whom it is almost automatically identified with
what a reviewer called 'a quality of seriousness', a quality he
attributes to those novelists who methodically build up their

temperaments into a manifesto advertising – by means of the plotting and ploys of fiction – a way of life. Hardy's fiction has no way of life, because it has no home to lead it in, and no consistent idiom to keep it before the reader and attach him to it. 'A quality of seriousness' (the phrase was used by Frederic Raphael of novelists like David Storey and Margaret Drabble) is found today in the pre-stressed and pre-formed fictional structure from which the novelist, as spokesman of feminity or celebrant of sterling local realities, looks smugly out. He knows that his own fantasies, efficiently built into the structure, give it a still greater rigidity of purpose and meaning.

The self that Hardy expresses in his recurrent themes and fantasies, escaping from or portraying with gloom the institutions of home and marriage (the fictional device of marriage just missed or evaded, or snapping behind one like a locked door, is used by him with fascinated relish) in no way resembles this modern fictional self, flaunting its burden of 'seriousness'. Nor is it the self of Montaigne, *ondoyant et divers,* interested both in its own nature and in the nature of that interest. One of the oldfashioned things about Hardy is that he does not come before us seeming to possess a self in any of the senses to which the romantic poets and theorists, the philosophers and the novelists, have accustomed us. His presence is much more indeterminately personal, self-delighting but not self-scrutinising, a tremulous tender fleeting entity, like the Emperor Hadrian's *'animula vagula blandula'* – a phrase which must have held an appeal for Hardy, for he quotes it more than once – haunting the pages of his prose. The disagreeableness of such a story as 'Barbara of the House of Grebe', in which all such intimate significance seems petrified into a deliberate impersonality, shows by contrast how sympathetic is this attraction of Hardy's presence elsewhere throughout his novels.

A presence with all the intimacy of a self but none of its proclamation, or insinuation. In every sadness, deprivation, or neutral tone and 'hap' of the novels there is still the unmistakable Miltonic assertion – 'For who would lose, though full of pain, this intellectual being'. And in the poems, equally pre-Words-worthian, is the 'delighted spirit' invoked by Claudio in

Measure for Measure, alive in the form of the verse, and itself a part of the event or association the verse discovers to us. So it is in such a poem as *Green Slates,* Hardy's presence being with them and the girl they remind him of:

> It happened once, before the duller
> Loomings of life defined them,
> I searched for slates of greenish colour
> A quarry where men mined them;

and now

> Green slates – seen high on roofs, or lower
> In wagon, truck, or lorry –
> Cry out: 'Our home is where you saw her
> Standing in the quarry;'

The sight of the girl is alive in those greenish slates, and they in their turn are as much alive as she, and more capable of speech and reminder. Meeting thus in consciousness gives a voice to all that meets, even to the dead, when meditation ('The slow, meditative lives of people who live in habitual solitude . . .') imagines a meeting with them in the churchyard. In 1890 Edward Clodd observed to Hardy, in the course of a conversation on comparative cultures, that Dorset peasants 'represented the barbaric idea that confuses persons and things'. Recording this in his diary Hardy added a note in parenthesis: 'This barbaric idea which confuses persons and things is, by the way, also common to the highest imaginative genius – that of the poet'.

It was certainly true of his imagination, in whose clarity persons and things have a much simpler life – and a life whose romance is more taken for granted – than in the world of Coleridge and Wordsworth. For Hardy consciousness was romanticism, 'which will exist in human nature', he notes, 'as long as human nature itself exists'. The encounters that for Wordsworth were admonishments from another world, 'types and symbols of eternity', were for him without other significance, too absolute to become part of a meaningful whole. All those he notes in diary or poems are at one with the order of perception in his novels, but not because they have any metaphysical coherence. They could go straight into his novels, in whose texture – like all that is there already – they would be neither relevant nor irrelevant, but engrossing, and disappointing. Sometimes the encounter is solitary, as when he sees Orion upside-down in a pool of water under an oak; sometimes with a consciousness which appears to extend into his own –

January 30. Sunday. Dr S. called as usual. I can by this time see all round his knowledge of my illness. He showed a lost manner on entering, as if among his many cases he had forgotten all about my case and me, which has to be revived in his mind by looking hard at me, when it all comes back.

In 1896 he visted Warwick church, where 'looking through a slit by chance' he saw the coffin of Lord Warwick, who had invited him some while back to visit the castle:

'Here am I at last', he said to the coffin as he looked; 'and here are you to receive me!' It made an impression on Hardy which he never forgot.

It impressed him, one can't help feeling, a great deal more than the recounted recollection in the *Life* impresses us. But that would not have bothered him. He was not in the least shy of obviousness, and encounters thrilled him that to us might seem a stagey imitation of Hamlet's and Yorick's.

The fact was what mattered to Hardy's romanticism, not what might be made of it; and this accounts for any discrepancy between his own response and ours, a discrepancy that Wordsworth and Coleridge would have dissolved away by the manner in which they order and shape our responses in sympathy with their own. Hardy's encounters, like the three I have referred to, remain in their own kind of rapt separation, hard and clear for him though not necessarily for us. In another area of encounters we might note that Gogol – and Dickens too in his different English way – apply the same sympathetic pressure as the earlier romantics to merge their experience into ours; to this end using language to swamp and demoralise the actuality of persons and objects rather than to intersect with and appraise it. This is true of the famous carriage-wheel on the first page of *Dead Souls,* which might have got to Moscow but definitely not as far as Kazan; and the young man with a tie pin in the shape of a pistol, who happens to walk past, and who is gone for good almost before we – or Gogol – know if we have really seen him. He was, in a sense, 'standing in the quarry', when the anomalous conveyance from which Gogol glimpses life's scattered phenomena happened along. But the moment does not define him – it does the opposite – even though it gives him the memorability in a Gogolian context that Hardy's meetings have in his own. His point is to suggest the nature of the novel (as we find looking back) and in a much more deliberate fashion than any encounter in Hardy would do.

Not that Hardy was not able, when he wanted, to employ the most careful – indeed the slyest – calculations of his own, as he tells us with his own kind of simplicity when talking about his early years in the *Life*:

Almost suddenly he became more practical, and queried of himself definitely how to achieve some tangible result from his desultory yet strenuous labours at literature during the previous four years. He considered that he knew fairly well both west-country life in its less explored recesses and the life of an isolated student cast upon the billows of London with no protection but his brains . . . The two contrasting experiences seemed to afford him abundant materials out of which to evolve a striking socialistic novel – not that he mentally defined it as such, for the word had probably never, or scarely ever, been heard of at that date.

The engaging vagueness which comes over the recollection is as striking as the shrewdness with which Hardy had obviously planned out at the time the possibilities of *The Poor Man and the Lady.* The word 'socialistic' is held at a slight distance, the attitude being somewhat quizzical. It is as if Hardy's simplicity becomes still more itself through being presented with this indulgent confession of intent. Out of an equable indifference to his present identity he recalls how his younger self invented one, to impress the publishers and the public. His hero, Will Strong, was an angry young man.

The story was, in fact, a sweeping dramatic satire of the squirearchy and nobility, London society, the vulgarity of the middle class, modern Christianity, church restoration, and political and social morals in general . . . the tendency of the writing being socialistic, not to say revolutionary; yet not argumentatively so, the style having the affected simplicity of Defoe's (which had long attracted Hardy, as it did Stevenson, years later, to imitation of it). This naïve realism in circumstantial details that were pure inventions was so well assumed that both Macmillan and Morley had perhaps been a little, or more than a little, deceived by its seeming actuality . . . Portions of the book, apparently taken in earnest by both his readers, had no foundation either in Hardy's beliefs or his experience.

Down with practically everything! Hardy goes on to say that he described in the first person an introduction to the mistress of an architect, who added to his income by designing pulpits, altars, and ecclesiastical furniture – 'the lady herself being a dancer at a music-hall when not engaged in designing Christian emblems – all told so plausibly as to seem actual proof of the degeneracy of the age'.

With a certain pride he opines that Meredith, who discussed the manuscript with him and advised against publication, was not taken in by 'the affected simplicity of the narrative.' But like Macmillan and Morley he thought it an 'aggressive and even dangerous' work, and advised the young author not to 'nail his colours to the mast' in this way. Obviously the young Hardy had not grasped the extent to which his calculation had succeeded with his elders; he had given the impression that he 'meant mischief', and had done this 'almost without knowing it, for his mind had been given in the main to poetry and other forms of pure literature'. The strategy of his fantasy was not always to be so conscious, but the relation between it, and the gravity with which it was received, was to be repeated years later when he commented in his diary on the *Quarterly*'s review of *Tess*. 'How strange that one may write a book without knowing what one puts into it – or rather, the reader reads into it'. Certainly it was very strange indeed for Hardy, much stranger than it would be for most novelists. In spite of – or perhaps because of – his first enterprise, he could never feel that he was committing himself by anything he wrote in a novel.

He is much more pinned down when he tries to be impersonal, than when his own 'animula', with all its revelations and withdrawals, is continuously present. 'Barbara of the House of Grebe' shows that. Even the noble ideals of J. S. Mill, which impressed him so deeply as a young man, were built into a concept of himself that was not himself, and which one can feel the text of novels and poems escaping from, as they escape – when he is fully present in them – from all other kinds of definition and identification. But Mill, and the thinker's 'duty to follow his intellect to whatever conclusions it may lead', were deeply congenial none the less to what I have called the literalism in Hardy: so much so that when in May of 1906 he wrote to *The Times* on the occasion of Mill's centenary an account of how he first saw his hero, it is difficult not to feel that he is really presenting, for the first and last time, an image of himself, of how he would wish to appear to himself and to others:

The appearance of the author of the treatise *On Liberty* (which we students of that date knew almost by heart) was so different from the look of persons who usually address crowds in the open air that it held the attention of people for whom such a gathering in itself had little interest. Yet it was, primarily, that of a man out of place. The religious sincerity of his speech was jarred on by his environment – a group on the hustings who, with few exceptions, did not care to understand him fully, and a crowd below who could not. He stood bareheaded, and his vast pale brow, so thin-skinned as to show the blue veins, sloped back like a stretching upland, and conveyed to the observer a curious sense of perilous exposure. The picture of him as personified earnestness surrounded for the most part by careless curiosity derived an added piquancy – if it can be called such – from the fact that the cameo clearness of his face chanced to be in relief against the blue shadow of a church which, on its transcendental side, his doctrines antagonised. But it would not be right to say that the throng was absolutely unimpressed by his words; it felt that they were weighty, though it did not quite know why.

'A curious sense of perilous exposure' is indeed what Hardy often gives us, perhaps felt himself. But though it is a moving and graphic picture, very like Hardy's own public image, even like the image of Hardy the novelist, yet it still seems quite other

than the presence we actually meet in them, which even Mill
had no real hold over.

All his ideas and experiences go straight into his work, in the
same way as those 'socialistic' ideas born of his early time in
London. Yet he never got over his surprise at their reception, for
they too seemed to him to have been used as constructions and
'pure inventions', as opposed to 'poetry and other forms of pure
literature'. His fantasy and ingenuity was the most direct way of
using experience, and he could never adjust himself to his
readers' misunderstanding of the operation as he conceived it.
For him the 'purity' of poetry consisted in not having to take the
trouble to simulate and display, to fashion surprises and strong
conclusions. But perhaps he was not aware how often his prose
approached this condition of his poetry, even when apparently
intent on nothing but beguiling and surprising the reader. We
might compare a poem about a cottage where nothing
'happens', with a story about one in which a good deal does:

> When the inmate stirs, the birds retire discreetly
> From the window-ledge, whereon they whistled sweetly
>   And on the step of the door
>   In the misty morning hoar;
> But now the dweller is up they flee
> To the crooked neighbouring codlin tree;
>   And when he comes fully forth they seek the garden,
>   And call from the lofty costard, as pleading pardon
>   For shouting so near before
>   In their joy at being alive:—
> Meanwhile the hammering clock within goes five.
>
> I know a domicile of brown and green,
> Where for a hundred summers there have been
> Just such enactments, just such daybreaks seen.

'Pure literature' might be said to reveal itself here both in the
absolute pleasure of the event, and the steps, like those cut in a
box or yew hedge, which signal its observed stages. Those
formal insets in the lines also conduct the transit in the reader's
mind from freshness to commonplace, from the eager dawn to
the placid day, a transit interrupted by the remarkable impres-

sion conveyed in the word 'hammering', a vivid index of sound without contrasted with sound inside.

The story called *Enter a Dragoon* begins with the narrator going over a house which is about to be pulled down:

Some of the thatch, brown and rotten as the gills of old mushrooms, had, indeed, been removed before I walked over the building. Seeing that it was only a very small house – which is usually called a 'cottage-residence' – situated in a remote hamlet, and that it was not more than a hundred years old, if so much, I was led to think in my progress through the hollow rooms, with their cracked walls and sloping floors, what an exceptional number of abrupt family incidents had taken place therein – to reckon only those which had come to my own knowledge. And no doubt there were many more of which I had never heard.

It stood at the top of a garden stretching down to the lane or street that ran through a hermit-group of dwellings in Mellstock parish. From a green gate at the lower entrance, over which the thorn hedge had been shaped to an arch by constant clippings, a gravel path ascended between the box edges of once trim raspberry, strawberry, and vegetable plots, towards the front door. This was in colour an ancient and bleached green that could be rubbed off with the finger, and it bore a small long-featured brass knocker covered with verdigris in its crevices.

Hardy's imagination is so inseparable from place and event that identification is superfluous, but both cottages would seem to be based on the one at Upper Bockhampton. What is absorbing is the sense poetry and prose alike give us of the passage of life within it, and the prose syntax makes its point in a manner corresponding to the steps cut in the verse. Had it been a big house, and older than a mere hundred years – 'if so much' – more might have taken place; but the narrator is led to reflect on the number of things that have happened, because the house is small and *not* old. Hardy secures our attention on his narrative mood by the absent-minded expression of the prose contrasting with the attention of its gaze. The story that follows is of course an extraordinary happening, as befits a country anecdote, but its very unusualness is itself a kind of platitude, letting us down from this first sense of pleasurable concentration, but keeping it alive in expectation of the final crisis at the end.

II

THIS QUALITY IN THE WRITING OF BOTH ATTENTION
and inattention, shifting between the language itself and what it
describes, is an aspect of what could be called Hardy conscious
and unconscious; and our feeling is for the alternation of the
two. The Hardy who is on duty does not seem aware of the one
who unknowingly observes: this perceiver pays no regard to the
artificer and craftsman. The text is like a landscape of which the
constituent parts — cows, birds, trees, grass — pay no attention to
one another, although they appear as a total composition to the
beholder, the reader.

The metaphor does not quite do, but it may convey
something of the complex pleasure in attending to Hardy. The
conscious Hardy may not seem aware of the unconscious one,
but he is extremely sensitive to everything else, including the
main chance of the story and what response his readers may
show. The conscious Hardy is laborious in the pursuit of
literature and the exploitation of verbal effect and allusions,
erudite or worldly, meditative or melodramatic. This conscientiousness can give us the feeling of disappointment, of let-down,
but also the knowledge that the conscious Hardy augments the
unconscious. The two are mutually dependent, perhaps on
account of their seeming ignorance of each other.

A real let-down occurs, on the other hand, when we are
confronted not with the Hardy experience but with what might
be called the Hardy image. At such moments the powerful or
the picturesque or the pitying Hardy seems to be detached, and
displayed in isolation from the rest of him. Such an image
impresses itself on the public, and although Hardy rejected it he
had made his own contribution to it. He tells us how he did so
when he wrote *The Poor Man and the Lady*, in the guise of an
angry young socialist, and as we have seen Macmillan thought it

positively dangerous because – unlike Thackeray – it really 'meant mischief'. Such an adaptation of the author for his book is not uncommon, but in Hardy's case it could have been more addictive than he realised to get a leg up into a prospective work of fiction by seeming more positive and dedicated than he really was. Committed to being far from the madding crowd; or to satire on London drawing-rooms; to the worldly, the tragic, the pessimistic; to the cause of unmarried mothers or the unhappily married . . . to the pursuit of eternally vanishing and reincarnating feminine beauty.

These manifestations of Hardy on duty are all in their various ways 'simple', or unitary, and for that reason they lack the real simplicity of his text, which proceeds from a complex interaction. His 'greatness' inevitably tends itself to be a unitary concept. It is not something that can be extracted and exhibited on its own, particularly not by himself. Here too there is much more of Gogol than, say, of Goethe. Particularly Gogolian is the Preface to *Late Lyrics and Earlier,* in which he defends the 'philosophy' of the poems, usually reproved as 'queer' (the inverted commas are his), while at the same time withdrawing into much more indeterminate explanations, which are, very properly, not really explanations at all. He invokes Wordsworth's Preface, citing the poet's freedom not to enter into 'a formal engagement that he will gratify certain known habits of association'. And twice he emphasises Matthew Arnold's dictum on the duty of poets to apply 'ideas to life', adding the characteristic proviso that the famous writer could hardly have foreseen what was likely to happen if an enthusiastic disciple actually tried to put this high aim into practice.

In so far as it has a meaning at all, Arnold's dictum suggests the application to experience of a coherent and co-ordinated body of ideas, the kind that we meet in Wordsworth as in Shelley, in Eliot, in Arnold himself. And this is what Hardy seems to be disassociating himself from in the arguments of the Preface. He tells us for instance that his creed is not pessimism but 'evolutionary meliorism', and he cites a 'much earlier' poem, *In Tenebris,* to show that this has long been so: 'If way to the Better there be, it exacts a full look at the Worst.' A few, but not very many, poems from any of his collections might be said

to have some connection with this creed, if hardly to endorse it.
But Hardy is deprecating 'the stern pronouncement made
against me by my friend Mr Frederic Harrison', one of the
'so-called optimists', who had gone on record with the verdict
that 'Hardy's view of life is not mine'. His real escape from Mr
Harrison and his other critics, however, is to deny that he had
any definite views of things at all (he noted in his diary that
Arnold 'had a manner of having made up his mind upon
everything years ago') and that the views which Harrison
disapproved of are 'really a series of fugitive impressions which I
have never tried to co-ordinate'.

He thickens the smoke-screen by observing that the poems
are a mixture, disparate both from the moods they represent,
and because so many are resurrected from previous epochs of his
writing. This, he says, misleads the reviewer, who imagines that
poems with a comic intention are 'misfires', precisely because
'they raise the smile they were intended to raise, the journalist,
deaf to the sudden change of key, being unconscious that he is
laughing with the author and not at him'. This retort upon the
would-be sophisticated reviewer is very significant. Hardy
wants to have it both ways. His views of life, are not those
attributed to him, alike by the serious but unbelieving positivist,
or the devout Christian. And they are quite compatible, too,
with fugitive and provisional impulses, with a relish in comedy
and incongruity. It is here, he claims, that the reviewer is most
taken in –

I must trust for right note-catching to those finely-touched spirits who
can divine without half a whisper, whose intuitiveness is proof against
all the accidents of inconsequence.

The appeal to those 'who can divine without half a whisper'
makes us realise that nothing could in fact be more incongruous
than the idea of collusion – winks and nods of intimacy – between Hardy and the reader. His text is indeed full of
'inconsequence', and the possibility of misunderstanding is as
great as our need for intuitiveness, for no poet or novelist could
be less likely to look sidelong at the reader, and address him
either with openness or with that 'half a whisper' which would

involve both parties in a relation of cosy fellowship. Byron, as a
poet, depends on exaggerating the nudge and the intimacy;
while almost every Victorian novelist speaks out to the reader
loud and clear, exhorting or expounding, encouraging or
commiserating, the tone of narrative communication common – however variously – to Charlotte Brontë as to Thackeray, Henry James as to George Eliot. The method and tones of
Wuthering Heights suggest that Emily Brontë may have avoided
it deliberately. Hardy certainly does not do that: he employs it
with conscientious assiduity but is unable, as I said earlier, to
make it ring quite true. It seems the pretence of communication
rather than the real thing.

Keats who wanted 'to write fine things which cannot be
laughed at in any way' would have sympathised with Hardy's
desire to make the reviewers feel that the laugh, if any, was on
his side. But in fact many of Hardy's most poignant poems turn
on the difficulty of human communication, just as his novels
make use of every possible device for preventing, hindering, or
stultifying it. It would perhaps not be too impertinent to read
into this the signs of his own deepest disability.

God, we infer from a good number of poems, has the same
sort of difficulties. Hardy associates communication with
self-consciousness, and an image of consciousness evolving to its
present state, to the misfortune of mankind, is one of his salient
ideas. God, too, may become aware of what he has done, his
consciousness brought into being by that of his own creation,
and its efforts to get in touch with him. In a letter to Edward
Clodd in 1908, about *The Dynasts,* Hardy added a postscript,
'The idea of the Unconscious Will becoming conscious with
flux of time, is also, new, I think, whatever it may be worth. At
any rate I have never met with it anywhere'. God may one day
have the same sort of revelation that other poems record in
human terms – the power of realisation, about oneself and
others, that has come retrospectively, or too late.

Most moving and brief of the poems on this topic is *The
Self-Unseeing:*

> Here is the ancient floor,
> Footworn and hollowed and thin,

Here was the former door
Where the dead feet walked in.

She sat here in her chair
Smiling into the fire;
He who played stood there,
Bowing it higher and higher.

Childlike, I danced in a dream;
Blessings emblazoned that day;
Everything glowed with a gleam;
Yet we were looking away!

As often in the poems, emphasis is made typographically: by the concluding exclamation mark, not in the internal musing of the poem. Two verses are wholly absorbed by the exactness of position in recollection. The door was here (altered? bricked up?) father here, mother there. This mesmeric exactitude is not blurred but heightened by the possibility that the door's former *self* is being referred to, that this is the same door but totally altered by the change time has made in the look of the place. Preoccupation with the exactness of the past joins up with the vanished preoccupation of the child in dancing; and both are scattered by the return of consciousness at the end. No more than melancholy intentness is happy concentration aware of itself; no one knew it as a moment of blessing; the awareness comes years after, when, Hardy implies, it is no 'use'.

And about this awareness Hardy is at his most inconsistent; for he implies that consciousness, elsewhere in his poems such a burden to suffering mankind, should then have been fully present to him, so that he could have *known* how happy he was. Yet in this the craftsman and composer in the poem typically ignores its own apparent conclusion. The composer knows that the moment of memory and making is the moment of joy – not when it happened. The impulse born of the knowledge embodied in the point of exclamation that ends the poem is like that in Wordsworth's twenty-first sonnet in the River Duddon sequence:

From her unworthy seat, the cloudy stall
Of Time, breaks forth triumphant Memory . . .

or of Proust's access of unmotivated joy when he stumbles on the uneven stone, or hears a spoon accidentally tap a plate. But Hardy does not join things up as they do. His response is immediate and literal. For the self was unseeing; it could not communicate its joy to itself; consciousness was not on itself. This is cause for sorrow, but it is that of the man who is reflecting, not of the poet who is writing. The two come together at the moment in *A Night in November,* when the dead leaves blow into the bedroom:

> One leaf of them touched my hand,
> And I thought that it was you
> There stood as you used to stand,
> And saying at last you knew!

The exclamation again: and the understanding and communication withheld. The whole emotion of the poem, 'touching our hearts by revealing its own' (in Hardy's phrase) is that there was nothing special to know. It was shared understanding, mutuality of consciousness, that never were, until this imagined moment of visitation.

It happens often in a Hardy poem that the elements of separation are assembled in the poem itself, concentrated, almost stylised, so that the effect is correspondingly more striking –

> I leant upon a coppice gate
>   When Frost was spectre-gray,
> And winter's dregs made desolate
>   The weakening eye of day.
> The tangled bine-stems scored the sky
>   Like strings of broken lyres,
> And all mankind that haunted nigh
>   Had sought their household fires.
>
> The land's sharp features seemed to be
>   The Century's corpse outleant,
> His crypt the cloudy canopy,
>   The wind his death-lament.
> The ancient pulse of germ and birth
>   Was shrunken hard and dry
> And every spirit upon earth
>   Seemed fervourless as I.

At once a voice arose among
  The bleak twigs overhead
In a full-hearted evensong
  Of joy illimited;
An aged thrush, frail, gaunt, and small,
  In blast-beruffled plume,
Had chosen thus to fling his soul
  Upon the growing gloom.

So little cause for carolings
  Of such ecstatic sound
Was written on terrestrial things
  Afar or nigh around,
That I could think there trembled through
  His happy good-night air
Some blessed Hope, whereof he knew
  And I was unaware.

This famous anthology-piece was first published by Hardy in
The Times on the last day of 1900. It is a moving and wonderful
poem, whose secret element is the separation – that by now
familiar indifferency – between the things seen in it, and the
images and interpretations made out of them. The man who is
'used to notice such things' leans on a gate at the dead time of the
year and looks about him. In such a woodland scene the deadest
winter feature is the matted tangle of wild clematis – 'old man's
beard' – seemingly extinct of life, even their feathery tufts
diminished to nothing by gales and the frosts. The sight of them
is unmistakably recalled by 'the tangled bine-stems scored the
sky, like strings of broken lyres . . .' just as a phrase from another
poem – 'briar-meshed plantations' – calls up the exact appearance of the bramble tracts which are the sole things that will
grow among planted conifers. The emblem of the season is of
the scruffiest and most unromantic sort, its actuality in the poem
not in the least courting the reader's attention, but nonetheless
placing itself as collateral – through the plangent music
word – with a line of Shelley, 'Make me thy lyre, even as the
forest is . . .'

The century's corpse is laid out, sharpened features making a
relief under the shroud. Yet no, not laid out. 'Outleant' seems
eccentric even by Hardy's standards. It has something of the

apparent literalness, hard to scan exactly, which distinguishes
the 'former door' of *The Self-Unseeing*. (The door might be still
there? – its being at a previous time referred to?) A corpse
cannot itself lean on anything – on a flat surface it can only
lie – but its stiffness could *be* leant, say against a gate. With
another rhyme, 'outlaid' would produce a clearer association
with the general image, and yet be much less arresting. For the
century's corpse, when one comes to think of it, is leant in
reflective pose, much as Hardy himself is.

The use of all kinds of anthropomorphism saturates Hardy's
style, and is usually so open that one takes its more peculiar
presence here for granted. Naturally enough there is no
recognition between Hardy and the corpse, though each may be
in the same attitude, as, in their separate solitariness, may be
'every spirit upon earth'. The metaphors of the third and fourth
line seem as unaware of these two questionable figures as the
'broken lyres' are of the woodbine. In fact Hardy puts metaphor
and description in apposition, so that each ignores the other
instead of complementing it; and he himself appears as
unconscious of the process as its components of each other. The
association of 'dregs' and 'eye' in the third and fourth lines of the
first stanza seems almost Shakespearian in its arbitrariness,
though they have an unobtrusive relation to something
perfectly observed – the setting sun blurred by the frost-fog
coating the scene, as the last drops cling to a cup.

The thrush's song is the climax of this whole tendency; and
the thrush himself, in his shrivelled and unkempt physical
presence, its leading man. The metaphors are now of religion, of
joys and consolations; and we recognise that the poem itself, like
not a few of Hardy's, has come to suggest the progression and
cadence of a hymn. But the blessed hope appropriate to a hymn
is in complete obliviousness of such a *song* as the bird is
singing – its 'happy goodnight air' – a line whose unexpectedness, among the comparatively formal sobriety of the poem's
diction, always brings the tears to my eyes. Such an 'air' is quite
inapposite to 'blessed hopes' of the religious sort, as would be
the airs of 'Haste to the Wedding' or 'The Soldier's Joy', lively
fiddle tunes which the youthful Hardy had played at dances and
often mentions in novels and poems.

It is because the pathetic fallacy is so absolute that the thrush and his song remain wholly outside it. By first perceiving bird and song, as only he could do, and then desiderating the blessed hope, Hardy in some way ensures that the two are not connected. One must emphasise again that there cannot be any consciousness or intention about this. If he could be suspected of bringing the two together with a deliberately ironic purpose, the poem would not be what it is. John Berryman, Donald Davie and other critics, have variously suggested that Hardy *is* being ironic here; not least by emphasising in his quiet way what readers of *The Times* would like to hear. But this is to bring him into that kind of relation with his readers which another poet may need, and even solicit (Berryman himself is an example) but which just does not occur to Hardy. His prefaces and comments show this beyond much doubt: no ironist, with an intuitive grasp of his audience, could have written them. Still more important, nothing in the poem is aware of the possibility of being organised for purposes of irony; its participants are preoccupied with their own affairs, the poet not least.

'At the very close of the year Hardy's much admired poem on the Century's End, entitled "The Darkling Thrush", was published in a periodical'. Hardy could put it thus, no doubt, because he was pretending to be his second wife, and it was the kind of success Florence Hardy might have fondly recorded. But clearly the wholly favourable response of readers had pleased him, and perhaps surprised him. Donald Davie imagines *The Times* reader's gratification at feeling Hardy was saying: 'I, the well-known atheist and author of *Jude the Obscure*, feel quite humbled by the blessed hope voiced by this bird.'* A nice idea, but Davie implies that Hardy had manoeuvred for such a response, and this the nature of the poem refutes. It is not conscious of its own comfortableness; nothing in it is working towards the blessed hope which the audience greeted with such approval, unconcerned by the fact that Hardy's impulses do not recognise one another in his art, any more than do the separate constituents of both his poetry and his fiction.

Thus his art is indeed made up of numberless 'acts of inconsequence'. And one result of this is that even the humour

* *Thomas Hardy and British Poetry*, London, 1973.

in it must be of a solitary kind, smiling to itself rather than at the imagined response of an audience. Hardy may genuinely want us to laugh with him, as we might do over the poem about the two lexicographers Liddell and Scott, or sardonically over such a poem as *Channel Firing*; yet we may still feel that he does not want to *see* us doing it; his pleasure in no way depends on the confidence that we shall be amused.

The Darkling Thrush really can be said to give us, with a clarity correspondent to its small scale, a clue to the working of his whole process, in novels as well as in poems. Throughout his work, the ways in which we are absorbed into it, moved, delighted, are never co-ordinated, never really unified. One can suspect that the exasperation felt by so many of his readers at his 'philosophy', and the emphatic ways in which they drew attention to its anomaly, was because his effect on them – his power to move them in particular – did not really seem much connected with it. Such a hiatus irritated the late Victorian mind, accustomed to continuity between attitude, system and feeling, alike in Tennyson as in George Eliot. And not the Victorian mind only: the same kind of exasperation can equally be found in a generation of readers whose responses to art have been influenced by T. S. Eliot and D. H. Lawrence, and by F. R. Leavis. Though Leavis admires many of the poems, he and Eliot share a dislike of the novels which owes something to fastidiousness at the conventions of their plotting and melodrama; but more, it would appear, to a sense of the 'parochial' confusions in them, the radical disunity.

III

THIS MAY GO WITH HARDY'S SPECIAL KIND OF SOLI-
tariness. Writers whose works show a natural psychological
unity are usually, and perhaps in consequence, coterie writers.
And however far apart their ideology – it comes now in fact to
seem closer than it once did – Eliot and Leavis themselves have
both spoken on behalf of a coterie. But Hardy has never had a
coterie following, of the sort that exiles like Lawrence and James
Joyce attracted. His position in the public eye made for quite a
different species of isolation, more like that associated with poli-
ticians and public figures, the product not only of temperament
but of class and status, and their relation in his time. He seems
almost to accept, as normal even if part of the general unfitness of
things, a literary version of the class barrier as existing between
himself and his readers. Ultimately, class in England has become
a matter of preferring to keep yourself to yourself, a privilege
Hardy made the most of, just as he did of its other advantage:
feeling romantic about the members of another class. Class and
sex are always intermingled in his imagination and his dreams, as
if they were aspects of each other.

Keeping yourself to yourself, while at the same time
wondering about others, also seems to be the basis of Hardy's
curious and unique kind of anthropomorphism, of which *The
Darkling Thrush* is such a striking example. It makes in a way a
kind of anti-dialogue, as we soon come to realise; it is imagined
because we know it cannot take place. 'The President of the
Immortals' is an obvious case. The point about that gentleman,
as assumed in the text, is that he is no more able to make sport
with Tess than Tess in person can reproach him. It is the same,
mutatis mutandis, with Hardy's thrush. And with the lady of *The
Sunshade*, which the poet finds as 'a naked sheaf of wires' in the
crevice of a cliff:

> Is the fair woman who carried that sunshade
> A skeleton just as her property is,
> Laid in the chink that none may scan?
> And does she regret – if regret dust can –
> The vain things thought when she flourished this?

The point is that dust can't. We have grown so accustomed to
the pathetic fallacy as an artifice for unifying sensibility and
sympathy that it takes time to grasp that for Hardy it is no such
thing. Hardy was misunderstood, and the President of the
Immortals caused such a furore, because his imagination
functions so literally. He imagines the President, straight out of
Aeschylus as he pointed out, doing his office, which like all
fonctionnaires he enjoys. This outraged people for whom the
anthropomorphic meant something not only fanciful and
delicate, but tactfully in tune with the real mood and wishes of
the writer and his audience.

As they are in Wordsworth. Probably Hardy was imitating
his flowers, dancing in the light so that:

> . . . I must think, do all I can
> That there was pleasure there

in what he tells us was his first attempt at verse, at the age of
sixteen or seventeen. It was a description of the Bockhampton
cottage:

> Wild honeysucks
> Climb on the walls, and seem to sprout a wish
> (If we may fancy wish of trees and plants)
> To overtop the apple trees hard by.

The diction goes back through Wordsworth to the
eighteenth century, but with Hardy the device works a little like
the mediaeval *occupatio*. 'I am not going to tell you . . .' – after
which the author does so. Because we may 'fancy' it, it isn't the
case. Even in this early example we may feel that those trees and
plants are not linked to us, but cut off, by the invocation of that
'fancy'. They live in their own place, which our colloquy with
them makes all the more different from our own.

No doubt the solitariness of marriage came to make its own

contribution to Hardy's imaginary dialogues. Like T. S. Eliot's first wife, his wife Emma became his muse all the more definitively because in such a sad way. Just after the building of Max Gate he records in his journal a deep depression. And in January 1886 there occurs a revealing entry:

Misapprehension. The shrinking soul thinks its weak place is going to be laid bare, and shows its thought by a suddenly clipped manner. The other shrinking soul thinks the clipped manner of the first to be the result of its own weakness in some way, not of its strength, and shows its fear also by its constrained air! So they withdraw from each other and misunderstand.

Withdrawal and misunderstanding become in Hardy's method artistic assets of the first value. In this passage, which can only refer to his relations with his wife, Hardy feels round the kind of awareness he had already imagined in *The Return of the Native*. He was afraid of her strength, and she thought his constrained manner a silent criticism of her own inadequacy. A weaker woman would have known how to melt this impasse – 'Why did you not make war on me with those who weep like rain?' – but Hardy's anthropomorphic vision is of things divided by the uncompromising nature of their own being, however involuntary that lack of compromise may be. His knowledge of this gives its piercing simplicity to his power of pity, and also its total lack of sentiment. Emma and himself are mysteriously affiliated to the thrush and the listener, the sunshade and the lady, the notion of dust regretting its vanity – or regretting that it should have ever felt it?

This may seem a pretentious way of analysing something that is in essence very simple, very direct. But such simplicity is most open to misunderstanding. Hardy's world is much more one of stasis and acceptance than his public supposed, an acceptance based on his imagination of things and people, dead or alive, communicating with us only through the strength of their difference. This cast of his mind became more conscious as he thought more about art, and as public expectations of his art increased with fame. His own power of endowing things with their separate and separating being now occurred to him as a conscious policy, as an entry in the diary shows us. He was always interested in possible future techniques for the novel, and for himself as a novelist –

Novel writing as an art cannot go backward. Having reached the analytic stage it must transcend it by going further in the same direction. Why not by rendering as visible essences, spectres, *etc.,* the abstract thoughts of the analytic school?

This idea, he tells us, was not carried out in a novel, but 'through the much more appropriate medium of poetry, in the supernatural framework of *The Dynasts* as also in smaller poems'. It is hardly surprising that he could not do it deliberately in fiction, although his coincidences and portents often appear there almost as 'visible essences' and 'spectres', making visible what might in a novelist of the modern 'school' be analysis of character, or of an age's sense of itself.

His unpretentiousness is such that he has never any fear of being portentous. To cook up 'the spinner of the years', the 'spirits ironic' and all the rest of them, was only an extension of the terms his imagination had always used in poetry – ghosts, birds, dogs, trees, gravestones, the bodies in their coffins and the dust of the chancel – all animated in their separate functions and yet totally unanimistic, made free of his musings but not taken over by them. When they are formalised into choruses or philosophic notions they do not lose their independence and the lack of a unifying pretension which it gave them, but they become more conventional, less a part of the idiosyncratic homeliness of Hardy's world. They are as naturally of that world as the rustics of his novels, and have the same air of fitting in with nothing except their own selves; they are not concerned with the outside world.

Although Hardy calls up all these familiars, and peoples his experience with them, he does not – as it were – 'own' them. If he did he would share them with us; but they keep themselves to themselves, a stance more social than intellectual. Here again he seems very far away from the romantic and intellectual fellowship of Wordsworth and the nineteenth-century pantheists and positivists. 'All thinking things, all objects of all thought' were not by him impelled by one motion and spirit: very much the opposite. The workaday relation of his art with the dead in their graves, with the years, the rocks or the waves, mean that these things retain, in the teeth of anthropomorphism, the same independence and air of aesthetic detachment which his human actors possess – the farm-workers at Warren's malthouse or the masons in the Luxellian family vault. In 1890, at the age of fifty, Hardy wrote in his diary: 'I have been looking for God 50 years, and I think that if he had existed I should have discovered him. As an external personality, of course – the only true meaning of the word'.

As an external personality – that was indeed for Hardy the only true meaning of the word. God must exist, if he exists at all, in the same absolute and indifferent sense as the thrush and the winter's day, the years, the separate fields. No doubt when young he did think of God in this way, like the single cuckoo which the little boy in the poem imagines has come 'on purpose to visit England and him'. The little boy's son says: 'how stupid boys were in those days'. If he could have gone on believing in God as an external personality, Hardy would have become a parson. As it was the poems in which God *was* in some sense an external personality became for him substitutions of a very literal kind, in the refuge and consolation of art.

In the history of lost faith Hardy has a unique place. Right up to our time he has been patronised, it seems to me, for his inability to do what most other artists and thinkers, who lost theirs, did: intellectualise, moralise, build new theologies. He substitutes, it is true, but he substitutes creatures as literal as God ought to be. He could not substitute 'grounds of being', or George Eliot's humanist idealism, Bergson's vitalism, the pragmatism of William James, the rational hedonism and 'states of mind' of G. E. Moore and Bloomsbury.* He lacked the intellectual agility, trained in the satisfaction of its powers. Lawrence's and Forster's ideas would have earned his respect and interest, even his admiration, but he could no more have lived inside them than he found he could do in Arnold's temple of culture and ideas, or Vaihänger's 'philosophy of the "as if"'. Mill was a hero of his youth, a god almost, and continued to

* Hardy was studying Bergson and G. E. Moore's *Principia Ethica* in 1914, as he had in his time conscientiously studied every other theorist and thinker.

influence him, probably more than the Germans, but where Mill in his later writings is spare and sceptical, Hardy produces what is almost a parody of him, and of the Germans, in his anthropomorphic vision of unconscious will becoming conscious mind.

Hardy never gave up, but he was not interested in intellectual problems for their own sake. His vision refused to go past appearances, was stubbornly unsynthesising. It is typically bizarre that while he seems inadvertently to parody nineteenth-century anthropomorphism by his exaggeratedly literal use of it, he is also going back past Wordsworth and Coleridge and the nineteenth-century philosophers to a dualism more like that of Locke and the eighteenth-century sceptics. (As an amateur of the business he recognised his own dualistic tendencies, commenting on them in old age in a facetious poem.) Consciousness is one thing and the material world is another, at the moment very much unsuited to it. This of course does not stop trees groaning, wounding each other as they rock in despair, and so forth; for such a display of pseudo-consciousness only reveals how we impute our feelings to objects which are shown by this very process to have no connection with it. By 'confusing persons and things' his vision shows how complete is the dualism.

In his text, indeed, parts of persons can be things, like the red interior of Tess's mouth, to be noticed for itself, not connected with her. In *Silas Marner,* Silas's brown pot is almost a part of himself – 'his companion for twelve years, always standing on the same spot, always lending its handle to him in the early morning so that its form had an expression for him of willing helpfulness, and the impress of its handle on his palm gave a satisfaction . . .' George Eliot may well have been thinking of the dipper by the well at Margaret's cottage, in Wordsworth's poem, worn smooth with human use, but now

> subject only
> To the soft handling of the elements.

In both cases the human and the material slip into one another with a natural harmony and a kind of verbal ease which is quite unlike the relation of the two in Hardy. What makes Hardy so arresting is that the closer and the more satisfyingly he sees things, and the more 'humanity' he endows them with, the more cut off they are.

On the same page of the *Life* which tells of his looking for God as an external personality – 'the only true meaning of the word' – he describes how he saw a 'staid, worn, weak man at the railway station':

His back, his legs, his hands, his face, were longing to be out of the world. His brain was not longing to be, because, like the brain of most people, it was the last part of his body to realise a situation.

Consciousness is ironically unhoused, the mechanical parts given its desires and sense of things. In another writer the comment might seem heartless, or cursorily showing off – we should pass it by with impatience. Its arrestingness as a note of Hardy's is not only its wholly unemphatic humanity, but its inability – by no means a refusal – to pass beyond appearances and the plain evidence they show. Appearance does not give way to idea. Hardy is certainly applying ideas to life, though they have none of the shaping and controlling power which Arnold assumed about ideas and expected of them. Notes like that from his diary, as well as the poems, make us realise how close Hardy's art is not to ideas but to daily impressions; and also to wonder what other poets – Rossetti say, or Swinburne – actually looked at in the streets? How much, for them, were ideas and the music of language a barrier to appearances?

But if Hardy only looked closely at things and people, like a 'realist', we should have none of his peculiarity. This is where the anthropomorphism not only 'confuses persons and things' but mixes them up with figments of God as well. Although like all artists he in fact protects himself and us from the consequences of appearance, by his own version of what Robert Graves calls 'the cool web of language', he cannot go on to the kind of large-scale synthesis which nineteenth-century literature made a surrogate for God, whether in *The Ring and The Book,* or later in *A La Recherche du Temps Perdu.* Vanished days are for Hardy a procession of creatures each quite different from the other. *A Procession of Dead Days* is a poem of extraordinary

happiness, conveyed by the feel of each day in memory, and
their fortunate obliviousness of their fellows –

> I see the ghost of a perished day;
> I know his face and the feel of his dawn:
> 'Twas he who took me far away
>   To a spot strange and gray:
> Look at me, Day, and then pass on,
> But come again: yes, come anon!
>
> Enters another into view;
> His features are not cold or white,
> But rosy as a vein seen through:
>   Too soon he smiles adieu.
> Adieu, O ghost day of delight;
> But come and grace my dying sight.
>
> Enters the day that brought the kiss:
> He brought it in his foggy hand
> To where the mumbling river is,
>   And the high clematis . . .

The absorption is wonderfully endearing, yet as a phrase
like – 'Ah, this one. Yes, I know his name' – shows, it is the
kind of rapt and homely absorption that would once have
belonged to devotional poetry:

> In semblance of a face averse
> The phantom of the next one comes:
> I did not know what better or worse
>   Chancings might bless or curse
> When his original glossed the thrums
> Of ivy, bringing that which numbs.
>
> Yes; trees were turning in their sleep
> Upon their windy pillows of gray
> When he stole in. Silent his creep
>   On the grassed eastern steep . . .
> I shall not soon forget that day,
> And what his third hour took away!

The unnamed affliction borne by the last day does not cancel the feel of the others, hardly even sobers it indeed. Herbert and Crashaw would be at home with a day that brought a kiss in his foggy hand, but like the image of the last stanza – the trees turning in sleep on their pillows – only Hardy could have written it. The odd procession are not really even members one of another in the anthropomorphic fold. Yet that joyful reverence in the reception of the days is the tone of Herbert, and Stinsford was holy ground to Hardy as his church at Bemerton was to Herbert – except for the dogma the location rested in.

The fervour comes home to us as if we shared an essential orthodoxy, which in a sense we do, for Hardy is the reverse of heretical. He does not substitute a new belief or attitude but continues in the old one, having ceased to believe it. His poetry is an aspect of the liturgy, God having as solid an existence in his art as he did in the old worship. For the saints, and a saintly poet like Herbert, humour is part of a secure belief; and it is typical that Hardy still assumes this kind of security, the belief having gone. An analogy might be a crematorium service, where the element of comedy in such a disposal can be taken quite naturally so long as the traditional rubric and prayers are said. But in a 'humanist' service in such a place complete gravity is a must, a rigidity of demeanour attending on the kind of seriousness required by unbelief.

In Matthew Arnold's church, where religion is 'morality touched by emotion' we must not laugh. This is where Hardy's humour came unstuck with the public; reaction to it hurt and puzzled him, as his comments in the preface show. And oddly enough we may still find it as difficult to 'smile with him' as his original audience did, though for a different reason. His metaphysical mock-ups of God's activities and behaviour are no doubt humorous with intent – 'fanciful impressions' as he calls them in a letter of defensive protest to Alfred Noyes – but like all Hardy's fancies they seem as matter-of-fact to the reader as if he were standing in the nave, looking at the empty chancel and listening to the clock ticking in the tower. *God's Education* and *God's Funeral* are like this, as is the poem called *Fragment,* in which a vast crowd queue up 'waiting for God *to know it*' – to know, that is, as they already do from experience, the nature of the world he has created. To rationalist readers these may once have seemed childishly outlandish theories, to others jokes in bad taste. For us, today, they are too laborious to seem jokes at all, but their literalness remains. They seem, so to speak, earnest without being serious.

Like many another mover with the times Browning tried in his poetry about God – sometimes too hard we may feel – to be serious without being earnest. Hardy noted that the *Athenaeum*'s obituary on Browning stated that 'intellectual subtlety is the disturbing element in his art', and remarks that this 'is true, though not all the truth'. Although a lifelong admirer of Browning, he may have felt it was that air of worldly fellowship in subtlety and speculation which had made Browning 'all right', alike with intellectuals and believers. Blougram and others did not really disturb but glossed over, as – for all its apparent trenchancy – does the conclusion about the Christian faith and original sin in 'Gold Hair: A Story of Pornic'. It is Browning's God speech that now seems outmoded, while Hardy's lives by its refusal ('Tense, musty, unignorable', as Philip Larkin writes about the church in his poem *Church Going*) to first conjure up and then conjure away the grounds of debate.

In Hardy these remain as solid as old church furnishings. The same is true of the examples, like the unborn pauper child, whose existence makes God's position so anomalous, though no less literal for that. In *The Journeying Boy* Hardy modifies a line from Swinburne, in which he also describes his own early days in London – 'Save his own soul he hath no star':

> Knows your soul a sphere, O journeying boy,
>   Our rude realms far above,
> Whence with spacious vision you mark and mete
> This region of sin that you find you in,
>   But are not of?

The boy as a being does not belong to this world, a fancy seeming incarnated in fact by his indifference to where he is, and where going. In the same way *The Darkling Thrush* is a divine harbinger, and the blinded bird divinity itself –

Who hopeth, endureth all things?
Who thinketh no evil, but sings?
Who is divine? This bird.

The directness disturbs, and moves, because it is as uncompromising as the dogma it opposes. In *While Drawing in a
Churchyard*, the soughing of the yew reveals that the dead under
their stones are quite conscious, and perfectly pleased with their
quiet abode, but that instead of waiting in sure and certain hope
of resurrection

> That no God trumpets us to rise
>   We truly hope.
>
> I listened to his strange tale
> In the mood that stillness brings,
> And I grew to accept as the day wore pale
>   That show of things.

The pay-off of such poems should make them seem facile, but
such a possibility is discomforted by the way in which they cling
to the location of belief, far more devoutly than do its apologists
or modifiers.

This does not seem quite like 'fanciful impressions'. And in
fact Hardy may have shocked his readers by the smallness of the
change he made. Church and churchyard are as animistic
without God as with Him, or more so. The dead do not
disappear with the loss of belief in Him, but remain where they
were, awaiting the resurrection while hoping it won't come.
The reversal is indeed 'strange', and in his still way Hardy is
quite prepared to be challenging about it. His vision of the dead
is as absurd – as totally uncontemporary that is – as the old idea
of them waiting the Last Trump. This must have riled
conventional Christians by taking the business of bodily
resurrection more literally than they were accustomed to do;
while to enlightened believers and non-believers it seemed a
grotesque notion expressed with strangely inappropriate intensity.

The Darkling Thrush was no doubt a relief to them all (as
Hardy records) but it is actually the same kind of poem. Despite

Hardy's extreme interest in ideas and new theories, the objects of his imagination remained obstinately unaware of public opinion and the climate of change. How much so can be shown by another reference to *Church Going,* and its concluding lines. 'A serious house on serious earth it is', because human needs are ritualised there and cannot grow obsolete:

> Since someone will forever be surprising
> A hunger in himself to be more serious,
> And gravitating with it to this ground,
> Which, he once heard, was proper to grow wise in,
> If only that so many dead lie round.

Like many of Larkin's it seems a poem very much akin to Hardy, but its success in fact depends on a totally different tone. This is concentrated in the word 'serious', used of an instinct which still attracts people towards a church, which has nothing to do with belief, indeed is 'what remains when disbelief has gone'. The poem is faintly ironic about this reaction and yet wholly sympathetic to it, a combination in its quiet way highly collusive with the reader and rather flattering to him. We are dispossessed but sensitive people, humorous about our losses and our persisting nostalgias. In the metre and cadence there is an echo of *The Scholar Gipsy,* also a collusive poem with a wryly humorous note behind it, not so much in its tone as in the way it draws us into the higher intimacy with Matthew Arnold, as kindred souls who know and perceive as he does.

No wonder Hardy was not able to persuade readers into this kind of intimacy, and make them smile regretfully with him. Larkin's humour, and perhaps Arnold's too, is subtly successful in committing the reader to it before disclosing itself. It makes us realise how intimate is the kind of poetry with which Hardy seems to have most in common – going back to Wordworth and Cowper; and how careful to keep its tone, especially its humorous tone, such poetry usually is, even to the point of gratifying, as Larkin's does, 'known habits of association'. For better or worse, Hardy is always independent of such intimacy.

His verbal peculiarities are of course predictable – Max Beer-
bohm did an excellent verse parody – but his *tone* never quite is.

The thrush, for instance, crops up again in a comic poem about
one who has been caught by men, and hopes to learn from
them – 'How happy days are made to be'. But, escaped back to
the other birds, he has to report that this secret:

> Eludes great Man's sagacity
> No less than ours, O tribes in treen!
> Men know but little more than we
> How happy days are made to be.

As the portable ambiguity (made by whom?) suggests in the
refrain, Hardy enjoyed the 'scrabble' possibilities of the repetitions in these verse forms. In another, the villanelle becomes an
exceedingly ingenious triolet –

> Around the house the flakes fly faster
> And all the berries now are gone
> From holly and cotone-aster
> Around the house. The flakes fly – faster
> Shutting indoors that crumb-outcaster
> We used to see upon the lawn
> Around the house. The flakes fly faster,
> And all the berries now are gone.

Larkin follows Hardy in having joke poems among the serious
ones, but Hardy uses just the same sort of anthropomorphism in
poems of all kinds, thus further confounding and cutting off the
reader's expectations. The birds are treated as 'unseriously' as
religion, a fact all the more evident if we recall a famous poem of
Sassoon, another of Hardy's admirers – 'Everyone suddenly
burst out singing'. It is an emotional poem, the reader's emotion
readily following the poet's into the region where

> My heart was shaken with tears, and horror
> Drifted away

and where inarticulate beauty and a benighted world are all of a piece. The poem movingly succeeds, but in its atmosphere of wistfulness and elevation Hardy's ingenuities about feeding birds or talking birds would be quite out of the question.

The point seems to be that nothing is expected by Hardy of his animistic fancies: sometimes he attaches weight to them and sometimes they act as a playful statement. He and the poem are happy either way. This absence of discrimination is essential to his art, and to its disorientation of the reader. 'Seriousness' is equally definable in Arnold and Eliot as in Philip Larkin, but where does it fit in with Hardy? The answer seems to be that it is wholly taken for granted, and does not have to display its credentials, as modern seriousness usually feels it must. In Hardy seriousness and humanity are equally commonplace, as for Herbert again, or for a mediaeval poet. And yet nothing could be more typical of the best nineteenth-century thought than Hardy's humanity – 'an intensely humane man', like his own Gabriel Oak, and his poems intensely humane poems.

Another paradox arrives here. All I have been saying about his attitude to church, the gulf between his imagination and Arnold's religious culture, would suggest that he would be as much on the side of the old liturgy and traditional Anglican pieties as Eliot has been in our own time, or John Betjeman. Not a bit of it. His literalness revolted from the Creed and the General Confession: he wanted 'services with no affirmations or supplications'. He merely shrugged at the 'comic business' of church restoration, which he had worked on himself professionally (of an architect friend who had supervised the demolition of All Saints, Dorchester, because its buttresses interfered with the pavement, he observed that 'a milder-mannered man never scuttled a sacred edifice'). But he was earnestly on the side of 'rationalising' the rubric, and, curiously enough, he connects this in the *Life* with the Preface he wrote for *Late Lyrics and Earlier*. 'Some of his friends regretted it', he wrote, 'thinking it betrayed an oversensitiveness to criticism which it were better the world should not know'.

But sensitiveness was one of Hardy's chief characteristics, and without it his poems would never have been written, nor, indeed, the greatest of his novels. An interesting point in this Preface was his attitude to religion. There had been rumours for some years of a revised liturgy and his hopes were accordingly raised by the thought of making the established Church comprehensive enough to include the majority of thinkers of the previous hundred years who had lost all belief in the supernatural.

The new Prayer Book was a disappointment however; the revision had not been 'in a rationalistic direction, and from that time he lost all expectation of seeing the Church representative of modern thinking minds'.

But did he ever? – or at least could one possibly think so from the poems? They would not be at home – nor were they – in the company of 'modern thinking minds'. What seems odd here to us did not necessarily do so to Hardy, and we must allow for the subterfuge of writing the book in his wife's name, and all the pieties about himself he perhaps took a certain puckish pleasure in putting in. Even so, the impression his poems make is hardly that of a large-minded rationalist anxious to accommodate all men of good will under one roof. That kind of enfeebling good will is not alien to his intellectual temperament, but to his creative being. Whether on behalf of helpless animals, or 'hard-run humanity', Hardy's good will and pity are direct and total, but he shows no spirit of compromise or saving the appearances in matters of belief and the First Cause.

Even when he is handling the simplest of episodes from 'common life', Hardy's text – whether in prose or poetry – can be so absorbed in its subject as to be far from clear in relation to response – his or ours. Again, this may be because the writing part of him is not concerned with what we think. Take *The New Boots*, in *Winter Words*, which may be a poem of Hardy's old age, or from much earlier, or a re-working:

> 'They are his new boots,' she pursued;
> 'They have not been worn at all:
> They stay there hung on the wall,
> And are getting as stiff as wood.
> He bought them for the wet weather,
> And they are of waterproof leather.'

'Why does her husband,' said I,
'Never wear those boots bought new?'
To a neighbour of hers I knew;
Who answered: 'Ah, those boots. Aye,
He bought them to wear whenever
It rained. But there they hang ever.'

' "Yes," he laughed, as he hung them up,
"I've got them at last – a pair
I can walk in anywhere
Through rain and slush and slop.
For many a year I've been haunted
By thoughts of how much they were wanted."

'And she's not touched them or tried
To remove them. . . . Anyhow,
As you see them hanging now
They have hung ever since he died
The day after gaily declaring:
"Ha-ha! Now for wet wayfaring.
They're just the chaps for my wearing!" '

The metre is perfectly adjusted to the leisurely onset of
anticlimax in each stanza, and whatever our first impression the
poem may come to seem more effective whenever we re-read
it. The dialogue itself has the unfathomable quality of such
rustic exchanges. Whatever the two were talking about, when
an unrecorded query or glance prompted the explanation
'pursued' in the first line, it could not have been the husband. His
death has not been mentioned, nor is it now. Does the woman
take it for granted? – the narrator not like to ask? An elemental
tradition of closeness and formality is thus manifested in the first
stanza, and succeeded by the more relaxed dialogue of man and
man, narrator and neighbour by presumption. The question
must be pondered, not answered directly. 'Ah, those boots.
Aye'. The neighbour is a man whose pauses can be conveyed,
even in a rhyming poem, by the mimicry of the fullstops in
mid-line. In his report of it, the dead man had quite a different
style of speech, as naturally colourful as the idiom of Tranter
Dewy or Joseph Poorgrass – visions of boots – 'just the
chaps' – had 'haunted' him. The neighbour reproduces this

colourfulness with instinctive fidelity but also with a kind of conscious and sardonic grimness, as if fancy sentiments couldn't save you, although they are all that now survive of the deceased, hanging as a curiosity in a living memory, as the boots still do in the physical world.

The effectiveness of the poem is that it is written by a novelist. In various ways all Hardy's poems are. It is not pictorial or exhortatory – nothing of Van Gogh's expressive picture of the boots about it. The poem is in its way a detail in the close fabric of invention which includes all the poems and novels. This makes anthologies unsatisfactory, just as extracts from the works of fiction would be. Larkin has remarked that the poetry shows its peculiar qualities in the fact that one would not want to do without any bit of it – every new perusal produces good things never found before, and perhaps never found again, for their number and closeness means that it is as difficult to keep track among all the poems as it is among prose.

Even a good selection of them, like that of John Crowe Ransom, is misleading, in that it stresses a particular aspect (in his case what he calls the 'fables') rather in the same way that emphasis on 'powerful' scenes in the novels – fine passages, or tragic effects, in them – can also mislead. Like the novels the poems have a complete texture. Donald Davie points out that there has never been any concerted agreement about a best selection, and – though he does not say so – the reason may lie somewhere in their fictional skills and obfuscations. It is probably true, for instance, that the rule of thumb suggesting that the 'best' are the autobiographical poems written after the death of his first wife, does not really meet the case.

At the same time, readers who are enthusiastic about the same sort of scene in the novels are apt to draw the line at such a poem as *The New Boots*. This seems illogical to me, for the poem works in the same ways, and with the same complexities of observation, detachment, and sympathy, as the domestic scenes and exchanges in prose. Above all it is instinct with Hardy's 'animula', which seems pervasively present – whether in prose or verse – when the attitude of another writer to his material would be expected most to show. Hardy's personality is there, but not his attitude.

But the reader's expectations may be different where verse is concerned, and why not? He expects something the form, in its precedents, seems to promise. In Wordsworth he would get it, for we are accustomed there to finding such a form inherently meaningful, 'full of matter', as in *We are Seven* or *Advice to Fathers*. But Wordsworth would not get the inner scene and the detailed knowledge – acoustic knowledge in particular – which Hardy in his relaxed way commands. The poet's presence is both exact and normal: he is one of the neighbours, himself a private man, not a writer recounting something meaningful for our benefit. And he is really the same sort of person in the great poem *After A Journey:*

> Hereto I come to view a voiceless ghost;
>   Whither, O whither will its whim now draw me?

He enters the landscape of that poem, the landscape of his wife's old home, passing straight into the fictional as if from house to garden. His address to the ghost seems as oblivious of the reader as is Heathcliff of Lockwood in *Wuthering Heights,* when addressing the ghost of Cathy.

In one of his essays Eliot distinguishes between what he calls 'the three voices of poetry':

The first is the voice of the poet talking to himself, or to nobody. The second is the voice of the poet addressing an audience, whether large or small. The third is the voice of the poet when he attempts to create a dramatic character speaking in verse.

The three were important to Eliot, because he was in the habit of distinguishing so accurately between them. Hardy, we may feel, was not. Of course the effects in his verse were most carefully calculated, and he was put out when his readers assumed they weren't. He was obviously thinking of himself too when he wrote of Swinburne's poems:

> Fresh-fluted notes, yet from a minstrel who
> Blew them not naïvely, but as one who knew
>   Full well why thus he blew.

But he did not feel impelled to distinguish between himself and others when casting the plot of a poem. The shape and vocabulary of the poem is most carefully crafted, but not, in Eliot's sense, the scenario.

That is almost always a meeting, almost any kind of meeting; or a prospective one – 'a man was drawing near to me' – or one that did not occur. It may be three insects on a summer night meeting the poet on the page of his book. The record of encounter and what took place is the thing: though it may be striking enough, Hardy has no interest in *charging* the encounter with metaphysical energy and significance, as the young Hugo Von Hofmannsthal does in his remarkable poem *Die Bei-den* – 'The Pair' – which explores the ergonomics, as it were, of the meeting between a young man on a horse and a girl who brings him out wine from an inn. He reins in easily to take it; she lifts the brimming glass without spilling a drop, but at that moment

> . . . it was so much
> Too heavy for them both, they found,
> That each escaped the other's touch
> And dark wine spilt upon the ground.

Hardy, one feels, would have liked this poem; but done by him it would become a 'neutral-tinted hap', touching the origins of an anti-climax, although the sense of meeting would compel us just as much.

Something in his handling of meetings gives us the clue to the way Hardy fictionalises the self in his poetry, rather than dramatising it. That is to say he naturalises a self in a landscape or situation, instead of pointing up a situation to make a drama for the self. He makes no distinction between Eliot's three voices, and he never attempts to conceal his own self or transform it into a poet's persona. He can appear before us, as we shall see, with complete and startling candour, but there is no suggestion that he is doing so 'by special arrangement', as Browning does in the final poem of his 'Fifty Men and Women', presenting them to his wife with the sole comment he is ever going to make on their own relationship, such reluctance making it seem all the more exclusive.

The way fictions work in Hardy's poems becomes clearer if we compare them with those of a particularly subtle self-dramatist who greatly admired them – Robert Frost:

> The way a crow
> Shook down on me
> The dust of snow
> From a hemlock tree
>
> Has given my heart
> A change of mood
> And saved some part
> Of a day I had rued.

With allowance for a New England landscape, *Dust of Snow* could apparently have been written by Hardy. Its accomplishment does not pretend to make more than the simplest drop of point. Like Hardy in *The Wound,* or at the end of *A Procession of Dead Days,* Frost doesn't specify, but even on that scale he is able to make quite a thing out of *not* doing so. Donald Davie observes that Hardy 'imposes himself on the reader hardly at all'; that 'on page after page he bows and retires'. The metaphor of a stage appearance is well suited to Frost but not to Hardy, who never appears there before the reader in the first place. And Frost's careful settings-up can make us suspect he is himself inside a dramatic monologue, like that of the girl in *Wild Grapes,* with its arresting image of being pulled off her feet by a sapling:

> I had not taken the first step in knowledge;
> I had not learnt to let go with the hands,
> As still I have not learnt to with the heart,
> And have no wish to with the heart – nor need,
> That I can see.

We might note how firmly unobtrusive is the placing of 'heart' in *Dust of Snow*; and how that makes the repetition of the word here seem all the more likely to show the author refraining, in the same sort of way, from putting himself forward.

This cultivation of the personal touch is equally present in the Hardy-style turn of humour which ends *In A Disused Graveyard:*

> It would be easy to be clever
> And tell the stones; Men hate to die
> And have stopped dying now forever.
> I think they would believe the lie.

They would not if they were Hardy's stones. When Hardy speaks of the yew persuading him to 'that show of things', it is the dead who interest him, and us through him. By being clever, and deprecating the fact, Frost is fashioning the graveyard into an aspect of his own personality, making his poem equally effective but not a bit like Hardy. This may also suggest to us why Frost's rural tales in verse are much more exciting and compelling than Hardy's – marvellously compelling in some cases – for they have every intention of being so, and self-consciousness like an impresario makes the most out of them. By making positive and adroit all that in Hardy is negative and placid they not only 'score' for Frost (his own term) but augment his personality. One result of this is that it can be parodied. Hardy's, like all unconstructed personalities, cannot be, however much his diction and fabling may be open to such treatment.

In the scenario of one of his most memorable pieces, *Stopping by Woods on a Snowy Evening,* Frost's deprecative technique is especially marked; and Randall Jarrell's extremely witty change of a lower-case letter to a capital in its first stanza aims a point not at the poem but at 'the guy inside it', as Auden would say

> Whose woods are these I think I know.
> His house is in the village, though;
> He will not see me stopping here
> To watch his woods fill up with snow.

To read it as the colloquialism 'Village' – signifying Greenwich

Village for the artistic intelligentsia of the time – effects an instant scene-change; but only because the idea of some sophisticate with a snug property in these parts is quite in keeping with the actual theatre of the poem. Like all good parodic touches it brings out the way the magic works – what a careful, meticulous, *open* presence it reveals, and how deliberately the extreme simplicity invites the recognition that this is really a very complex thing. It is a masterpiece which fills up with more than snow, and Hardy would have much admired the technical way it is done – triplet rhymes in each quatrain with the blank word taken up in the next stanza, until the last buries every line with the same rhyme on 'deep'. Although the track of the poem is hidden in the sleep of snow, a complete domesticity in fact opens out from it, and it is this domesticity, set in a personal theatre, which becomes in the 'life studies' of Lowell and Berryman the most effective and as it seems the most native tradition in American poetry.

Our intimacy with Hardy is certainly not domestic, and has none of that disclosure which conceals nothing but offers an unfenced relationship. The fictionalised self of Hardy can, as it were, only be known by conventional social means, on the same terms as it knows itself the objects it invents. He is on familiar terms with his ghosts and gods, his meetings and misfortunes, but not familiar with them: it is because he isn't that he can invent and converse with them, as the poet converses with the widow in *The New Boots*. This is the importance of the difference from Frost, which I have been analysing with some labour. With Frost, as with Lowell and Berryman, there is finality in the achieved self-dramatisation; because there are no restraints and separations the picture can be complete, down to the fact, as Frost puts it in another memorable poem, that there may be 'no expression, nothing to express'. Hardy's boredoms are never as blank as this, for he writes not to 'score' but to sustain himself, and the lack of challenge in the things he writes about makes their day-by-day acceptability as subjects all the greater.

Imagining himself as other selves, and in other situations, Hardy also remains himself naturally present among these fictions. It is at least possible, though we cannot know, that

Shakespeare's Sonnets work in a somewhat similar way. Some of the misunderstanding about them may arise from the fact that they are made for pleasure as fictions of the self as well as realities – neither true nor 'made-up' but both – and that the tension of a sustained relational drama in them is illusory. Certainly in temperaments like Hardy's, and probably Shakespeare's, the artist's need to make direct use of emotion and experience has none of the fascination of self-scrutiny. Candour might equally apply to a fictional emotion, but when candid about himself Hardy does not always use fiction. We know how he felt at times about his relations with Emma, and in poems like *Had You Wept, We Sat at the Window,* and *Love Lost,* we can see with what clarity he expressed them. The autobiographical fallacy about the poems, put forward by Weber, or by Coleman and Deacon, assumes that since some poems are personal, many more must be. But we are entitled to see Hardy writing of Emma, since we know past any doubt, and from other sources, of their relation: since we have no facts about others in his life we are not entitled to deduce them from other poems.

Coleman and Deacon's researches are certainly of interest, and they may well be right that a relation closer than was supposed before existed between Hardy and his kinswoman, Tryphena Sparks; but there are far too many meetings and partings imagined in verse, and declarations or forebodings of pregnancy, to recognise his actual experience among them. We can certainly feel that *The Wind's Prophecy,* in which an 'I' travels through a coastal landscape, graphically evoked, away from a woman with dark hair whom he knows, and towards a fair-haired one he does not, must have been written after he met Emma, perhaps years after. Its emphasis is on the power of fate and the unforeseen, and the 'I' is as vigorously stylised as the landscape is rendered with relish and attack. Though detective critics make much of it, it seems a particularly clear instance of Hardy's fictionalising of the self, using his own and Everyman's experience to realise the idea that decisive moments in one's life are often like appointments in Samarra. Hardy, like Everyman, would be likely to know *some* woman well, when unconscious he was about to meet his fate with another one. Just the same

thing happens in a poem of which even more has been
made – *On A Heath:*

> There was another looming
> Whose life we did not see . . .

Even Hardy's recent biographer, Robert Gittings*, thinks this
must refer to a child who will be born, though he discounts all
external evidence that it could be Hardy's and Tryphena's. But
it is clear from the poem that the 'child' is in all likelihood a
more unspecified threat from the future, another portent of the
unknown life that has yet to impinge on one's own.

One may doubt if Hardy was the marrying kind: his younger
sisters and brother never took the step. And it is possible to
wonder whether the privacy which is the peculiar strength of
this poetry may not have been, in daily married life, a factor that
made for estrangement. It seems the certainty of privacy that
enables the poet to turn from equable and decorative narration
to intense and blunt analysis. Poems suddenly concentrate on
the poet's inability to see a wife as she is in herself, and the most
moving thing about those written after her death is how this has
been humbly accepted –

> All's past amend
> Unchangeable. It must go.

But *Love Lost,* seen from her point of view, is also a generalised
and fictionalised poem, and so is *Without, Not Within, Her* –

> It was what you bore with you, Woman,
> Not inly were,
> That throned you from all else human,
> However fair!
>
> It was that strange freshness you carried
> Into a soul
> Whereon no thought of yours tarried
> Two moments at all.

---

* *The Young Thomas Hardy,* London, 1974.

And out from his spirit flew death,
  And bale, and ban,
Like the corn chaff under the breath
  Of the winnowing-fan.

Two readings are possible, and it seems likely that both are close to Hardy's own experience. The woman could be his wife, or someone the speaker fell in love with, she remaining unknowing and indifferent. Across both possibilities the poem takes for granted the lack of understanding, which both inspired love and led to trouble. Perhaps it is the wife who suffers from the cruelty an unrequited affair brings out in the man? – perhaps it is the woman fallen for? The power to inspire but not to admit a passion brings woes all round; with its more sombre suggestiveness the simile recalls Shakespeare's compressed dual image of 'the bellows and the fan', that at once kindles and calms the ardours of Cleopatra. The deliberation, conveyed as so often in punctuation – the commas after 'bale' and 'ban' – underlines the intense and withdrawn violence in the poem.

It seems unlikely that these perturbations of feeling would be recorded as they are, had it not been for the narrative habit Hardy built up in his verse and made a part of his daily consciousness. Of the poems written after Emma's death Irving Howe has this to say:

. . . they show how a man learns not to tamper with his grief and not even to seek forgiveness in his own eyes. The kindness Hardy characteristically shows to all creatures he does not deny to himself, for he is free of that version of pride which consists in relentless self-accusation.

That is certainly true, but though not relentless it still *is* self-accusation; and it is a very Hardyan paradox that at such moments of self-reproach or self-analysis he seems least like his own self – that compendious 'animula' – but colourlessly and grimly impersonal. As in the Sonnets, the intimacy of such moments seems to enhance their anonymity, make them at once seen as a general part of human experience.

In general, though, Hardy's poetry loses in intensity what it gains in variety; and intensity in our time means keeping up the form and pressure of the poet's own being. 'Nature is a haunted house' said Emily Dickinson, 'and art a house that tries to be haunted' – a comment that suggests very well the area of intensity which her poems – and Frost's, and Lowell's – set up, and their *unremitting* quality, the avoidance of that relaxation which for Hardy is the area not of 'persona' but 'animula'.

He creates hauntings in every poem, but where nature and consciousness seem to have a timely and accepted meeting-place. Even so, his variety can be as disconcerting as another poet's intensity: there can be something positively eerie about his own disposability when invention suits. Some of the poems written in the first war take some evil to be deplored – such as the dividing of Germans from their English kinsmen by a few villains filled with 'Empery's insatiate lust of power' – measure the theme with the experienced eye of Marty South about to split a gad, and turn it out neatly divided into sonnet or quatrains. Thus *In Time of 'The Breaking of Nations'* ('Only a man harrowing clods . . .') reverses the platitude of its fellow poem, *In Time of Wars and Tumults,* each being technically as sufficient as the other, as characteristically marked and grained. A poem written two years later, in 1917, takes another commonplace of the time – 'if only I were young enough':

> Would years but let me stir as once I stirred
> At many a dawn to take the forward track,
> And with a stride plunged on to enterprize,
>
> I now would speed like yester wind that whirred
> Through yielding pines; and serve with never a slack,
> So loud for promptness all around outcries!

It seems useless to ask if this is how Hardy really felt, or if at that time of conscription and war-weariness he did not intuit what was happening to those who, in Wilfred Owen's words, 'die as cattle': and be glad to be out of it. A poet who strove for exigence in the self would ask that question, as Yeats was to do in one of his civil war poems, and by asking it inevitably make the question seem more important – in and *as* the poem – than any general response to the war. Hardy's poem is moving because it says what many older people were feeling; without losing any of its own quiddity his animula enters into a common and deeply felt emotion. The awkwardness is a sign that he is at home, and having taken the tone of Milton for his template, as it were, he still sounds like himself, and writes a moving poem in which the pines at Max Gate, or on the heath, identify his own privacy, which the poem otherwise sets aside. It is instinct with the same kind of presence that the novels have. And it is this presence which is lacking in *Wessex Heights,* to which – most uncharacteristically – he gave a date – 1896.

Wessex Heights is a defiantly personal poem, and all the more uncomfortable for it. The date records it as just after *Jude the Obscure* had come out, when Hardy was feeling persecuted and upset. The hills of Wessex, he tells us in the poem, become his refuge on such an occasion –

In the towns I am tracked by phantoms having weird detective ways –
Shadows of beings who fellowed with myself of earlier days:
They hang about at places, and they say harsh heavy things –
Men with a wintry sneer, and women with tart disparagings.

Down there I seem to be false to myself, my simple self that was,
And is not now, and I see him watching, wondering what crass cause
Can have merged him in such a strange continuator as this,
Who yet has something in common with himself, my chrysalis.

Although the poem is touching in what it reveals of Hardy's sense of having become 'a strange continuator' of 'my simple self that was', it is also depersonalised, in the way I noted about the story 'Barbara of the House of Grebe'. Of course the reason is quite different, but in both cases the fantasy, or animosity, which impels the work seems disastrously detached from its author. *Wessex Heights* might be appropriate to Hilaire Belloc, or even (particularly in its metre) to Kipling in the manic mood of many of his verses. When Hardy is stung into this kind of bravado he becomes, in a dispiriting sense, like other writers. And it is significant that the 'detectives' whom he mentions pounce on this poem for evidence of what he was up to, and for the identity of the 'rare fair woman' he refers to –

Yet my love for her in its fulness she herself even did not know;
Well, time cures hearts of tenderness, and now I can let her go.

That has not the piercing note of Hardy's rare analysis, but one
that is in the bad sense ordinary. The cliché poem about war has
all of Hardy in it: the personal one about his reactions to coldness
or to criticism has mysteriously little.

This may seem a perverse way of trying to get at the nature of
his originality, but I feel it gives us the clue; and that Donald
Davie has hold of the wrong end of the stick when he says that a
great poet could not be content with saying so little, and that
'the honesty of the honest journeyman is dishonest in the
master'. This means, I take it, that Hardy was betraying his real
talent when he wrote trivial things. I would feel that he did so
only when he wrote things like *Wessex Heights,* which has a
resentment that anyone might feel, but which in expression
takes away the quality of Hardy's personal being. It is true that
Wessex Heights gives a disarming account of his sense of lost
identity ('my simple self that was') under the spur of this
resentment, but in describing his loss of this Hardy also forfeits
the kind of consciousness which gives him – for us – that
identity.

It is something that is most there the more indifferent he is
about whether there is anything of interest or originality –
either in prose or verse – in what he is saying. At no time of his
life does this necessarily correspond with his own intentions. His
early verse naturally assumes a dramatic pose. The Browning-
style sonnets, *She, To Him,* which were written in 1866, and
about which he tells us that only a few survived, have a young
man's pleasure in the dramatic role, and enter with zest into the
congenial pose of saying something penetrating about female
psychology. In this they strikingly succeed, and are all the more
accomplished from the obvious influence of Browning's *Any
Wife to Any Husband.* The dramatic process throws the light
back, as with Browning, on the poet's powers of sympathy and
perception; and Hardy is revealed as a promising young man
with plenty of both. But the fictional process does much more
than just show what a good psychologist the poet is. Many years
and several novels later Hardy wrote *Expectation and Experience:*

'I had a holiday once', said the woman –
    Her name I did not know –
'And I thought that where I'd like to go
Of all the places for being jolly,
And getting rid of melancholy
    Would be to a good big fair:
And I went. And it rained in torrents, drenching
Every horse, and sheep, and yeoman,
    And my shoulders, face and hair;
And I found that I was the single woman
    In the field – and looked quite odd there!
Everything was spirit-quenching:
I crept and stood in the lew of a wall
To think, and could not tell at all
    What on earth made me plod there!'

This is a masterly fiction. There is no apparent intelligence,
either in the poem or behind it, only an absolute sense of the
woman's experience; and what brings it before us is not
sympathy and perception, dramatically displayed, but a nearly
invisible technique that has its firm touch on syntax and rhythm,
stops and restarts. The remorseless banality promised by the title
is fully borne out in the text, but, as in *The New Boots,* the real
interest of the poem is in the nature of its narrative continuity,
which gives the slow ellipses of country speech ('. . . a good big
fair: And I went.') an individual intensity of recall ('my
shoulders, face and hair') that contrasts with all absence of
pleasure in being the only woman there – advantage in singularity being merely drowned out.

   Such a poem shows how wide of the mark is Irving Howe's
comment that Hardy has an uncertain ear, and that his lines tend
to 'crumble' towards the close of a stanza or verse paragraph.
The awkward lack of congruence between the last line, and its
rhyme-partner four lines before, is clearly as deliberate as it is
effective: Hardy wearied of pointing out that these seemingly
slipshod rhythms were produced by care for a purpose. The
kind of reality they have is not only that of his prose fiction, but
an added undercurrent of humour – an aspect of the apparently
banal treatment of poetic form – as if Hardy was well aware of

the possibilities of making a joke out of his own literalness, as well as out of the obscure niceties of his technique. Implicit in this humour, 'animula' fills with its presence even such a bald and circumstantial narrative as that of the woman drowned out at the fair.

The kind of humour which records the woman's keen recollection of the fair, and herself at it, is directed by Hardy at himself in the poem which gives him the posthumous sobriquet of the 'man who used to notice such things'. He can touch us in a very simple way while also presenting the observations that do so in a manner that suggests a deliberate hint of the ludicrous. He seems willing to share a joke with us, while lacking the psychological equipment needed – the gift of bonhomie – and this can be baffling. Again there is a kind of split in the mode of communication: those who are touched simply by the art are not the audience who would respond to the traditions of rural humour. In so far as it assumes anything, the verse assumes the latter rather than the former response. 'I had been, as I thought', he remarks of the poems in *Human Shows,* 'rather too free in admitting flippant, not to say farcical, pieces into the collection'. And he seems to have recognised the sort of man he regarded as his right audience in a monk who once showed him the relics in a Roman church. 'Perhaps there is something in my appearance which made him think me a humorist also'. That he is a humorist – even too much of one – is his defence against critics who don't know a joke when they see it.

As a pose this could be far from attractive. But in fact Hardy's occasional emphasis on it only suggests a nature incorrigibly isolated and unpretending. When the humorist is obviously 'on duty' in his fictions – as in the scenes at the malt house in *Far from the Madding Crowd,* or in the church vault in *A Pair of Blue Eyes,* he has no trouble in making clear that 'his natural port was comick', as Dr Johnson said of Shakespeare. He was liberated by working in a medium he had taken on professionally, and he could get across to readers at home in the same medium. Even so, among the rustic humours of fiction, the fun is not exactly gregarious: every man enjoys his own.

In his fiction, as in general, humour can be a way for the author to defend himself, to be a public character. It is their unpublic and vulnerable nature that makes the humour in Hardy's poems hard to familiarise. But the unexpected thing is that just as many of them took historical tales for a model, in the manner of Scott and Southey, so his other first attempts – including probably those he originally intended to print in the text of *The Poor Man and The Lady* – have a hard brio which makes their drive and purpose immediately clear. They are lively, but unhumorous, with plenty of those flourishes of the knowing grotesque which are so effective in Browning's monologues. The poor man and the lady plight their troth together with a ring 'in the sight of God', but

> I was a striver with deeds to do,
> And little enough to do them with,
> And a comely woman of noble kith,
> With a courtly match to make, were you;

and inevitably she must in time have someone of her own class to be 'my husband *really*. You, Dear, weren't so'. Although the tone and the dash are Browning's, the emphatic sense of social necessity is Hardy's own; and in his poem it is not solved in the way in which fiction demanded when he came to write *An Indiscretion in the Life of an Heiress*, based on his first unpublished novel. The upshot of the poem is just, one feels, what would have happened:

> The track of a high
> Sweet, liberal lady you've doubtless trod.
> – All's past! No heart was burst thereby,
> And no one knew, unless it was God.

The story has to opt for, and make the best of, one of the most conventional of fictional endings – the mismatched heroine dying after committing herself wholly to her humble hero. But though the end of *The Poor Man and the Lady* poem, which Hardy printed late and described as revised 'from an old draft', is so tersely plausible, Hardy stylises it by bringing God into the last line, as Browning so often does. When he was young, and first in London, he probably felt most keenly the sting of his situation, as a non-gentleman strongly attracted, sexually and socially, to a culture over which the idea of the gentry presided; and not least for those champions of emancipated thought who would be his heroes, men like Mill and Arnold and Leslie Stephen. This was to remain both a hurt and an inspiration to him, but in the early days he was able to make use of it, as the novel suggests, and the early poems as well.

This, as well as their derivativeness, protects them from the vulnerability which was to be the most natural and characteristic part of his genius; it only shows when he moves from the dramatic technique to the fictional, together with the style of humour which is its odd but constant companion. If the self-dramatisation of the very early poems shows Hardy under Browning's tutelage, it did not last long. However much it owes to *May and Death* and *Two in the Campagna,* and possibly Rossetti's *The Woodspurge* as well, *Neutral Tones,* dated 1867, is already a complete Hardy poem:

> We stood by a pond that winter day,
> And the sun was white, as though chidden of God,
> And a few leaves lay on the starving sod;
>   – They had fallen from an ash, and were gray.
>
> Your eyes on me were as eyes that rove
> Over tedious riddles of years ago;
> And some words played between us to and fro
>   On which lost the more by our love.
>
> The smile on your mouth was the deadest thing
> Alive enough to have strength to die;
> And a grin of bitterness swept thereby
>   Like an ominous bird awing. . . .
>
> Since then keen lessons that love deceives,
> And wrings with wrong, have shaped to me
> Your face, and the God-curst sun, and a tree,
>   And a pond edged with grayish leaves.

I used to take it for granted, as I suppose most readers do, that the speaker was a man, the poet himself, however much the situation might be 'made up'. So he could be, although a girl would fit the case as well or better, and Hardy was often to imagine one in it, but the lack of emphasis in the poem extends to identities, as it blurs distinction between the invented and the real. Nerve and feeling, the power to resolve and act, are submerged in a clarity of enervation. The fidelity of texture to mood may make us aware, by contrast, of an incongruity in the positive *bustle* of rumination in Browning's *Two in the Campagna*; while Rossetti in *The Woodspurge* seems chiefly assiduous to make sure that we grasp the total *unity* of the experience – '*For perfect grief there need not be / Wisdom or even memory.*' Even when he is being his most subtle and sympathetic, Browning arrives at sententiousness as if it were the true goal, which for his poetry it indeed is. Success with him is in the energy with which he establishes what he set out to do, however deliberately off-key or oblique. Response in that vigorous world, even if a stunned one to grief, must indeed be 'perfect', whether it is the reaction of Childe Roland –

> I asked one draught of earlier, happier sights,
> Ere fitly I could hope to play my part . . .

or the wry conclusion of *Youth and art,* after the young singer and sculptor have missed their chance to love through concentrating on their ambitions

> This could but have happened once,
> And we missed it, lost it for ever.

For the poet, as for his characters, 'playing the part' is indeed the point, as Hardy plays it at the end of the Poor Man and Lady poem. 'No heart was burst thereby / And no one knew, unless it was God'.

This is the right quality of dramatic poetry, but the feel of fiction must correspond to its event. *Neutral Tones* shows that the tone even of Hardy's early poetry, like the textures of the prose, can be radically different from anything in its Victorian origins, more at home in the world of Chekhov or Pound or Virginia Woolf. There is no resolution between the participants of Hardy's poem, as there is none between the components of its tone and style. These are as effective together, yet as separated, as those in *The Darkling Thrush,* written thirty-five years or so later.

Such a poem has no centre in the poet, or his dramatised representative, with components grouped to lead all our attention back to him. Here he is only one among a number of characters, who may be 'persons', or 'things'. Any central focus to the poem is lost in the generalisation of the speaker's identity, which could be that of any one of Hardy's heroes and heroines, himself included. Notwithstanding the statement of the last verse, the 'I' is not the determinant of the poem, in which its events and conclusions are resolved. The narrators in Hardy's poems sometimes have a much odder relation to himself, the result of his making no effort to keep them at a dramatic distance. In *The Woman I Met,* written in 1918, the 'I' walks through West End streets and encounters a prostitute whose face he recalls, but who is now a ghost 'in a shroud that furs half-hid'. She avers she had loved him then because of his simplicity – 'a fresh bland boy of no assurance' – and reminds him that she had once on the pavement held up 'a costly flower' to his face. Years earlier Hardy had noted in his diary how a young girl had held a narcissus to his nose on a spring evening in Piccadilly. Characteristic is the memory of a meeting, fashioned into a poem by the device of the *revenant,* and the absence of awareness about how the poet's role in the affair might strike the reader. Rossetti was much more crafty in *Jenny,* his poem about a girl of the streets. With its usual simplicity Hardy's fantasy imagines such a girl madly in love with him; but in his contemplation of the episode, and his invention of a story in it, he seems unconscious of any oddity in the way he presents his day-dream.

Neutral Tones has phrases whose stageyness – 'chidden of God', 'ominous bird', 'God-curst sun' – make no contact with the feel of the occasion, but are related to it only through the Hardyan law of separation: as if the poet needed such concepts, as he will need ghosts and convergences, and talking birds and trees, to respond in art to the anti-climax of existence. Whether it is of apology, pathos, or embarrassment, that smile suggests only in retrospect anything so positive as the grin it hardly rose to at the time. Only in retrospect could it be dignified with the 'ominous bird' metaphor:

> And some words played between us to and fro
> On which lost the more by our love.

Both in syntax and rhythm these are the decisive lines. The sentence does indeed 'crumble', in the most effective manner possible, making the sense opaque at first, until we see that 'on' means 'as to', but more suitably, for the words exchanged are indeed *on* a subject, in detachment. It is an instance of the difference we noted between 'remissness' in Hardy's poetry and in his prose. The apparent lapse in the syntax here makes the sense more compact, not less. No doubt the words were as limp in fact as the lines pretend to be in art. There is a significant contrast with the Browning-like bravura in what might have been the similar poem of *The Poor Man and the Lady*. For whichever here is the 'I' of the poem, the concern of the lovers is concentrated in a numbed, unromantic way on the penal-ties – in a very practical and worldly sense – which each may incur from their relation. And both share a corresponding awareness of the workaday gloom of the occasion – a 'hap' gray rather than neutral tinted – even though only one will record it, or perhaps recollect it.

Many anecdotal moments emphasise a curiosity, a mild wonder noted in rustic lore or perpetuated in the poet's own mythology – in such a poem as *The Slow Nature* for instance – but the humour of *Neutral Tones* is not in the tale itself but in the telling: probably the first poem about which this is so, as it will be in *The New Boots* and *Expectation and Experience*. They had fallen from *an* ash, and were gray . . . The other sense of 'ash' hovers in the background, in characteristic separation from the tree, further isolated here by the curious precision of the indefinite article. The collapse, rather than fall, of the large straggling leaves round a single ash-tree is indeed a memorable sight. They look like the victims of an accident, and they are still more closely defined in the last line as 'grayish'. Hardy was quite capable of constructing the whole episode from this one sight alone, piecing together out of memory and imagination a story appropriate to the spectacle.

Early as it is, the poem shows how complete is the divorce between Hardy's sense of, and use of, nature, and that of the English romantic poets and their Victorian successors. In his textual language the objects of the world appear in disturbing or tranquillising isolation, unrelated to humanity, however populous with it. This is the basis of the humour of life, as of its impossibility.

IV

NO DOUBT HE ENJOYED THE HUMOUR. IT WAS ONE OF the ways in which consciousness made existence tolerable. So perhaps was imagining being in love when he saw a girl, and constructing a fantasy in verse or prose out of such possibilities. He enjoyed making something technical in rhyme out of a day-dream. I. A. Richards remarks that a poet who writes verses as Hardy did, 'as a method of sustaining and enriching his imaginings, will know how readily the technical interest of the chosen form can supplant and elbow out the poet's creative aim'. But no, Hardy shows no sign of either knowing about or caring about this. With him it is right that the tail should sometimes wag the dog; that the subtleties and not the *donnée* of the poem should determine the impression it leaves. In the same way we may be more at home in the space, time and texture of his novels than when we are receiving the whole impression of their scope and plan. For technical ingenuity with Hardy is actually an aspect of his vulnerability, that uneager reception that leads us deeper into the inside of the poem, its humour and its story, which makes the sudden sprawl of felled ash-leaves on a sunless day seem the expression of human pain, parting and indifference; all the vicissitudes that must – in getting through life – be taken on like responsibilities.

That responsibility had always depressed Hardy. *Childhood Among the Ferns,* probably an early poem in some form, although not collected until *Winter Words,* shows his attitude in the matter. In the *Life* he recalls pulling his straw hat over his face on a summer day, looking at the light between the chinks, and reflecting that experience had taught him not to want to grow up. The poem makes a small work of art out of the same kind of experience. Alone and sheltered, the child crouches in a shower under the tall green bracken, even when the rain begins to penetrate – 'making pretence I was not rained upon':

77

And queried in the green rays as I sate:
Why should I have to grow to man's estate,
And this afar-noised world perambulate?

That laborious last line is surely intended to recreate the forlorn
pomposity of childhood, at least of so precocious a child. In the
Life Hardy notes he confided to his mother, at about this time of
his childhood, his conclusions on existence – 'thinking she
would enter into his views' –

But to his great surprise she was very much hurt, which was natural
enough considering she had been near death's door in bringing him
forth. And she never forgot what he had said, a source of much regret
to him in after years.

Like his mother, Hardy did not forget the reception of this first
confidence. He may have been surprised, too, at his mother's
non-recognition of the fact that it was the happiness of his
childhood that prompted this disquiet about the life to come.
'Little Father Time' himself is created out of the humour of this
self-importance in the young, embodied in the last line of the
'Ferns' poem, as much as out of their bewildered pathos.

At moments the relation between subject and poet and
reader, for all its natural intimacy, is not unlike that Hardy
records between the parson at Stinsford church, and the little
boy Thomas who began to imagine that the parson was
'preaching mockingly', and that there was a humorous twitch
in the corners of his mouth, as if he could hardly keep from
laughter. Mockingly is never the word, but his art continues to
show a persistent recall of that early clerical context, diction
corresponding in some degree with its equivocal rubric. What
are we to make of Hardy beginning his poetic apprenticeship at
Westbourne Villas by attempting a rendering of Ecclesiastes in
Spenserian stanzas, until 'finding the original unmatchable he
abandoned the task'? A twitch of the mouth there? Certainly
our relation is more like the unpredictable one of congregation
and parson than the romantic or the Victorian relation of poet to
reader, or the modern one (bequeathed from Baudelaire) of
kindred spirits, fellow-bores or fellow-neurotics. Charles Mor-

gan observed that Hardy had 'the formal subtlety peculiar to his generation', which suggests the attitude of a particular epoch, between that of the poet as 'a man speaking to men' and as a man revealing his private history.

By turns droll and glum, Larkin often plays the parson, but with Hardy it seems not a role but a kind of conditioned recollection. The boy who studied the mouth of the Stinsford curate with such intentness was also unconsciously adept in the tones of the pulpit, hints of which reveal themselves in many poems. In the rural life of the time a sermon still had a curious status: its hearers expected little and yet could be keenly critical; and the form could equally produce impersonal nothingnesses or personal outbursts, both equally acceptable if blent with some care as a work of art.

The cadence is audible, together with psalm and hymn, in the openings of poems:

> At last I put off love,
> For twice ten years
> The daysman of my thought,
> And hope, and doing . . .

'Daysman' appears in context as the kind of church word a congregation might expect: even the punctuation suggests the pause they are used to. And the cadence is sad, but unperturbed, the two words Hardy noted as the parsonical tone in *Far from the Madding Crowd*. A sermon can also be refurbished and delivered again; Hardy tells us that he was quite glad later on that editors had rejected the poems he wrote in the sixties, which he retouched here and there and issued many years later.

While keeping the congregation in play the sermonist can think his own thoughts, which may emerge at moments with an unexpectedness that bothers nobody. Donald Davie makes a point of Hardy's expertise as technician, a sort of Victorian engineer in verbalising. Of the poem called *Overlooking the River Stour* he says that it is 'the work of a superb technician who dismays us precisely by his *superbia*'. The criticism takes for granted that Hardy is not only a technically ingenious talent but a wholly secular one. But though his verbal skills may resemble those of engineer or draughtsman, the way in which he organises his poems is often more like that of a cleric accustomed to his office. Davie makes what sounds like a cogent objection: that this poem 'provides more components than it uses or takes account of'; but that is just what a sermon was apt to do. The 'components' are both public and private aspects of performance, the doctrine and the individual presentation.

The River Stour scene is presented with great descriptive ingenuity. Swallows fly 'in the curves of an eight / like little crossbows animate', and a moorhen darts out, 'planing up shavings of crystal spray'. These bright animations held the poet's gaze, and he did not turn round – 'to see the more behind my back'. The upshot of the piece indicates that certain other things – domestic and personal – might have had his attention –

> O never I turned, but let, alack,
> These less things hold my gaze.

That is the homily, the vicar's voice pointing out how we fail in our duties, and giving a lively image of the sort of secular enticements which may make us do so. Davie, however, requires a drama, with 'the human presence, Emma's, in the room behind'; and he thinks that though the poet professes awareness of his neglect, he is still unaware of how much his own virtuosity, and his absorption in it, really means to the poem, the reader being distracted from the hypothetical Emma and the meaning she should bring to the poem, just as the poet was.

But does the poem work in the way Davie thinks it ought to? Hardy certainly did write miniature dramas, like *The Frozen Greenhouse* and *Lost Love,* which are both expertly cantilevered and adjusted naturally to personal experience. But the tone of fiction, and of the sermon, is more complex. What is the relation of these 'less things' that held his gaze to the jeweller's images he sets them in? The relation of memory to visual or physical impression always fascinated him. He described it in a sentence probably left over from *The Poor Man and The Lady* as 'a state of mind which takes cognisance of little things, without at the time being conscious of them, though they return vividly upon the memory long after'. In *Desperate Remedies* and *Far from the Madding Crowd* this idea receives graphic illustration, as we shall see, and is the most important way in which Hardy gets inside some of his characters, without either analysing or taking them over. The wry humour hidden in the River Stour poem is in the relation between the original dreamy Coleridgean contemplation of the scene, and the phrases now used to describe it. Their virtuosity comes after the experience, and their vividness is not due to the things in themselves but to memory. The poet was not phrase-making as he gazed at the moorhen and the swallows, but it is them he now remembers, because of the state of mind engendered by inattention to human matters, and it is them he now celebrates in precision-turned images.

The parson draws the open moral, the poet makes a more secret pilgrimage and a mental connection. The process is related to that whereby Hardy renders, in the 'Ferns' poem, the child's forlorn and solemn sense of the future with a laboriousness appropriately adult, touching it with a gentle comedy of retrospection. Associations of place and language have an inner meaning for him, as appears in the poem *By the Barrows*, impossible as always to date, but probably early, though it was printed in 1909 in *Time's Laughingstocks*. What it says is plain and forceful:

> Not far from Mellstock – so tradition saith –
> Where barrows, bulging as they bosoms were
> Of Multimammia stretched supinely there,
> Catch night and noon the tempest's wanton breath,
>
> A battle, desperate doubtless unto death,
> Was one time fought. The outlook lone and bare,
> The towering hawk and passing raven share,
> And all the upland round is called 'The He'th'.
>
> Here once a woman, in our modern age,
> Fought singlehandedly to shield a child –
> One not her own – from a man's senseless rage.
> And to my mind no patriots' bones there piled
> So consecrate the silence as her deed
> Of stoic and devoted self-unheed.

It grows on one, like so many, and shows how his central simplicities can move all the more for having the detachment of the sermon about them, its offical phrases co-existing with ones much more intimate to the poet's pleasure. We may remember that at the end of *The Return of the Native*, Clym Yeobright, Hardy's favourite among his heroes, takes to preaching, on Egdon and roundabout, on 'morally unimpeachable subjects'. Crabbe and Barnes were real clergymen where Hardy was not, and although not at all clerical their poetic utterance is much more uniform than his. Neither uses phrases so obviously sermon-worthy as 'desperate doubtless unto death' – 'in our modern age' – 'and to my mind'. There is no element of parody in these: they are completely natural to Hardy's conditioning; yet they are quite separate from the phrases of his own private imagining. Without meaning to, they have the unperturbed quality that marks off the treatment of the poem's subject from the more familiar kind of romantic or humanist sententious-ness – Wordsworth's again, and George Eliot's. Like so many of Hardy's, the poem's information moves us while its expression is intriguing us on a quite different plane. The woman's deed is greater to Hardy's mind than that of the 'patriots' who have left their bones under the heath, but his antiquarian pleasure is in the thought of the two events succeeding one another, across a great interval of years.

'Multimammia' is an appropriate image for the woman – the child *not* her own – but it is also more subtly agreeable to his own sense of the landscape. This comes out in his repetition of the phrase (unless the poem is later, which seems unlikely) towards the end of *The Mayor of Casterbridge*. Henchard leaves the town for the last time, and takes his way past the north side of Egdon, where tumuli, 'dun and shagged with heather, jutted roundly into the sky from the uplands, as though they were the full breasts of Diana Multimammia supinely extended there'. In the novel, as in the poem, the reference seems a kind of separate pleasure to Hardy, and through him to us, for it has no connection with Henchard. It draws attention to the private side of the novel, a private side all the more marked, in such touches as this, because the novel is in its general case and aspect so decidedly public. Hardy borrows Lear for his official image of

Henchard's destiny and ending; yet it is not Henchard but Elizabeth-Jane – not his daughter although at one time he thinks she is – who is seeking for him past the barrows when Hardy makes his comment on them. And she is the novel's most private person.

Almost the identical phrase is repeated when Tess is travelling over the uplands of Wessex, seeking the farm work she eventually finds in the bleak environs of Flintcomb Ash:

Towards the second evening she reached the irregular chalk table-land or plateau, bosomed with semi-globular tumuli – as if Cybele the Many-Breasted were supinely extended there – which stretched between the valley of her birth and the valley of her love.

In the context this seems an echo rather fatigued and mechanical, an attempt to get some more – and more pressingly symbolic – service out of Cybele: here joined in an association with Tess's birth and love that, like much else in the novel, insists too much on its meaning. To query the symbol is to find it will hardly do, for the many-breasted is situated in this purgatorial and inhospitable land, away from the valleys of fulfilment. This is no matter, but what is depressing is the absence of that privacy of pleasure which we shared in the other contexts, and which expands and aerates the whole narrative. In *Tess* there is little of what is elsewhere such a typically Hardyan contrast between the public and the private.

In *The Mayor of Casterbridge* we have it both in style and form. Henchard has no intimacy, with his own mind or any other's. His unseeing power is suited to the most impressive kind of representational treatment, Lear being invoked in parallels full of meaning. But the Multimammia image comes from the other and more intimate side of the book – Hardy's and Elizabeth-Jane's side as it were – for Henchard is all the more impressive a figure in that he is cut off from Hardy himself. Hardy does not seek to enter into the character that is the man's destiny. He knows he is not close enough to do so, and that gives his hero the isolation which is so effective a part of the artistic treatment. It is Elizabeth-Jane's consciousness, with all it has discovered of sorrow and learnt by self-improvement, which brings the novel to its end –

The finer movements of her nature found scope in discovering to the narrow-lived ones around her the secret (as she had once learnt it) of making limited opportunities endurable; which she deemed to consist in the cunning enlargement, by a species of microscopic treatment, of those minute forms of satisfaction that offer themselves to every person not in positive pain; which, thus handled, have much the same inspiriting effect upon life as wider interests cursorily embraced.

'Finer movements . . .' the cunning enlargement of 'minute forms of satisfaction . . .' 'inspiriting effect upon life . . .' this seems very like the recipe for, and the point of, Hardy's own verses, perhaps his art in general? 'Minute forms' of private satisfaction are passed on to the reader; and the comparison involving the Egdon tumuli is one of them. In considering Elizabeth-Jane's consciousness, and its relation to Hardy's, we might remember her prolonged visit to the museum, sent thither by Lucetta to get her out of the way when Henchard is coming, and Lucetta's mild gibe that she will find all the old stuff so interesting she won't be able to tear herself away. Such things form the unobtrusive inward part of the novel whose front is dominated by the figure of Henchard, and of Lucetta and Farfrae too, kinds of consciousness to whom author and reader have no inner access.

One of our major pleasures in Hardy is not only the museum of his mind, but his own attitude towards it. In one sense it connects with his parsonical side: he shows us what he knows with the relish of a sermonist proving himself agile in scriptural text and interpretation. His passion for painting and literature is infectious, and his communication of it wins the sympathetic reader completely. At the same time something in him does not want to share or display it, like a child who keeps favourite things secret, so they shall not lose their power and fascination over him. 'Because we are *ourselves*', as he remarks near the opening of *Desperate Remedies,* our future seems to us altogether special, no matter how it may seem to resemble that of many others, and so do our possessions. His apprehension of this is like no other writer's.

The case is put with delightful simplicity in the case of Egbert

Mayne, the ingenuous young hero of *An Indiscretion in the Life of An Heiress*. This *nouvelle* Hardy abstracted from the body of his unpublished first novel, but though it appeared in English and American magazines in 1878 he did not allow its inclusion in his collected works. Mayne's reflections, as he sets out to make name and fortune in London, may well be identical with those of Will Strong, the hero of the vanished novel:

. . . several habits which he had at one time condemned in the ambitious classes now became his own. His original fondness for art, literature and science was getting quenched by his slowly increasing habit of looking upon each and all of these as machinery wherewith to affect a purpose.

A new feeling began to animate all his studies. He had not the old interest in them for their own sakes, but a breathless interest in them as factors in the game of sink or swim. He entered picture galleries, not, as formerly, because it was humour to dream pleasantly over the images therein expressed, but to be able to talk on demand about painters and their peculiarities. He examined Correggio to criticise his flesh shades; Angelico, to speak technically of the pink faces of his saints; Murillo, to say fastidiously that there was a certain silliness in the look of his old men; Rubens for his sensuous women; Turner for his Turneresqueness . . .Bonozzi Gozzoli was better worth study than Rafaelle, since the former's name was a learned sound to utter, and all knowledge got up about him would tell.

What is engaging about this would-be cynical statement is that we know its author was in fact still feeling the same private joy in the objects of study and contemplation. Gozzoli's name may be a learned sound to utter (which does not stop Hardy and his hero from spelling his first name wrong) but we suspect that neither of them enjoy him the less for showing off. Such a desire to impress is the opposite of snobbery; for the snob, whether in art or society, is concerned to follow the fashion and say and do the right thing, because he has no natural feeling for what it is. Such a feeling Hardy, and Egbert, possess overwhelmingly, yet we may say that the author was as painfully conscious as his hero of the difficulties they faced socially and intellectually; and what Egbert finds to be 'the evil when a man of his unequal history was possessed of a keen susceptibility'.

Keen delight in art and culture is sharpened by the sense of how to use them as assets, in pursuit not only of fame and fortune but of love itself. Egbert knows that he is not only in love but making use of being in love. The challenge of sex and class enhance each other, as does the feeling for books and pictures, and the realisation of how to make use of it.

The candour and intensity that survives in *An Indiscretion* exhibit a remarkable understanding of the behaviour and mental state of a young man so situated. Egbert finds a particular pleasure in calling his beloved Geraldine Allenville 'Madam', because it both suggests the majesty of her social position far above him – the social equivalent of Raphael and Gozzoli in art – while by 'using it at the warmest moments it seemed to change its nature from that of a mere title to a soft pet sound'. If indeed it survives almost unchanged from the vanished *Poor Man,* Hardy's delineation of the young persons' feeling for each other is remarkable for its shrewdness. Egbert 'even wished that he might own her, not exactly as a wife, but as a being superior to himself – in the sense in which a servant may be said to own a master'. For all his reading it seems unlikely that Hardy at this point had happened on the section in Hegel's Phenomenology entitled 'Master and Slave', but here he shows his own sense of what such relations involved; and subsumes them by implication, it seems to me, not only under the category of a human relation but with those of art and culture too. He both reveres and 'owns' the objects of his artistic and cultural pursuit.

When discussing *Tess* and the later novels I shall return to Hardy's presentation of social difference, but the point to notice here seems to me the very Hardyan relation of unobtrusive 'satisfaction' – of the Elizabeth-Jane kind – with sexual awareness and ambition. Hardy can both love and make use of art, however much the practice may smack of the 'ambitious classes', but he is well aware of how little the reality of other human beings is susceptible to these processes. He came to know – to put it in its crudest terms – how wide was the gap between the reality of Emma and the sense of her he had conceived, as Egbert does of Geraldine, and Clym of Eustacia. So that, to simplify for our immediate argument an obscurely and richly devious process, his characters divide into those who are aware, like Elizabeth-Jane, of the conditions which life seems to demand of them, and of the kind of rewards it offers; and of those who 'love it desperately', however little they may be aware of the fact, and who are for that reason outside – more or less – the kind of consciousness which Hardy disposed of, the kind of which he is the master in his poems. It is typical of him, and one of the signs of his uniqueness among novelists, that he has more interest in this unknowing class of person, than in those in whom he recognises, and to whom he gives his own sense of the 'show of things'.

In his account of this class there often appears a curious mingling of those two impulses which Egbert Mayne noted in himself – the natural fondness and the new deliberative animation – which distinguishes his way of bringing characters before us. It is not enough that Eustacia Vye, for instance, should appeal to him: he must expend all his artifice on 'learned' and ingenious means of describing that appeal. The result is inimitably characteristic. Eustacia is a 'Queen of Night', with 'Pagan eyes, full of nocturnal mysteries', and everyone remembers with what thoroughness Hardy sets about conveying the impression her appearance makes – or might be said to make if any of the cultivated readers whom he has in mind, and is presumably hoping to impress, had set eyes on her:

Her presence brought memories of such things as Bourbon roses, rubies, and tropical midnights; her moods recalled lotus-eaters and the march in 'Athalie'; her motions, the ebb and flow of the sea; her voice, the viola. In a dim light, and with a slight rearrangement of her hair, her general figure might have stood for that of either of the higher female deities. The new moon behind her head, an old helmet upon it, a diadem of accidental dewdrops round her brow, would have been adjuncts sufficient to strike the note of Artemis, Athena, or Hera respectively, with as close an approximation to the antique as that which passes muster on many respected canvases.

All this knowledge got up is intended to tell. But in the preceding paragraph there is much more of the 'humour to dream pleasantly' which was native to the young Egbert –

The mouth seemed formed less to speak than to quiver, less to quiver than to kiss. Some might have added, less to kiss than to curl. Viewed sideways, the closing-line of her lips formed, with almost geometric precision, the curve so well known in the arts of design as the cima-recta, or ogee. The sight of such a flexible bend as that on grim Egdon was quite an apparition. It was felt at once that that mouth did not come over from Sleswig with a band of Saxon pirates whose lips met like the two halves of a muffin. One had fancied that such lip-curves were mostly lurking underground in the South as fragments of forgotten marbles.

Those Sleswig pirates undoubtedly have the same status as the Diana Multimammia of the other contexts. Hardy is musing as himself, and the effect of his musing is an odd one for our image of Eustacia. We realise from it a pathos and involuntary comedy, even though we accept, too, that 'a true Tartarean dignity sat upon her brow, and not factitiously, or with marks of constraint, for it had grown in her with years'. This is not incongruity as a careful writer is able to administer it, but the lack of realisation, as between her appearance and her sense of herself at one time or another, which must be true of a living person but is extraordinarily difficult for a novelist to render with intent. Tolstoy contrives it of Anna Karenina though not, we may feel, with Natasha Rostov in *War and Peace*. In his exhaustive method over Emma Bovary, Flaubert could not possibly have arranged for such exuberance to catch him unawares, although he too might well have recorded something about Emma's physical being in the same objective spirit with which Hardy, a little earlier, notices Eustacia's hair. 'If, in passing under one of the Egdon banks, any of its thick skeins were caught, as they sometimes were, by a prickly tuft of the large Ulex Europoeus – which will act as a sort of hairbrush – she would go back a few steps and pass it again a second time'.

By these means Eustacia makes her impression; but the variations between them are such that she escapes any definition by the author, he seeming able, but hardly willing, to focus them and show them to us. So extremely literary is he about Eustacia that he is in the end not literary at all, in the sense that such a portrait in fiction would in general proffer a clear-cut

image of what the artist saw his portrait as representing. J. I. M.
Stewart sees the build-up of Eustacia

as an attempt – balancing the attempt to create a Clym Yeobright of
the highest representational significance for an entire world-view – to
give her inches, or a stature, which she has not, as it were, the hard
bone to carry . . . We are not quite sure what Hardy feels – or designs
us to feel.*

Is she, like Emma Bovary in James's view, too mean a
consciousness to justify the parade? But Stewart concludes that
though all the references to French roses and dramas, 'which
would sink most heroines for good' do not matter in the least
with so vigorous a concept as Eustacia shapes to be, we must and
do realise that she is 'only an ignorant and wayward girl who
plays at high passion, sees her fantasies fade in the bleak air of
Egdon, and is rescued from insignificance by a capacity for
suffering'.

The nature of Hardy's success is to make us realise nothing of
the kind. That blood-sport image of the 'hard bone' is apposite
to something in our impression of her, but if we were not sure
what Hardy feels, or designs us to feel, we would still not go
over his head, as it were, to conclude that Eustacia is only the
Emma Bovary of Egdon Heath. Hardy may indeed have his
Emma Bovary, as we shall see, but she does not live on Egdon.
And where Eustacia is concerned, the nature of her presentment
gives us no wish to help Hardy out by defining her ourselves: it
doesn't matter here that neither he nor we should be 'sure' of
what we feel. Hardy's sense of a place, and the person there, is
what matters; and this appears the more absorbingly factual the
more he loads it with literary suggestion. It is the literari-
ness – its intimate and Egbert-like quality – that neutralises the
movement towards 'representational significance', for it means
that what is carefully attributed, by Flaubert, to Emma
Bovary's literary idea of herself, is found in the romantic image
of Eustacia shared by her creator and readers.

Hardy sees her both with the charmed attraction with which
Egbert might have seen her before he embarked on his literary

* *Thomas Hardy*, London, 1971.

'sink or swim', and as he might have described her after. He always has the first kind of fascinated curiosity, watching her retrace her steps to let the tufts of gorse comb again through her hair (perhaps he once saw a girl do this). The result is a disintegrated portrait, such as only he was capable of, disintegration appearing not in our image of Eustacia, which is graphic and complete enough, but in the sense of romance and objectivity jostling each other without summation or issue. Emma Bovary is placed by her day-dreams: Eustacia is, so to speak, displaced and undefined by Hardy's. The images we get of her are as uncognisant of each other as the brain, back, and arms and legs of the old man at the railway station. Putting up her chin to her husband, Clym, to have her bonnet tied, she is for once unmindful of her appearance, because of his alienation from her. When drowned and laid out – 'the expression of her finely carved mouth was pleasant, as if a sense of dignity had just compelled her to leave off speaking'. 'Pleasant' – the unlikeliest word for the stormy Eustacia, is here strangely touching.

Certainly Eustacia, and Clym too, are not in any sense 'conceptions', of a Jamesian or Flaubertian kind. James would have spotted that Hardy was aiming, none the less, for something big in the way of a conception, as he was to do in *Tess,* and would have considered the result a facile and muddled failure. But she does not, as Stewart suggests, escape as a real person from under a weight of portentous verbal decoration. That decoration *is* her, both as she sees and as she is seen. It is right that she should remain an 'unadjusted impression', like one of the poems. The same is true – as we shall see – of Clym himself, and of Wildeve: all three have the provisional aspect which is the singularity of Hardy's success in such cases, and which comes from the relation – so unexpectedly harmonious in practice – between what was for Egbert Mayne a devoted simplicity of response, and his 'increasing habit' of looking at things 'as machinery wherewith to effect a purpose', the purposes of literature.

Literature, the display and evidence of it, the sight of its being laboured on in public, is not in Hardy a process that sinks or deadens or constricts, but has a wholly liberating effect: and all the more evident if we think of novelists – Faulkner, Patrick

White – who really may be felt to be imprisoned by the weight of their own literary process. Their extensive worlds may strike many readers now as constructed on an entirely literary basis, and to cling grimly to a style and purpose determined by it. Their characters are indeed conceptions, determined as much by uniformity of style as by the studied creation of a significant and typical socety, that of the American south or of Australia, in which they have their being. On the other hand, such a character as Conrad's Lord Jim could be said to owe much of his memorableness to a process not so very different from Hardy's. He remains unresolved because Conrad has to give him back ultimately, as it were, to literature, to a novelish ending. But he has made his mark as a kind of primary being, and even as the combination fails to realise him properly it adds to his interest, and to the kinds of importance and memorableness he possesses for the reader. Of course Lord Jim is utterly different from any Hardy character, but he may be said to benefit in something of the same way from the strength of his author's primary feeling for him, coupled with the wish to make use of him for 'effecting the purposes' of a study and a tale.

The two impulses in Hardy which he so candidly, almost ingenuously, allowed Egbert Mayne to expound, can also be secretive, as if they were hiding not only from us but from each other. If it were not so we should not have that sense of a relation between a silent man and a man who impelled himself into speech, and indeed into loquacity. The relation of the two can have its uneasy, almost painfully droll side, which comes out in the preface to *Late Lyrics and Earlier*; yet the duality in the novels, when the conscious Hardy does not seem aware of the preoccupied one, though he is intent on making us aware of everything else – is their most satisfying and singular quality.

At their most unsurprising his observations and comments draw from this background something that always seems out-of-the-way, a distance and detachment from the common-place, even when and as they aver it. The 'catenary curve' formed by the reins of the carrier's van which we encounter at the opening of *The Woodlanders*, is a wholly gratuitous piece of Egbertian knowledge, and yet it does make us feel the presence of the van, in the context of road and journey. In his *Notebooks* Hardy jotted many details of the itinerary of the Dorchester–London coach, which used to pass near Bockhampton, and the personality of its driver. He would not have bothered with catenary curves in those bits of recollection, but the novel does increase our feeling of the habitual nature of a van's journey, by way of a visual image of necessity in the lines of those reins. He must be the only author with whom displayed learning increases the clarity and simplicity of the picture, instead of blurring it. Anyone who imitates him, or learns from him, as later novelists of country life have done, gives the impression of being pleased with himself about his knowledge of country matters, and assiduous to impress us with them. Hardy somehow avoids this, and the reason is his dualistic approach, with its odd partnership of reluctance and exhibitionism. 'Our old friend Dualism', as he called it in that facetious poem from *Winter Words,* is certainly a 'tough old chap'.

In his art Hardy corresponds to his own God, the concept of whom as 'an external personality' is the corner-stone of dualism. Consciousness can never be at one with the world it inhabits. The writer is never at one with the observer, nor with the observed, and though their relations are never predictable we are always participating with them in an essentially dualistic world. It is especially marked in the earlier work; much less so in the two last novels, as if Hardy grew more aware of it as he grew older – as the *Winter Words* poem suggests. Egbert Mayne's discovery is a superficial sign of it, recognised with a youthful version of the facetiousness the elderly author put in his poem.

Desperate Remedies, his first published novel, has scenes which show its most relaxed and yet rewarding operation, like this passage from chapter nine. With problems on his mind which the complications of the plot have only just begun to indicate, the hero-villain Manston is returning to his house on the estate of Knapwater, where he has just taken up the position of steward:

After walking under the dense shade of the inky boughs for a few minutes, he fancied he had mistaken the path, which as yet was scarcely familiar to him. This was proved directly afterwards by his coming at right angles upon some obstruction, which careful feeling with outstretched hands soon told him to be a rail fence. However, as the wood was not large, he experienced no alarm about finding the path again, and with some sense of pleasure halted awhile against the rails, to listen to the intensely melancholy yet musical wail of the fir-tops, and as the wind passed on, the prompt moan of an adjacent plantation in reply. He could just dimly discern the airy summits of the two or three trees nearest him waving restlessly backwards and forwards, and stretching out their boughs like hairy arms into the dull sky. The scene, from its striking and emphatic loneliness, began to grow congenial to his mood; all of human kind seemed at the antipodes.

A sudden rattle on his right hand caused him to start from his reverie, and turn in that direction. There, before him, he saw rise up from among the trees a fountain of sparks and smoke, then a red glare of light coming forward towards him; then a flashing panorama of illuminated oblong pictures; then the old darkness, more impressive than ever.

The surprise, which had owed its origin to his imperfect acquaintance with the topographical features of that end of the estate, had been but momentary; the disturbance, a well-known one to dwellers by a railway, being caused by the 6.50 down-train passing along a shallow cutting in the midst of the wood immediately below where he stood, the driver having the fire-door of the engine open at the minute of going by. The train had, when passing him, already considerably slackened speed, and now a whistle was heard, announcing that Carriford Road Station was not far in its van.

But contrary to the natural order of things, the discovery that it was only a commonplace train had not caused Manston to stir from his position of facing the railway.

If the 6.50 down-train had been a flash of forked lightning transfixing him to the earth, he could scarely have remained in a more trance-like state. He still leant against the railings, his right hand still continued pressing on his walking-stick, his weight on one foot, his other heel raised, his eyes wide open towards the blackness of the cutting. The only movement in him was a slight dropping of the lower jaw, separating his previously closed lips a little way, as when a strange conviction rushes home suddenly upon a man. A new surprise, not nearly so trivial as the first, had taken possession of him.

It was on this account. At one of the illuminated windows of a second-class carriage in the series gone by, he had seen a pale face, reclining upon one hand, the light from the lamp falling full upon it. The face was a woman's.

In the earlier fiction the relation of such scenes to the whole is marginal, but none the less intimately satisfying. We have no trouble, while this action proceeds, in virtually becoming Manston himself, a state we share with both Hardys. Two of the four drop out, as it were, when it becomes necessary for the conscious Hardy to get on with 'effecting his purpose', and to propel Manston in the direction determined by the ingenuities of the plot. We are quietly dispossessed, and taste, rather than suffer, the characteristic disappointment. In this case it is the physical reality that leaves us – that 'careful feeling with outstretched hands', that 'sense of pleasure'. Manston realises that the woman he has just seen is his wife, who has found out his whereabouts by means yet unknown, and about whose existence he has so far neglected to inform either the young heroine with whom he has fallen in love, or his employer (who will later turn out to be his mother.) But both he and the silent unconscious observing Hardy will soon, we know, be back; and the pleasure of this knowledge accompanies our curiosity about the story, and sinks its ingenuities in a different and denser medium.

This relation with people, or a person – now unhesitatingly and congenially intimate, now merely docile and detached – is as typical as it is unobtrusive: once we become addicted we hardly notice what is going on. The natural, unconscious Hardy seems to know that place has the only stability, and that human beings are briefly real only when the intentness of the author focuses them as a part of it. Tess, however real to herself, is only 'a passing thought in other minds', and those must be the minds of her author and his readers. We become conscious of place through the presence of the character, who is not just a convenience for Hardy's ambulant awareness of things. For much of their other life depends on their creator's zealous facility with a plot; and thus Tess must be not just a consciousness but a prototype of the wronged maiden: Manston, or Wildeve, that of the rake and unscrupulous seducer. A natural incongruity arises, which we have already noted in more complex form in Eustacia's case; and we may feel, too, that their consciousness could not seem so clear at moments if it were not in abeyance for so much of the time, while other fictional tasks are going forward. There are consequences which I must try to analyse later, but the main point is that consciousness comes and goes, in a compelling rhythm; and that our sense of it in the characters is most present when the plot is momentarily at a stand.

Desperate Remedies gives the impression of a gap between the plot's determined progress, and the tenor of the prose, which gropes its way forward from exploratory touch to touch, like Manston feeling his way in the dark. In the passage quoted there is no sense of a preconceived climax, of the kind in *The Woman in White*. Neither is there any contrast, like that which Wordsworth contrives in Peter Bell, between the startling apparition and its natural explanation. The train itself, its fire-door, the woodland cutting and the imminent arrival at the halt, seem to mean more to Hardy's imagination than the sudden strangeness of the phenomenon itself. There is a typical cunning, too, but this time of the 'sink or swim' young author's kind, in the way in which Manston's attention is arrested at the moment when a natural sequence of events might have caused it to lose interest, by the figure he glimpses in the setting of those 'illuminated oblong pictures'. The commonplace and the sensational are fused; the excitement of being a kind of voyeur is mixed for Manston – and for ourselves – with the passive meditational aspects of the night and the trees, so that the observed and inhabited space of the novel becomes virtually at one with its melodrama. Not quite, as the graph of our involvement and disappointment reveals, for after two more paragraphs the chapter ends thus:

As he neared home, the anxiety lately written in his face merged by degrees into a grimly humorous smile, which hung long upon his lips, and he quoted aloud a line from the book of Jeremiah –
A woman shall compass a man.

This is not the Manston with whom we and the author have been in the silent relation of different entities in the companionship of nature at night, but the lay figure to be duly furnished with quotations from Hardy's well-stocked store. Yet even here Hardy's sense of physical continuity is evident, in the relation between walking and expression, the latter taking its meaning from the slow tempo of the former.

It is not likely that Hardy used the light and dark effects of Caravaggio and La Tour, whom he much admired, just because 'all knowledge got up about them would tell'. Like Multimammia and the Sleswig pirates they appealed for their own sake, and the scene foreshadowed in *Desperate Remedies* reaches its perfection in the meeting by night, after the shearing-supper, between Bathsheba and Sergeant Troy:

Her way back to the house was by a path through a young plantation of tapering firs, which had been planted some years earlier to shelter the premises from the north wind. By reason of the density of the interwoven foliage overhead it was gloomy there at cloudless noontide, twilight in the evening, dark as midnight at dusk, and black as the ninth plague of Egypt at midnight. To describe the spot is to call it a vast, low, naturally formed hall, the plumy ceiling of which was supported by slender pillars of living wood, the floor being covered with a soft dun carpet of dead spikelets and mildewed cones, with a tuft of grass-blades here and there.

This bit of the path was always the crux of the night's ramble, though, before starting, her apprehensions of danger were not vivid enough to lead her to take a companion. Slipping along here covertly as Time, Bathsheba fancied she could hear footsteps entering the track at the opposite end. It was certainly a rustle of footsteps. Her own instantly fell as gently as snowflakes. She reassured herself by a remembrance that the path was public, and that the traveller was probably some villager returning home; regretting, at the same time, that the meeting should be about to occur in the darkest point of her route, even though only just outside her own door.

The noise approached, came close, and a figure was apparently on the point of gliding past her when something tugged at her skirt and pinned it forcibly to the ground. The instantaneous check nearly threw Bathsheba off her balance. In recovering she struck against warm clothes and buttons.

'A rum start, upon my soul!' said a masculine voice, a foot or so above her head. 'Have I hurt you, mate?'

'No,' said Bathsheba, attempting to shrink away.

'We have got hitched together somehow, I think.'

'Yes.'

'Are you a woman?'

'Yes.'

'A lady, I should have said.'

'It doesn't matter.'

'I am a man.'

'Oh!'

Bathsheba softly tugged again, but to no purpose.

'Is that a dark lantern you have? I fancy so,' said the man.

'Yes.'

'If you'll allow me I'll open it, and set you free.'

A hand seized the lantern, the door was opened, the rays burst out from their prison, and Bathsheba beheld her position with astonishment.

The man to whom she was hooked was brilliant in brass and scarlet. He was a soldier. His sudden appearance was to darkness what the sound of a trumpet is to silence. Gloom, the *genius loci* at all times hitherto, was now totally overthrown, less by the lantern-light than by what the lantern lighted. The contrast of this revelation with her anticipations of some sinister figure in sombre garb was so great that it had upon her the effect of a fairy transformation.

Their exchange is a mixture of the shrewdly social ('A lady, I should have said') with the comedy biblical, as one can only call it ('I am a man'). After her monosyllables in the total darkness, Troy would have known what the fact was, but have instinctively wanted to proclaim her femininity in front of them both, while his own statement – 'I am a man' – is, in him, equally plausible. Moreover the same element of surprise repeated, which kept Manston motionless in the cutting, after his first surprise was over, is used again with much greater effect. Bathsheba's bizarre entanglement in the dark is now explained; she is only irritated and embarrassed; but the real astonishment is still to come, when darkness is overthrown – 'less by the lantern-light than by what the lantern lighted'. Her apprehension of finding herself tediously enmeshed with some local poacher is resolved in 'a fairy transformation'.

We fully share her astonishment. Like the cloak of the pantomime demon, Troy emerges out of the darkness in the scarlet regimentals which he will always, somewhat improbably, wear – he even has them on at the harvest supper after he is married and out of the army. It is the jacket that will vanish 'like a brand swiftly waved', after he has shown Bathsheba the sword-exercise and left her breathless and motionless in the ferny hollow. But where Manston was attached to the sensible and physical world by his own sense of it – that of Hardy and the reader – Troy is much more strikingly and dramatically a part of it. He seems as much a native of the plumy darkness of the fir coppice as he will be to the hollow amid the fern where he demonstrates his sword to Bathsheba. And it is very noticeable that the image of Troy shrugs off, as it were, the curlicues of literary analogy with which Hardy decorates the picture. At first indeed there are none of them; and we scarcely bother to notice when Troy leads out the inebriated farmhands at the end of the harvest supper, and the night of storm and stress for Gabriel and Bathsheba that followed it, in 'a procession which was not unlike Flaxman's group of the suitors tottering on towards the infernal regions under the conduct of Mercury'. We take correspondingly small notice when, in *The Return of the Native,* Hardy throws out the suggestion, after we have known Wildeve for quite a while, that he might be called 'the Rousseau of Egdon Heath'.

This observation sounds important, but isn't. Hardy is doing his not uncommon thing of creating a character in one kind of way and then talking about him in another. The manuscript of the earlier serial version of the novel makes clear that he started off with a standard type of villain seducer, and then diversified him into various sorts of weakness, good nature, and fastidious dislike of his rough rural surroundings – insipid male equivalents of the stormy and passionate female feelings of Eustacia, and sound psychological grounds for her contempt for Wildeve as unworthy to be her lord and master. As the manuscript of the serial indicates, Hardy became more deliberately ambitious as the novel went on, determining to give it a larger and more meaningful tragic tone than when he first conceived it. At one point he succeeds: the family tragedy involving Clym and his mother, and the misunderstanding between them, is worthy of the highest intention, but the corresponding drama of the passions in which Wildeve should be involved, is less successful. The Rousseau of Egdon may be a phrase to prepare him for a role he was not up to sustaining, but it is just as likely to have been thrown off by Hardy quite gratuitously.

Wildeve's trouble is that, like Manston, he is only intermittently present in his surroundings, although those are among the most notable of any Hardy fiction. The night scene, when Venn and he gamble by the light of glow-worms for Mrs Yeobright's guineas, is not, for all its memorableness, on the same level of achievement as the nocturnal encounter in the plantation. That establishes Troy once for all, whereas the gambling scene, in itself equally worthy of Caravaggio or La Tour, fails to identify further either of its participants. Wildeve lacks both Hardy's consciousness of things, which, as we have seen, Manston fitfully possesses in the intervals of his hard work as a villain, and the objectivity with which Troy is revealed in dramatic spectacle. Our real sense of him is not in the big scenes or in his role with Eustacia, but in his need to remain superior to the peasantry at the inn, and his relations with Thomasin. Her simple desire for more of his company gives a not unsubtle impression of a man less wild than he would like to be, who needs domesticity as much as he is bored by it.

The story of Troy and Bathsheba gripped Hardy too much as he went along for him to try to put the kind of 'representational significance' into it that he attempted in that of Eustacia and Clym; and this is probably just as well. But it does not matter much either way. We do not think of Wildeve as the Rousseau of Egdon, any more than of Troy as Mercury, leading the suitors in a study by Flaxman. 'Representational significance' was something Hardy went in for from early days – there is plenty of it in *The Hand of Ethelberta* and *A Laodicean* – and in this, as in the insertion of 'knowledge that would tell' he is conscientiously following such an example as Meredith's. But the significant character tried for could never be so effective as the one he saw, merely, as if in a poem. Such creation startles us into a pure apprehension of the naïve. Its intensity is the paradoxical one of the passive voyeur, who has no purpose, only a sense of the other person. Out of this modest compass Hardy's strength smokes up like a djinn. When he watches the Baron wad Marjorie's jacket into a ball about as big as an apple dumpling, the pair at once begin to exist, not as representative persons but as individuals unlike any other.

Hardy's realisation of character not only squares, in general, with his need to make it into something representative, but acts in concert with this literary duty. With Tess the process works on the largest scale. *Her* representational significance is there all right, but her equally undoubted physical presence is manifested at intervals, as when with Troy the slide of the dark lantern is drawn back. Meredith's commentary on a character is comprehensive: Hardy's exists beside the facts of his person and story, in seeming separation from them. Troy, like Henchard later, does not need Hardy's observations to be himself. He is seen first, discussed later. The significance of this is obvious when we see what happens to minor characters whom Hardy hits off at once in Egbertian vein. He does not look at Mrs Leat, the postmistress of *Desperate Remedies,* but gives her a narrow hand 'which would have been an unmitigated delight to the pencil of Carlo Crivelli'. At the shearing in the great barn Maryann has 'the mellow hue of an old sketch in oils – notably some of Nicholas Poussin's'.

Eustacia, and Bathsheba, can shrug off any such comparisons. When the latter consents to delight the company after the shearing-feast, a knowing reference is made to her rendering, as a popular finale, of 'The Banks of Allan Water':

> For his bride a soldier sought her,
> And a winning tongue had he . . .

'Subsequent events' the author observes, 'caused one of the verses to be remembered for many months, and even years, by more than one of those who were gathered there'.

The comment falls flat. Hardy usually does when he makes such a conscious pronouncement, and here it recalls us rather too sharply to the pretension of the work. The song has been much too well chosen by the author. Yet by insisting, like an officious scribe, on getting everything at the party 'right', Hardy seems to convey how little the assembly are concerned with him, or with each other either. Like most great creators Henry James was incapable of extending critical sympathy to a method so far from his own – his comments on *War and Peace* and on *Sons and Lovers* show that – and his review of *Far from the*

Madding Crowd shows not the faintest awareness of its genius. But, strangely enough, it is the case among Hardy's novels which shows most clearly a resemblance between Hardy's portrayal of character and James's own.

For neither claim to know their characters by any other than social means. With James this forbearance becomes deliberate, almost mystical, and by the time of his later novels has become a principle, not only of characterisation but of the rules for enquiry and discovery. He was, moreover, in conscious reaction against the omniscience practised both by George Eliot and the French realists. Hardy had no such scruples; he was, in all probability, not conscious of using a method at all. And yet it is particularly true of this novel that it knows its characters only socially, in James's fashion, although they may not belong to anything that James would recognise as 'society'.

It is the secret of its success with the rustics, with whom Hardy never claims to be specially intimate or to have expert knowledge of, as a modern writer proud of a genuine working-class background might do. About Farmer Boldwood he makes no claim to knowledge at all, not even appearing to have been introduced to him by his first name. He enters easily into an in-between world of surnames, a no-man's-land where different kinds of folk are found not unwarily meeting – bailiffs, stewards, senior domestics, tenant farmers and parish officials. The scenes among these in *Desperate Remedies* are some of the best he ever wrote, and there is a particular delicacy in the way he introduces its heroine among them, and in her relation to the hero's father, Mr Springrove, a smallholder and keeper of a decayed inn. Other novelists treating of rustic life, and anxious to avoid the anthropological tone, often use the expedient of a pedantic or innocent young go-between, whose function is to reveal *localness* – its disregard for outsiders and concentration on its own affairs – without the writer having to do it directly. Merimée does this in his Lithuanian tales, as Tolstoy does in *The Cossacks*: the same device is brilliantly used when Lockwood arrives at Wuthering Heights. The variety of his tones, and the way one aspect of narrative ignores another, make this no problem for Hardy.

Nor is the way he can go on to muse and moralise about a

character he has introduced us to, as he does with Sergeant Troy in the chapter, 'The New Acquaintance described', for he seems to have no more grounds to base a judgement on than ordinary social acquaintance, and his assumption of knowledge resembles that of a man speculating about an arresting new one:

He was a man to whom memories were an incumbrance, and anticipations a superfluity. Simply feeling, considering, and caring for what was before his eyes, he was vulnerable only in the present. His outlook upon time was as a transient flash of the eye now and then: that projection of consciousness into days gone by and to come, which makes the past a synonym for the pathetic and the future a word for circumspection, was foreign to Troy. With him the past was yesterday; the future, to-morrow; never, the day after.

On this account he might, in certain lights, have been regarded as one of the most fortunate of his order. For it may be argued with great plausibility that reminiscence is less an endowment than a disease, and that expectation in its only comfortable form – that of absolute faith – is practically an impossibility; whilst in the form of hope and the secondary compounds, patience, impatience, resolve, curiosity, it is a constant fluctuation between pleasure and pain.

Sergeant Troy, being entirely innocent of the practice of expectation, was never disappointed. To set against this negative gain there may have been some positive losses from a certain narrowing of the higher tastes and sensations which it entailed. But limitation of the capacity is never recognized as a loss by the loser therefrom: in this attribute moral or æsthetic poverty contrasts plausibly with material, since those who suffer do not mind it, whilst those who mind it soon cease to suffer. It is not a denial of anything to have been always without it, and what Troy had never enjoyed he did not miss; but, being fully conscious that what sober people missed he enjoyed, his capacity, though really less, seemed greater than theirs.

The tone is self-consciously knowledgeable, but it is also oddly abstracted and incomplete, the contrast of 'moral and aesthetic' with 'material' poverty as offhand as the way in which Hardy noticed the mildewed fircones and the meagre grasstufts, in the dark wood where we met Troy. The comments no more define him in theoretic outline than these things did symbolically, for Troy's force is so obviously distinct from his author, as distinct as the mute force gathered in those observed natural objects.

This is perhaps the most remarkable feature of Hardy's style at this vigorous period: whether noticing or commenting, it has at one moment no eye for itself, as it seems, while at the next it is assiduously concocting effects.

As it happens there is no one in this novel with whom Hardy is not on these purely 'social' terms. But even with Tess, with whom he is in a quite different relation, his powers of observation can occasionally surprise themselves, as it were, by their own objectivity. Abruptly he seems to see her as a new social phenomenon, as he saw Troy. Tess descends to the dairy after 'the usual afternoon nap of an hour or so which the exceedingly early hours kept in summer-time rendered a necessity'. Angel Clare is there. 'She was yawning, and he saw the red interior of her mouth as if it had been a snake's.' Hardy is very close to Tess, the relation altogether different than that to Bathsheba or Eustacia, but at this moment he sees something in her which has the mesmeric attraction of the wholly separate and strange. Nothing about Tess is like a snake except the inside of her mouth, seen at that moment. Troy has such a separateness entirely, whether he is being seen by Hardy, or commented on by him. He is, like Tess's mouth seen at this moment, 'vulnerable only in the present'; and by implication such a sensibility is foreign to that of the writer, and the reader. That may be why the passage ends with one of those obscure and quiet ironies which are as typical as they are effective: Troy's vividness to others makes his capacity for consciousness, which it seems should be greater than that of most persons, really less.

Troy has the advantage over Manston in that he never becomes a part of the receptive consciousness the author shares with us. And the same is true of the others most involved in the passions of the rural drama – Fanny Robin, Farmer Boldwood, and Bathsheba herself. There is greater conformity between Hardy's idiosyncratic genius, and the traditional folk ways of recounting such a drama, than there exists in *Desperate Remedies* between his own sensibility and a Wilkie Collins-type mystery. At the same time it is typical of Hardy, and of the perverse way in which his effectiveness creeps round normal standards of judgement, that however much of a dislocation may exist between the informing consciousness of his first published novel, and its mystery specification, neither suffers: both indeed may be said to benefit, in the ways I have suggested. So the superior equilibrium in the later tale might not in itself be an asset; success with Hardy usually goes with anomaly of some sort, and in *Far from the Madding Crowd* it depends on the figure of Gabriel Oak, whose close association with the author makes him in many ways as improbable a farmer and smallholder as Manston is an implausible schemer and villain.

But before we come to Gabriel's position, and what it involves, it is worth seeing how well the meeting with Troy has been prepared for in the genre of pastoral drama, a model which Hardy sets out to 'overgo' as deliberately as he did that of the complex mystery tale in *Desperate Remedies*. Pastoral gold is alchemised in the shearing and the shearing feast. Every possible *topos* is made avail of, down to Jan Coggan's echo of Polonius in his encouragement of the song by Joseph Poorgrass. We may miss Hardy's more factual and low-keyed narration, like the apple-pressing scene in Farmer Springrove's yard in his first novel. Homeric idealisation makes this world appear too happy in its happiness, whereupon we may feel that Hardy has anticipated precisely such a reaction. This comes out not so much in the hint of troubles to come, prefigured by the singing of 'Allen Water', and the reference to those who would recall its words, but in something more physical and inevitable, more wrought into the scheme of things. For Bathsheba, latterly knitting at her end of the table, has been as indifferent to the harmony of the occasion as if she were a hawk or a heron perched beside a scene of extreme natural beauty. Her moment comes when the shearers depart and Boldwood makes his declaration of love – a moment of triumph for her but 'a triumph which had rather been contemplated than desired'. Her instinct is for an absolute such as her own nature requires, a need quite different from that of the rustics who find it reclining over the bowl together like Homer's gods.

But Boldwood cannot offer it, and the scene with him lacks the consummate and appropriate life of the impending times with Troy. Boldwood has his own natural and absolute kind of being, which is not that of a lover. As a lover he wears now in her eyes 'the sorry look of a grand bird without the feathers that makes it grand'. And in giving his literary version of this rustic cliché, Hardy has already sealed it with his own sense of the physical in bodily displacement, here awkward:

She was standing behind a low arm-chair, from which she had just risen, and he was kneeling in it – inclining himself over its back towards her, and holding her hand in both his own. His body moved restlessly, and it was with what Keats daintily calls a too happy happiness.

Boldwood should have the uninsistent dignity of a natural creature:

This unwonted abstraction by love of all dignity from a man of whom it had ever seemed the chief component, was, in its distressing incongruity, a pain to her which quenched much of the pleasure she derived from the proof that she was idolised.

The reference to Keats is as apposite as could be, even more so perhaps than Hardy intends (he aptly misremembers the Nightingale Ode, in which the poet had expressed himself too happy in the *bird*'s happiness). 'Daintily', a Keatsian word, itself perfectly conveys the 'distressing incongruity' of the man in this position; and Bathsheba responds to his devotion as many readers have responded to similar kinds of awkward devoutness in Keats's own lines. The reference shows, if that were needed, how close the texture of Hardy's prose style can be to Keats's poetic one, in what each can encompass of the physical, in all its awkwardness and richness.

The Keatsian and the Shakespearian have everything in common except awkwardness, and there is nothing awkward in the articulation of these scenes. We turn from one kind of engrossment to another by turning, as in *A Midsummer Night's Dream*, from the nature of one kind of being to another. Even the pastoral harmony of the shearing is marked by touches of separateness more than appropriateness (the 'unctuous' fleeces as superior to anything *woollen* as cream is to milk and water) like the old maltster's denunciation of a mere sixty-year-old ('Weren't I stale in wedlock afore ye were out of arms?') or old Maryann's query for 'a crooked man or a lame, or any second-hand fellow at all that would do for poor me'. Like Shakespeare in full flow, such things seem thrown off by association, not intention, and are as far as possible from the carefully mellow tableau of humours that George Eliot can produce. Even so, it was not unreasonable in the *Spectator* reviewer to opine, after the appearance of the novel's first instalment in the *Cornhill,* that it could be an anonymous work of hers. But Hardy was not flattered. He remarked later in the *Life* that her own pastoral showed more of 'a woman's wit cast in country dialogue rather than real country humour . . . of the Shakespeare and Fielding sort'; and he went on to observe with mild shrewdness that she 'was not a born story-teller by any means'. That indeed is the crux of the matter: a pastoral drama cannot afford still life, like the tableau in the Rainbow Inn in *Silas Marner*; it must be in constant motion. When composing his *Life,* Hardy must have known he had been a 'born story-teller' – he spoke of 'the something' in *Far from the Madding Crowd* 'which I could not have put there if I had been older'.

Engrossment and disappointment, of the wholly peculiar sort we experience with him, make him in fact quite the most accomplished of nineteenth-century story-tellers, and his popular power reflects the first audience's acceptance of anomalies by which narration is sustained, for example the gulling of Boldwood by Troy after his secret marriage to Bathsheba, which, as J. I. M Stewart points out, could well occur in an Elizabethan play. So much so, that it does not seem in any sense 'out of character'; literature, as usual, has a liberating effect. Life, on the authority of this novel, proceeds in a series of jerks – galvanic in their operation on different species of mortal at different moments – rather than by any slow maturing process. Life, that is, as this narration undertakes to view it, is a drama of choice before the monotony of determined existence has begun.

And the mode of art reinforces the message. Insensible change and slow process are subsumed under Hardy's private consciousness and sense of the show of things, but his judgement on *this* rustic drama is as impersonal as it is practical and shrewd –

Bathsheba loved Troy in the way that only self-reliant women love when they abandon their self-reliance. When a strong woman recklessly throws away her strength she is worse than a weak woman who has never had any strength to throw away.

In such a case the tone of the author is hardly distinguishable from that of the characters themselves. It is not precisely what Mark, Jan and Joseph would say, but it corresponds pretty closely to their apprehension of things. There is an amazing difference between the tone of it, and that on which Hardy will end chapter fifty of *Tess* –

Thus the Durbeyfields, once d'Urbervilles, saw descending upon them the destiny which, no doubt, when they were among the Olympians of the county, they had caused to descend many a time, and severely enough, upon the heads of such landless ones as they themselves were now. So do flux and reflux – the rhythm of change – alternate and persist in everything under the sky.

By then Hardy had himself become in some sense an Olympian, not exactly identifying with the fallen grandees, but creating his own particular image of their state, and embodying his own isolation in its being a fallen one.

His intimacy, or reticence, for the two seem at times indistinguishable, can be such that a perfectly ordinary comment or generalisation, at the period of *Far from the Madding Crowd,* may seem to stand out of the page, solely because of its lack of point in the context of what we may feel to be his own personality. This too could not occur by the time of *Tess* or *Jude.* As the storm is about to break Gabriel reckons up the value of the unprotected stacks in a sum which Hardy places on the page:

Oak returned to the stackyard. All was silent here, and the conical tips of the ricks jutted darkly into the sky. There were five wheat-ricks in this yard, and three stacks of barley. The wheat when threshed would average about thirty quarters to each stack; the barley, at least forty. Their value to Bathsheba, and indeed to anybody, Oak mentally estimated by the following simple calculation:—

$$5 \times 30 = 150 \text{ quarters} = 500l.$$
$$3 \times 40 = 120 \text{ quarters} = 250l.$$
$$\text{Total} \qquad 750l.$$

Seven hundred and fifty pounds in the divinest form that money can wear – that of necessary food for man and beast: should the risk be run of deteriorating this bulk of corn to less than half its value, because of the instability of a woman? 'Never, if I can prevent it!' said Gabriel.

Such was the argument that Oak set outwardly before him. But man, even to himself, is a palimpsest, having an ostensible writing, and another beneath the lines. It is possible that there was this golden legend under the utilitarian one: 'I will help to my last effort the woman I have loved so dearly.'

The paragraphs following the figure seem to waver into an instability remarkable even for Hardy. The authority of the calculation set out is as complete and as effective as the signs noted of the coming storm: the large toad accidentally kicked on the path near Oak's door; the 'serpentine sheen' on his table, 'as if a brush of varnish had been lightly dragged across it', leading to a huge brown garden slug, 'come indoors tonight for reasons of its own'. And the palimpsest with its golden legend is in the same fellowship of fancy with Multimammia and those Sleswig pirates. But there is something jauntily and yet uneasily impersonal in the preceding sentiment about 'the divinest form that money can wear'. This, in its context, sticks out as the sentiment and tone of an inferior writer, almost any inferior writer, having nothing in common with thoughts probable either in Hardy or in Oak. Not only is 'animula' absent from such sentences, but their nullity shows that the relation between these two – who are neither at one nor separate – is not easy to adjust.

For Oak is part of the Homeric scene, and his two main functions – fidelity in love and skill in husbandry – are as absolute as its scale requires. He can not only play the flute but 'pipe with an Arcadian sweetness'. His determination to save the corn, and the words he is given to express it, are as heroic as the sentiment: 'I will help to my last effort the woman I have loved so dearly'. But to use a memorable phrase of Hardy's in a different context, the heroic passes into the homely without mingling with it. Any attempt at such mingling produces phrases like 'the divinest form that money can wear' – conspicuous in a total lack of Hardyan meaning. This is the closest he comes to real weakness in his tricky relation with Oak, for

unlike the other characters Oak is not seen quite objectively.
When he stops to watch the small birds, who take no notice of
him till he does so, he is rather obviously mingled with his
author. But in this the Hardy animula is present, whereas 'the
divinest form that money can wear' is a narrative convenience
which produces what Balzac would call a *déflocquement,* an
inertia replacing the individuality vital to the language of
Hardy's feeling. It is a tiny instance of the process of taking
cover behind a persona, which is so depressing in a tale like
'Barbara of the House of Grebe'.

But it is rare: found only when Hardy is in a difficult relation
with a character. Oak's handling seems to present difficulties not
found in the more mature creation of Giles Winterborne. The
awkwardness is apparent when Oak contemplates the stars, on
which Hardy himself has just commented so memorably –

Being a man not without a frequent consciousness that there was some
charm in this life he led, he stood still after looking at the sky as a useful
instrument, and regarded it in an appreciative spirit, as a work of art
supremely beautiful.

The labour of the opening phrase both suggests embarrassment
in making this attribution, and saves itself by so doing. Hardy
must not patronise Oak – he never patronises – but he seems
aware here of the possibility, and patronage exists in ignorance.
When disaster strikes and the sheep are all killed we hear that
'Oak was an intensely humane man . . . a shadow in his life had
always been that his flock ended in mutton – that a day came
and found every shepherd an arrant traitor to his defenceless
sheep'. Again this is objectively believable, however close it
comes to Hardy himself, and the more so because of the
cumbrous phrase that intervenes, telling us that Oak's humanity
'often tore in pieces any politic intentions of his which bordered
on strategy, and carried him on as by gravitation'. Hardy then
introduces Oak into a composition of the 'Neutral Tones' kind,
as he had done with Cytherea Graye, the heroine of *Desperate
Remedies,* at a similar moment of horror. The dawn shows 'the
attenuated skeleton of a chrome-yellow moon . . . the morning
star dogging her on the left hand', and an oval pool that
'glittered like a dead man's eye'. 'All this Oak saw and

remembered'. So had Cytherea, in her context, and there is a
kind of humility in the fact that Hardy himself did not presume
to have a moment of horror to recall in his poem, but only an
unforgettable listlessness in association. He objectifies his characters by giving them the stature joined to disasters more suited
to novels.

Literature, that is, which includes notes of the epic as well as
melodrama and pastoral romance. Realism may require Oak to
be an 'arrant traitor' to his sheep, but he will never be one to his
lady love. Hardy is remarkably skilful at tucking in together the
ends of the different conventions, however incongruous they
might seem. In the Homeric scale the dance played in the barn,
'The Soldier's Joy', must be the most 'immortal' of tunes, and
the thunderstorm that follows the most spectacular of storms;
even the toad and the snail whose activities are one of the
portents of its coming, must be the largest of their kind. The
huge dog who helps Fanny Robin on the last stage of her
journey to the Casterbridge workhouse is 'the ideal embodiment of canine greatness.'

These touches are not in themselves intrusive, but they point
to the method of the whole, into which Oak fits exactly. After
Bathsheba refuses him he becomes a personification of devotion,
acquiring an ever greater authority in that role until the end of
the novel, when he stands on the verge of diminishment into the
commonplace of married life, when Bathsheba will no longer
be for him 'the embodiment of all that was sweet and bright and
hopeless'. Boldwood stands for obsession, in its extremest form;
Troy for sexual attraction at its most spell-binding.

The climax of Bathsheba's marriage is similarly of unexam-
pled vehemence – the *tetelestai* of her union with Troy being a
'cry of measureless despair and indignation such as had never
before been heard within those old-inhabited walls.' The
reference to Christ's last words from the cross is sufficiently
extreme, but characteristically this display of Hardy's knowledge of the Greek testament makes no great impression on the
reader, not so much as the gospel phrase – 'It is finished' – would have done. It shows, though, how thoroughly an
instinct for the epic scale in the story's specification had taken
hold of him, and something important in our conception of his

powers must follow from this. They are in no sense 'natural' but worked up, on the basis not of a 'vision of life' but of what is appropriate to an achieved narration.

I shall return to this question of the form appropriate to each novel: it seems to me the best way of appreciating them. But we should notice now that even the epic specification here is not stable. It can lead to an occasional vulgarity in the texture, unique in Hardy, which may remind us of nothing so much as Kipling, in such an epic tale as *Captains Courageous*. That is also a masterpiece, in its way, and it too works to the formula of everything being 'the best of its kind' – the ship, captain, crew, even the self-made millionaire who is the hero's father, and the record train journey across America he makes to find his son. But the epic superlatives are often mechanical, as sometimes in Hardy. We have seen how, although Oak's calculations are wholly literal, they are about something 'in the divinest form that money can wear – that of necessary food for man and beast'. That is not Hardy's kind of badness, not his style. A similar lapse occurs in the fine evocation of the great barn. 'The defence and salvation of the body by daily bread is still a study, a religion, and a desire'. That is not Hardy the sermonist, with the 'unperturbed' cadence which goes into so many commonplaces in the poems, but the vacant hyperbole of a *Times*' third leader; and it is noticeable that such mere perkiness seems the result of Hardy aiming too deliberately at a total effect, not the effect he gets when noticing 'the misty chestnut work of the rafters'; nor when he is giving out the sermon theme that four centuries had 'neither proved it to be founded on a mistake', nor 'inspired any hatred of its purpose'.

The instinct that suggested the emphasis on 'the best of its kind' as a formal principle in *Far from the Madding Crowd* (and we might remember Kipling's comment that his story too celebrated the ideal life of a rapidly vanishing community) may have made a comparable principle in *The Return of the Native* out of solitude, alienation, and estrangement. Formalists might argue that these two novels are Hardy's most successful, because in them the criteria of formalism are most effectively demonstrated: both novels get the most out of a self-justifying specification, which makes further query about purpose and viewpoint irrelevant. All, from Troy's swordsmanship onwards, excels in its class in the earlier novel: while all is estranged from itself and its class in the later one. There would be a good deal in this, for Hardy's earlier novels, like his poems, can indeed best be seen in terms of a craft specification rather than a vehicle for themes and ideas. Of course the two cannot be separated out, but the distinction would none the less be valid, for Hardy himself and his own intentions, as well as for the outcome of the work itself.

The intentions are always of the first importance, even if we may agree to disregard them or to feel the novel has achieved some sort of independence of them. It is customary for critics not to pay much attention to Hardy's own comment on 'the original conception of the story', which 'did not design a marriage between Thomasin and Venn', and which was to end with the reddleman disappearing from the heath, 'retaining his isolated and weird character to the last'. Serial publication is the reason given for a change of plan, and we are invited to choose between the two endings, Hardy rather obviously loading the issue by remarking that those of us with an austere artistic code can assume the more consistent conclusion to be the true one. 'Consistent with what?' we may ask, for nothing in the plot of any of Hardy's novels could be said to make sense of such a term. In their context, nobody objects to the drama of Clym's discovery and Eustacia's death being followed by the marriage of Thomasin and Diggory Venn. Indeed the more we accept that Hardy's tragic effects and the power of many of his scenes are compatible with the humblest sort of fictional device and requirement, the less seriously we may be inclined to take these remarks of his.

'Tragic powers' are now too much taken for granted in estimates of his work. What may have concerned him is something different – the problem of *formal* consistency which had been so well if inconspicuously solved in *Far from the Madding Crowd*. That devotion there should get its reward is right and proper, however much it has been an epitome of all that is 'faithful and true'; and the same consolation can succeed the infatuation of Bathsheba and the 'measureless despair and indignation' which ended it. But if Diggory Venn is to have the role of an Oak in alienation, a mysterious vindicator of the heaths, and of the estranged and isolated fates of those that live there, he must remain isolated himself. Or so Hardy may have felt. And the possibility may give us an insight into the controlling principles of the two novels.

He came near to making the same mistake about Troy that he felt he had to make about Venn. Troy was to have engaged in skulduggery on the farm making quick money dishonestly by feeding the sheep so that they seemed fatter and readier for market than they were. Oak was to have exposed this. Leslie Stephen, the editor of *The Cornhill* and very much Hardy's mentor at the time, may well have demurred, as he did at such other details in the submitted copy as an anecdote from the dishonest bailiff Pennyways at the shearing supper. Troy must not engage in agriculture – Oak's pursuit – and Oak must not undermine Troy's romantic superiority (beside Troy Oak has a tendency to look 'like a candle beside gas'). The principle of separation, and of each protagonist being top in his own line, would have been blurred, its drama diminished. Hardy hurries on the climax, the flower-planting on Fanny's grave – the same order of experience as the sword exhibition – and the doings of the gurgoyle, after which Troy 'simply threw up his cards and forswore his game for that time and always'. That game was a 'faint reversal of his life's course', a 'trembling and critical attempt' to be something else than 'the hero of his story, without whom there would have been no story at all for him'.

A curious thing about Hardy's chequered methods is that they *can* make for consistency of tone; of the sort, for instance, that makes it impossible for the gurgoyle episode to have occurred to any other man than Troy. And it is this consistency that Venn cannot have. Had he disappeared at the end we should have known no more about him than his role as the chief spirit and emblem of estrangement, which is as absolute as any of those in the earlier novel – more so indeed. This is brought out by a shrewd remark of Derwent May – 'Thomasin winds up with a far more difficult husband than Wildeve would ever have been',* On the evidence of Venn's previous behaviour the

* Introduction to new edition, London 1970.

critic's case is indeed a strong one: however chivalrous his motives Venn has behaved in a manner for which neurosis would seem too mild a term. And this brings out Hardy's inability to adjust such a concept to the ordinary accommodations of the novel, as he accommodated Oak and Boldwood and Troy. Venn is so determined a figure that to draw attention to the kinds of psychological oddity and perversity that might be said to lurk in him is merely to draw attention to the inherent limitations of the concept. Apparently one of the most striking of Hardy's creations he is actually, as he stands, the weakest of all. Hardy hints as much in his reflections on the book's ending. He would have confined Venn to a strictly formal role.

Venn's redness has the same function as Troy's red jacket: to separate him from other people. Troy without his coat becomes more Troy than ever, as we shall see Hardy showing us, but the reddleman can become quite normal again when it suits, for like Oak he is supposed to be a humane man. As we have seen, Hardy has some trouble with Oak's mind, and its relations with his own, but on the whole he solves this well. With Venn he does not attempt to solve it at all. He implies that such a mind is there, with a devotion much like Oak's, and thus he compromises Venn as an exterior personality. The secret of both novels is the creation and separation of such personalities, instead of their mingling together in one genre group, as in *Under the Greenwood Tree,* or *The Trumpet-Major*; and their relation to the authorial consciousness is an ambiguous one.

Bathsheba and Troy are prime instances of how effective it can none the less be. Absorbed as they are in their own selves, it is right they should lend their sensations to a certain coarseness of treatment when these are required to register a detailed consciousness of the outside world. We can feel in the text how Hardy renders it, and at some length. When Bathsheba rushes out of the house after the climactic scene with her husband beside the coffin of Fanny Robin, she sinks down like a wounded animal in a thicket near the farm. It proves to be a brake of ferns – 'beautiful yellowing ferns with their feathery arms' – the best place for refuge and protection. She gives no sign of recalling, as the reader does, the hollow in the ferns where Troy first showed her the sword exercise: she is too exhausted. In the morning a series of sounds presents itself to her listless consciousness, in sequence and with precision, like a farm ledger; first a sparrow's chatter, then the soft hoarse note of a finch, last the call of a ploughboy bringing her own horses to the pond. She shakes her dress to get rid of the leaves which have fallen about her overnight, and they flutter away 'like ghosts from an enchanter fleeing'. Shelley at this point is hardly suited to Bathsheba: the quotation is so obviously wasted on her, as none of Hardy's culture is on Eustacia, that it seems to bring out the stunned alienation of her responses. The swamp hollow she finds herself beside, with its fungi resembling torn or putrid flesh, is symbolically appropriate to the quality of her outraged consciousness, as are for Grace in *The Woodlanders* the autumn fungi she sees near her refuge in the saturated woods.

The last item of the ledger is a schoolboy, conning the collect of the day by rote:

In the worst attacks of trouble there appears to be always a superficial film of consciousness which is left disengaged and open to the notice of trifles, and Bathsheba was faintly amused at the boy's method, till he too passed on.

That faint amusement seems wholly characteristic of her, not of Hardy; and the reader may recall Joseph Poorgrass's comment on her father, who 'would box the charity boys' ears if they laughed in church, till they could hardly stand upright, and do other deeds of piety natural to the saintly inclined'. These things are succeeded by the arrival of Liddy Smallbury, Bathsheba's maid, who approaches the swamp to come to her mistress. Bathsheba has lost her voice from the dampness of the night air; she cannot utter a warning, but the little maid contrives to tread across without sinking –

Bathsheba never forgot that transient little picture of Liddy crossing the swamp to her there in the morning light. Iridescent bubbles of dank subterranean breath rose from the sweating sod beside the waiting-maid's feet as she trod, hissing as they burst and expanded away to join the vapoury firmament above. Liddy did not sink, as Bathsheba had anticipated.

The swamp, associated for Bathsheba with disillusion and decay, now takes on for her a biblical and Bunyanesque air, a slough which the innocent may travel without knowing the danger, revealing in the act for all time the value of a relation – Liddy's to Bathsheba – which has been taken for granted. The scene which Oak never forgot was appropriately more stark, simple and literal; more obviously akin, too, to Hardy's own pervasive sense of things. By contrast Bathsheba's experience seems entirely her own, and it seems felt by her – in a fashion that is like her – and not described or attributed.

Troy's parallel experiences are more seen than apprehended, and yet we can feel him responding to them in his own way too. He is 'so unlike himself now in look, word and deed, that *the want of likeness was perceptible even to his own consciousness*' (italics mine). Where the consciousness of the numbed Bathsheba is indicated in the nature of her successive experiences, passively received, and by the sense of almost religious comfort brought by Liddy, the shock to Troy is registered in actions of desperate self-assertion. The flower-planting may be described by Hardy as 'a trembling and critical attempt' to be something other than himself; but to us it seems much more like an attempt to be again the self which his consciousness has registered as absent. Hardy is expansive here, borrowing the notions of science in the study of national difference which were then in fashion. He observes that Troy's methodical thoroughness shows the English side of him, and 'that blindness to the line where sentiment verged on mawkishness, the French'. This dubious generalisation is in fact amply justified by what he does, but it also shows the gap between the author's commentary and the actual impression of Troy we are getting.

It is here the gurgoyle comes in, not as an engine of malignant fate contrived by Hardy but a manifestation of that side of Troy previously invisible to himself – the 'coral reef' of destructiveness, of others and of himself – which had been, as Hardy puts it, just below the surface of his sea. Now it is fully visible, Troy hates himself. And this takes a characteristic form: to escape at once from the places and happenings – the fir wood, the fern hollow, Fanny Robin's grave – which have made him his own hero, and which by Hardy's method have established his reality.

He sets out blindly to walk, and in walking he reaches a new
dimension of Wessex, as removed from Weatherbury's con-
tours of farm and pasture as the heathland where Henchard goes
to die is different from near-by Casterbridge. Toiling in the
'garish' afternoon up the slopes of Purbeck he glimpses the
vastness of the channel and descends to the sea at Lulworth
Cove. 'Troy's nature freshened within him.' The memorable
phrase is implicit with the irony of his need to become himself
again. The return to Weatherbury after adventures in the New
World is not only required by the plot but is a literal return to
his old self, now hardened by vicissitude. The only change is the
loss of the red coat, which once gave him the gallantry as well as
the dangerousness of a soldier.

Troy is the opposite of a Jamesian *conscience,* and it is not
surprising that James, in his review of the novel, should have
singled him out for special depreciation as an item of crude
melodrama, as – for him – Bathsheba is only an item of crude
feminine instinct. In fact, together with Henchard the Mayor of
Casterbridge, he is Hardy's most successful portrayal of a man
wholly alien to his own consciousness; as he is also the most
striking instance of personality created by means of place and
event, and their intersection. Ironically, because he himself is 'a
man to whom memories were an encumbrance' – the antithesis
of Hardyan man. Looking away, Hardy cuts the Gordian knot
of *conscience,* and its location in observer or observed, by his
apparently random alternation of comment – often literary
– with his sense, in the case of Bathsheba or Troy, of
consciousness operating on its surroundings, familiar or unfamiliar, in ways that are all the more striking because they are subtly
and yet uncompromisingly different from his own awareness of
things.

But the pair are only like this when seen in alienation from each
other and themselves. In the most striking scene in the
novel – perhaps in any novel of Hardy's – their preoccupation
with each other enables him to watch them wholly from
outside. This is the exhibition of the sword exercise in the
hollow amid the ferns. The nineteenth-century novel is full of
scenes of sexual symbolism, many of them quite unperceived as

such, as it seems, by their authors. Hardy knew quite well here what he was up to, one imagines, as he does in other novels, but his text saves him from any appearance of intention or insistency. Diversity is here unlike anything it usually means about the style of a narration. Tolstoy, for example, relates in a multiplicity of ways, now generalising about history and human nature, now describing in great detail what Turgenev in humorous exasperation called 'how N.N. held his left arm'. And Jane Austen also organises diversity, using a fluttered grammar of individual reflection as well as the measured symmetries of irony and amusement. But in them as in other novelists we may feel that such differentiations all work like a team, the members of which are mutually supportive, and aware of each others' duties.

Diversity in Hardy is quite unlike this. As with the poems, component parts of the prose seen unconscious of each other's presence, and this is especially true of so absorbing a scene as the one amid the ferns. A more or less appropriate comparison would not be that of a team but of a landscape: the close proximity of trees and other living things in a wood at night, where each sound or movement conveys the unheedingness of each to the other. Hardy himself describes such a situation often, numbering with pleasure the different responses of leaves, plants and grasses to wind and rain. The reader – with an equal pleasure – is made aware of all, though no effect is definitively in charge. It seems to be our own activities among the constituent parts of the writing that give us our sense of what is going on.

To be effectively symbolic of a sexual relation the scene would require purposive unity, such as D. H. Lawrence would have given it. It would not have been explicit, but a scene by him would have left no doubt of its significance. To be fair, many of Hardy's own Victorian contemporaries could have done the same if they wanted to. Alma Tadema had a painter's licence to do nude figures in conventional or classic settings, but apart from that he is also methodically suggestive in his sex symbolism. So, in her curious way, is Christina Rossetti in *Goblin Market*. And such sexual suggestiveness requires a greater degree of organisation than Hardy's prose texture knows about, or cares about.

This may explain why the sexual iconography of the hollow in the ferns, although it may have been apparent to Hardy, does not appear to come into the purview of his noticing and meditating faculty, which has other and more important things to absorb it. A Renaissance poet would nudge us insistently, as would a modern novelist, and as even Tennyson does – however unknowingly – in that extraordinary opening of *Maud* ('I hate the dreadful hollow behind the little wood'). But Hardy is fascinated by the scene's *romance,* just as his heroine is; and like him she also feels a great deal of curiosity at the novelty, like a fair or a new game. He loved artefacts and mechanical techniques of all sorts as much as natural objects (as an architect he had been ingenious in devising cheap and durable materials for decorating brickwork) and he would have been equally interested in the methods devised to train recruits in the art of striking accurately and effectively with a sword in the confusion of battle. Long experience would be required to make this instinctive, just as it would be for the labourer who used scythe, thatching spar or shearing iron.

But any such comparison is tacit. And even the syntax of the scene, as is not uncommon in Hardy, seems not to know what other clauses and phrases are about –

Standing in the centre, the sky overhead was met by a circular horizon of fern: this grew nearly to the bottom of the slope and then abruptly ceased. The middle within the belt of verdure was floored with a thick flossy carpet of moss and grass intermingled, so yielding that the foot was half-buried within it.

'Standing', a hanging participle, has lost the human actor and got attached to the sky itself, and the dialect word 'flossy', which also occurs in *Tess,* is equally out of tonal context. So is Troy's speech ('Infantry cuts and guards are more interesting than ours, to my mind, but they are not so swashing'), when compared with the force and timing of his desires and his play. Hardy's own interest in the technique of the movements is as exclusive of the rest of the scene as it is when Troy is swept by the current out beyond Lulworth cliffs, and attempts to keep afloat by various technical expedients – 'swimming several inches deeper than his wont, keeping up his breathing entirely by his nostrils, turning upon his back a dozen times over, swimming *en papillon,* and so on'. In his young days Hardy, the admirer of Defoe, had jotted down from a book of 'Curious Facts' both the details of the sword exercise and the swimming motions.

The tone changes again as the tension increases and the banality of the couple's exchange sharpens into a simplicity more dire than the speaker knows, and again as Hardy wheels out the full apparatus of pastoral and heroic mythology, where Hector is greatest of heroes and hyperbole the appropriate commonplace:

Never since the broadsword became the national weapon had there been more dexterity shown in its management than by the hands of Sergeant Troy, and never had he been in such splendid temper for the performance as now in the evening sunshine among the ferns with Bathsheba. It may safely be asserted with respect to the closeness of his cuts, that had it been possible for the edge of the sword to leave in the air a permanent substance wherever it flew past, the space left untouched would have been almost a mould of Bathsheba's figure.

The domestic placidity 'In the evening sunshine among the ferns with Bathsheba') and the canny laboriousness of that 'It may be safely asserted with respect to . . .' are not so much incongruous with the hyperbole as unconscious of it.

With a final stroke Troy trims off a lock of Bathsheba's hair, and a climactic thrust neatly splits a caterpillar which has crawled out of the fern on to the bosom of her dress.

She asks how he could have cut off her hair with a sword with no edge –

'No edge! This sword will shave like a razor. Look here.'
He touched the palm of his hand with the blade, and then lifting it, showed her a thin shaving of scarf-skin dangling therefrom.

That 'thin shaving of scarf-skin' banishes at a stroke the hyperbolic fantasy of the sword play, replacing it with the absolute and deadly texture of fact, fact which goes side by side with the imaginary mould of Bathsheba's figure created by the motions of the sword. That image drops us with perfect equanimity over the edge of the farcical, as any such exchange between the sexes, however intense and poetic, must do if it is to be true to the nature of the thing in life.

Hardy is unrivalled at conveying the clumsiness of such exchanges, and doing so very touchingly and delicately, as in *A Pair of Blue Eyes*. But in the relation of Troy and Bathsheba he set himself to convey the intensest kind of attraction, passion on the one side and performance on the other, between two remarkable people. It was, if I am right, part of his intention for making everything in the book magnificent of its kind, and 'measureless' in its operation. All the more remarkable, then, that he comes to the edge of the ridiculous without the slightest concern, and without any loss of poetry and romance. An element of the ridiculous is of course no more deliberate here than is a sexual symbolism, and indeed perhaps it is the wrong word to use, because it suggests an inadvertence which goes with an ambitious effect that has failed to come off. That is certainly not the case with this: it is one of the greatest scenes in English fiction. It becomes so because it contains all the most original and characteristic elements in Hardy's style, not fused together but assembled in their separate peculiarity.

Bathsheba is compelled by an attraction on the physical level, and also on that of fantasy. Animal submission, and the domination instinct in Troy's compressed lips, alternate with the charm of romance ('she saw his scarlet form disappear amid the ferny thicket, almost in a flash, like a brand swiftly waved') which couples Bathsheba's sense of it with Hardy's own reading in Scott or Harrison Ainsworth. And for both another kind of literature comes in as well. The sensual relaxation and relief which succeed the display are mingled, at Troy's parting kiss, with a biblical sense of guilt, as if she was 'aflame to the very hollows of her feet', a phrase only Hardy could have written.

Our emotional sense of Bathsheba becomes at this moment an historical sense too. She is a woman of the mid-nineteenth century, reared in the conviction of sin, and especially the sinfulness of the body. Where the summons, as well as the pleasures of scripture are concerned, she and Hardy are on the same ground, together with Boldwood and Oak and Joseph

Poorgrass. Hardy the church-goer is reminding the reader of familiar truths. His attitude towards the meeting of the pair is orthodox, in the sense that every reader would be excited by it as a novel-reader and disapprove as a church-goer. There is no private excitement in the scene, for though many of Hardy's characters are voyeurs this is so common a fictional device of the period that it is natural the author and his audience should have the same licence.

On the other hand it is typical that Hardy, by reason of his intentness on the scene, should fail to grasp the extent to which readers – and reviewers – might pronounce it grotesque and overdone. Fortunately he had no tact, or idea of when to stop, other than his own innate refinement, which was rarely the same as that of his readers and critics. For the irony of the thing is that he had much more natural refinement – innocence even – than most readers of novels; the kind of refinement, not uncommon then in the country, which accepts without question its uninhibited speech – 'the broad jests of our grand-fathers and grandmothers, now unquotable' – as he comments in the *Life*. The conditioned hypocrisy of Mudie's readers, which had to be deferred to by Morley and Leslie Stephen (the former reported on the 'disgusting and absurd outrage' on which the plot of *Desperate Remedies* depended) was something Hardy grew to accept but never got used to.

At Leslie Stephen's request, for example, he removed the mention of Fanny's baby beside her in the coffin, the convexity of its small head like 'a dawn mushroom'. What Stephen objected to, one imagines, was not the existence of the child itself, which the plot required, even though he had shaken his head over the whole business of Fanny's seduction by Troy, but this simile about its appearance. That this could be 'in bad taste' would never have occurred to Hardy the noticer and separator; but when Stephen hinted as much he removed the passage at once, and he did not restore it when the story came out in book form. T. S. Eliot shrank from Bathsheba's matter-of-fact femininity as much as James had done; he singles out the moment when she resolves to open Fanny's coffin and satisfy her curiosity as to whether it was 'true that there are two of you', as evidence of Hardy's inherent morbidity. In fact Hardy is as much at home with this down-to-earth behaviour in his heroine as he is with her name itself – that of Solomon's mother – and with the two references he makes to the fact. She is not only 'feared at tea-parties', but the stuff of which great men's mothers are made. And it must have pleased Hardy in *The Return of the Native* to refer to the passage about that mother in the book of Kings, the text which Clym gave out on Rainbarrow when he began his career as an itinerant preacher.

V

CYTHEREA GRAYE, THE HEROINE OF *Desperate Remedies,* is a young girl of the professional middle class. But the awareness Hardy devotes to her is largely that of the world he understood from early childhood, the world where mother and aunts had been in service below stairs, or ladies' maids. Upper-class convention, and this more direct kind of understanding work together with the Gothic element in the tale to produce a girl as convincing as any he drew, a composite heroine where Bathsheba is all of a piece. She shows Hardy's remarkable flair, already developed, for realising the physical identity of a heroine by a mixture of personal day-dream and copious literary analogy, a heroine nestled in his imagination and in 'the lap of legends old'.

The immediate vitality of his first heroine is complemented – in fact enhanced – by the sense he is equally immediately the master of, in a way no other novelist has equalled – the dullness of things, the unswerving nature of the daily round. He even manages to suggest it in the ingenious melodrama of the chapter headings – 'The Events of Thirty Years', 'The Events of Three Hours', 'The Events of A Day and A Night' – as well as in the demure epigraph from Scott – 'the province of the romance-writer being artificial, there is more required from him than a mere compliance with the simplicity of reality'. That simplicity is none the less there, from page five, the section of the chapter headed 'October the Twelfth, 1863'. It is the first of Hardy's 'scenes' – scenes in which the simplicity of fact is pushed to its extremest interest by observation and contrivance – and it is by no means the least remarkable of them. The plot requires no more than the death of the heroine's father, so that she and her brother should be launched on the uncertainties and hazards of the novel's path, but this is achieved in no

ordinary way: by means of it Cytherea herself, in her
consciousness and physical being, becomes wholly realised for
us.

First in relation to boredom. The country town of Hocbridge
(Banbury probably) has organised a reading of Shakespeare in
the town hall –

The weather was sunny and dry, but the ancient borough was to be
seen wearing one of its least attractive aspects. First on account of the
time. It was that stagnant hour of the twenty-four when the practical
garishness of Day, having escaped from the fresh long shadows and
enlivening newness of the morning, has not yet made any perceptible
advance towards acquiring those mellow and soothing tones which
grace its decline. Next, it was that stage in the progress of the week
when business – which, carried on under the gables of an old country
place, is not devoid of a romantic sparkle – was wellnigh ext-
inguished. Lastly, the town was intentionally bent upon being
attractive by exhibiting to an influx of visitors the local talent for
dramatic recitation, and provincial towns trying to be lively are the
dullest of dull things.

Little towns are like little children in this respect, that they interest
most when they are enacting native peculiarities unconscious of
beholders.

This is a version of the same point that Hardy will make about
mumming in *The Return of the Native*.

The survival is carried on with a stolidity and absence of stir which sets
one wondering why a thing that is done so perfunctorily should be
kept up at all . . . the agents seem moved by an inner compulsion to
say and do their allotted parts, whether they will or no. This
unweeting manner of performance is the true ring by which, in this
refurbishing age, a fossilised survival may be known from a spurious
reproduction.

It is possible to wish that Shakespeare producers in our own
day might take these comments about self-consciousness to
heart. But in any case, neither Hardy, nor his heroine and
ourselves, are much concerned with the performance: it is a
background both to her 'listlessness', and to attention of another
kind. 'To attempt to gain a view of her – or indeed of any
fascinating woman – from a measured category, is as difficult as

to appreciate the effect of a landscape by exploring it at night with a lantern.' What is fastened on is that 'motion was her speciality', and that when her fellow-children fell over, she went through sundry 'oscillations and whirls' to keep upright. A sense of balance is a useful capability for a heroine in melodrama, but Hardy typically gives the impression that he has settled on the trait simply for its own sake, as if this matter of her physical balance were the 'simplicity of reality' correspondent to the novel's artifice. It has immediate relevance, however, to the drama about to take place on the church tower outside the window, where Cytherea's father, an architect, is supervising repairs –

That the top of this spire should be visible from her position in the room was a fact which Cytherea's idling eyes had discovered with some interest, and she was now engaged in watching the scene that was being enacted about its airy summit. Round the conical stonework rose a cage of scaffolding against the blue sky, and upon this stood five men – four in clothes as white as the new erection close beneath their hands, the fifth in the ordinary dark suit of a gentleman.

The four working-men in white were three masons and a mason's labourer. The fifth man was the architect, Mr. Graye. He had been giving directions as it seemed, and retiring as far as the narrow footway allowed, stood perfectly still.

The picture thus presented to a spectator in the Town Hall was curious and striking. It was an illuminated miniature, framed in by the dark margin of the window, the keen-edged shadiness of which emphasized by contrast the softness of the objects enclosed.

The height of the spire was about one hundred and twenty feet, and the five men engaged thereon seemed entirely removed from the sphere and experiences of ordinary human beings. They appeared little larger than pigeons, and made their tiny movements with a soft, spirit-like silentness. One idea above all others was conveyed to the mind of a person on the ground by their aspect, namely, concentration of purpose: that they were indifferent to – even unconscious of – the distracted world beneath them, and all that moved upon it. They never looked off the scaffolding.

Then one of them turned; it was Mr. Graye. Again he stood motionless, with attention to the operations of the others. He appeared to be lost in reflection, and had directed his face towards a new stone they were lifting.

'Why does he stand like that?' the young lady thought at
length – up to that moment as listless and careless as one of the ancient
Tarentines, who, on such an afternoon as this, watched from the
Theatre the entry into their Harbour of a power that overturned the
State.

She moved herself uneasily. 'I wish he would come down,' she
whispered, still gazing at the sky-backed picture. 'It is so dangerous to
be absent-minded up there.'

When she had done murmuring the words her father indecisively
laid hold of one of the scaffold-poles, as if to test its strength, then let it
go and stepped back. In stepping, his foot slipped. An instant of
doubling forward and sideways, and he reeled off into the air,
immediately disappearing downwards.

The way the scene is stage-managed by Hardy makes it one of
the most astonishing in any of his novels. There is no doubt it is
an accident, but Mr Graye is in deep financial trouble, as his son
and daughter soon find out, and he is the first of Hardy's
characters to have his dilemma and his nature externalised in a
striking tableau, like Clym Yeobright's singing a French song as
he cuts furze on Egdon Heath, Troy's swordsmanship display,
and his flower-planting erased by the gurgoyle. As much, or
more, compelling, is the way in which the scene is first framed
pictorially in a static Pre-Raphaelite way, the four white and one
dark figures moving 'with a soft, spirit-like silentness' in 'an
illuminated miniature' and then transposed into dynamic terms
in which gravity itself acquires a grotesque unexpectedness. In
terms of the spirit-like picture, Mr Graye could easily, it
appears, have vanished *upwards,* and the macabre emphasis upon
the inevitable direction of his descent suggests both something
like a Kafka-type execution (the four white and one black
figures) and the switch from the passive contemplation of the
aesthetic to the brute irruption of fact. It is like Troy shaving off
a morsel of his skin with the sword which has just surrounded
Bathsheba with 'the luminous streams of an *aurora militaris*'.
However many and elaborate Hardy's pictorial analogies, he
can always go beyond them into the world which words rather
than paint can make us realise – the world of physical causation.

Violent movement recalls the aspect of Cytherea singled out
by Hardy – 'the oscillations and whirls for the preservation of

her balance' – and connects it with her father's 'doubling forward and sideways' before he 'reeled off into the air'. The picture frame jumps out into kinetic and magnetic forces: lines of force are drawn about the girl in the town-hall, transmitted to the 'entirely removed' scene outside, and after the accident to the sky itself. Such a transmission, as we might expect, leaves all the stronger impression of objects held apart. As Cytherea is carried into the house she sees 'white sunlight shining in shaft-like lines from a rift in a slaty cloud'. And the chapter section ends with one of those Hardyan sentences, like the one quoted from 'Enter a Dragon', which have to read two or three times before we see just what he is getting at –

Ever after that time any mental agony brought less vividly to Cytherea's mind the scene from the Town Hall windows than sunlight streaming in shaft-like lines.

The scene includes us in a kind of intimacy with author and heroine, of a kind quite unique to Hardy, and here already fully and apparently artlessly established, an intimacy cemented by the train journey she and her brother take in the dog days from Hocbridge to Budmouth Regis. It seems her artless young voice, melted into Hardy's, that we hear in the sentence about the 'sunlight streaming in shaft-like lines'; and that we continue to hear in the account of the different layers of country they pass through from the Midlands to the sea. This heroine is very different from the distressed damsel in Wilkie Collin's *No Name,* the novel from which Hardy quite evidently obtained the idea of her.

True, she does not stay wholly with us: the novel is too much for her, though she is still very much a part of its response to impressions and oddities of sight and sound. But she is too involved in Hardy's own perceptions, as those successfully sustained heroines, Elfride and Bathsheba, are not; and the dream-like lack of effort in the arrival of her personality is made more commonplace towards the novel's end by a real dream in which she is being attacked with a whip by Manston, as demon bridegroom, and awakes on her wedding-morning to a scene of climatic peculiarity such as Hardy loved to depict, a drizzle having frozen overnight and covered the tapping branches with thick ice –

'I never could have believed it possible' she thought, surveying the bowed-down branches, 'that trees would bend so far out of their true positions without breaking'. 'Or that I could so exactly have imitated them', she continued.

That 'true positions' combines in a droll way Hardy's sense of things with a stilted exemplar, as if from an emblem-book. The acoustic feel of Cytherea's speech has given way to formalism. But like all kinds of disappointment in Hardy this brings its own meaning, a meaning established in more auspicious sequences: for in her trouble the girl would indeed be different, stiff and withdrawn to herself and to us. In this way Hardy manages to humanise even the gothic nightmare, as Shakespeare did a similar kind of convention.

This lack of intimacy is variegated and reinforced by the admirable genre humours of the kitchen at Knapwater House on the morning of the wedding melodrama, and the simple pathos of the rejected lover's appearance. Both *A Pair of Blue Eyes* and *A Laodicean* follow, though less obviously, a similar pattern, from an inward to an outer grasp of the heroine. Although the type of both the later girls is more robustly conceived, they share with Cytherea the same immediate freshness of imprint – 'standing in the quarry' as it were – which modifies into an objectively related interest, the material of a study, and a different kind of admiration. In the case of Paula Power this comes to very little – Hardy set himself to complete *A Laodicean* while recovering from a serious illness – but Elfride married to Lord Luxellian, whose little girls had become so much attached to her, and then herself dying of a miscarriage, remains a most moving image; set in perspective by Knight's behaviour, and its cruel response to the fatal clumsiness of her innocence – 'the very innocence of Elfride in reading her little fault as one so grave was what had fatally misled him'.

In all these cases Hardy the noticer is succeeded by Hardy the reflective commentator, and the result is a characteristic separation between the image of the girl nestled in his imagination, and her fate and being objectively seen. She grows up, as it were, overnight, and becomes subject to all the impersonal sadness of things, no matter whether the plot arranges for her to be happy, as with Cytherea, or to die, as in Elfride's case. The transition may remind us in some way of Keats's 'milk-white lamb', and the exclamation in his letters about women dying of cancer. Certainly their separation means that there is no incongruity between the two images, only an added effect. Cytherea's dream, and the iced twigs beating against the window, are only a clumsy repetition of what was fresh and strange in our first acquaintance; but Hardy's comments on how she reacts to the despair of her wedding morning are of a different order. At such moments of anguish 'indescribable by men's words', a woman, he says, 'moves among her acquaintances much as before, and contrives so to cast her actions in the old moulds that she is only considered to be rather duller than usual'. This is the process by which Bathsheba will suddenly change, an appearance both of exaltation and diminution, when she holds Troy, her dead husband, and appears for the first time 'of the stuff of which great men's mothers are made' . . . 'indispensable to high generation, hated at tea-parties, feared in shops, and loved at crises'. Hardy's process takes in with great simplicity the way in which shock and suffering can make people appear dull and ordinary, even as their real strength of character appears, a strength that ends their differentiation as personalities in fiction.

Desperate Remedies has no strong characters in it, which makes a novel all the more intimate in the Hardy sense, and one lacking in that characteristic space in the later ones – but before the *Tess* and *Jude* era – between the people who are inside, and outside, Hardy's private sense of things. In a simpler way it has just the same specification as its successors: the closed circuit plot and the open area of observation. This formula continues until *Tess,* when the areas of plot and observation ominously converge and unite with one another. The open area is more neutral in *Desperate Remedies* than in *Far from the Madding Crowd,* or *The Return of the Native,* because its characters are more passive, and because form in the two later novels engrosses the observed area in the interests of epic scale, or of brooding isolation.

An open area in the first published novel appears in a sort of gentle and detached scientific delicacy, whether it concerns Farmer Springrove at work among his apples, or Mr Graye falling to his death from the scaffolding on Hocbridge church tower. The death of Mr Graye is more an exercise in the mechanics and aesthetics of disaster than a true dire event. It has much in common with that scene in *A Laodicean* where Paula and Somerset are nearly run over by a train as they stand at the mouth of a railway-tunnel built by Paula's father. Or with the more famous account in *A Pair of Blue Eyes* of Knight's investigation at a cliff's edge of the effect on physical bodies of up- and down-draughts. Retrieving his hat he slips over the brow of the 'cliff without a name', and while Elfride takes off her underthings to make a rope to rescue him, he hangs eye to eye with a fossil trilobite embedded in the rock, on the verge of that eternity which he conceives it as inhabiting.

When Hardy is fascinated by a technical question – in this case the effect of a *brief* shower of rain in making slippery a normally safe inclined surface leading to the cliff's edge – a kind of eroticism seems diffused in the very mode of concentration. The atmosphere is both absorbed and passive, like Bathsheba during the sword-exercise. Timing is important – seldom in the second half of the novel: for when what might have been such a scene is used mechanically and out of season towards the end of *The Woodlanders* its effect is unnatural. The episode of the man-trap intended for Fitzpiers, which nearly catches his wife Grace and deprives her of her skirt, is memorable enough, certainly, but oddly coarse by Hardy's standards. It attempts too obviously to provide a bizarre accident as an occasion for husband and wife to 'fall in love' again. We miss the concentration which generates its own kind of expectancy and awareness, an awareness as of physical surfaces and intimacies, at once thinking and sensitive to thought. But *Desperate Remedies* or *A Pair of Blue Eyes* have of course a great deal more of this kind of sensibility in them than *The Woodlanders*; their pleasures are those of a more essentially Hardyan text.

It is notable that these scenes which are literal, sometimes inordinately so, and yet highly fictionalised as well, should have more 'animula' in them than the starker and simpler dramas, like the deaths of Eustacia, Fanny Robin, Henchard and Winterborne, the griefs and the losses. In the closer text of Hardy there is an analogy with the world of Keats's poetry, and with the way in which his language becomes the more down-to-earth the more he is daydreaming. Hardy uses Keats's line about Madeline – 'As though a rose should shut and be a bud again' – about Bathsheba before her second wedding; and the Shakespeare epigraph for Tess is almost as Keatsian. 'Poor wounded name! My bosom as a bed / Shall lodge thee'. It is worth commenting on the fact, however, that Tess, for all her impressiveness as a late and a powerfully 'representative' heroine, really belongs to that mode of femininity so congenial to Hardy as to be almost a part of him. She is sister to Cytherea and Elfride and Elizabeth-Jane; whereas, for all his admiration of them, Hardy regards Bathsheba and Eustacia from outside, as he does Troy or Henchard; vessels of emotion, with all its ignorance and its power. They are persons of character, whom Hardy does not presume to feel for with the simplicity with which he enters into Cytherea's misery on the morning of her marriage to Manston, Elfride's troubles with her two suitors, and Tess's with Alec and Angel Clare.

So unconsciously dominant are the literary echoes in *Desperate Remedies* that Hardy may not have realised how the name of his heroine recalled Iachimo's words about Imogen, as he steals out of the trunk in her bed-chamber. 'Cytherea, how bravely thou becoms't thy bed'. The submerged quotation may none the less have taken a hand in turning the plot. The scene in which her employer, Miss Aldclyffe, asks to come into Cytherea's bed, does not, I would say, reflect gossip about lesbianism which Hardy might have heard from his cousin Martha Sparks, who had been a lady's maid in town houses. That conjecture of Gittings is as unnecessary as the comments by Stewart, and other critics who notice the passage, that Hardy had an eye for and an interest in odd goings-on. In fact, being as literary as he was literal, Hardy is probably recalling an incident he had read in *Pendennis,* an irreproachably domestic source, and which he might have found mention of in many other novels. For members of the same sex to share a bed was too common a practice then to raise eyebrows; it could thus be taken advantage of, as Courbet's academy-style picture 'Sleep' suggests, and Hardy's opportunity – like the picture's – lay not in the relationship but in the legitimate excuse to be a voyeur. Attendance on Miss Aldclyffe justifies our attendance on Cytherea's own disrobing when she goes to bed, tired out with her employer's exactions:

All these preparations completed, she began to undress, her mind unconsciously drifting away to the contemplation of her late surprises. To look in the glass for an instant at the reflection of her own magnificent resources in face and bosom, and to mark their attractiveness unadorned, was perhaps but the natural action of a young woman who had so lately been chidden whilst passing through the harassing experience of decorating an older beauty of Miss Aldclyffe's temper.

But she feels sympathy too. She has discovered that her father was once in love with Miss Aldclyffe, and that they share, in consequence, the same unusual Christian name. All this is the stock-in-trade of an ingenious plot, which none the less depends on a genuine commonplace of the period – a woman whose early seduction means that she has taken elaborate steps to conceal her past. It is typical of Hardy that an extravagant device seems to bring him a greater access of sober reality; because he strikes one, despite all the ingenuity, as not being really 'in charge' and not concerned to be. He seems to be investigating an actual situation he has heard of, not making it up, as Wilkie Collins would so obviously and emphatically be doing. Hence what seems a simple realism in the work, a realism only available to the great age of the novel – the age of cast-iron social standard and convention. Hardy is romantic, but not in the least sentimental: in Balzac the two adjectives would be synonymous. The sympathies with which the business of the night is described are unnoticed by the steady chronology of its intentness. Miss Aldclyffe torments Cytherea with questions about her lover ('Find a girl, if you can, whose mouth and ears have not been made a regular highway of by some man or other . . . a girl whose heart has not been *had* . . .') She first abuses the girl and is then comforted by her – the mother and daughter relations reversed, so that the older woman goes to sleep 'as if the maiden at her side afforded her a protection against dangers which had menaced her for years'.

In the sequence that follows, the relation of the two women, absorbing as it is to Hardy, gives place to one that absorbs him still more: the language of sounds. 'Sounds were in the ascendant that night'.

The first sound is of a water-fall, 'brought from its source to the unwonted distance of the House by a faint breeze which made it distinctly perceptible by reason of the utter absence of all disturbing noises'.

the second was quite different from the first – a kind of intermittent whistle it seemed primarily: no, a creak, a metallic creak, ever and anon, like a plough or a rusty wheelbarrow, or at least a wheel of some kind.

She remembers that there is a water-wheel in an outhouse in the shrubbery, and 'to imagine the inside of the engine-house, whence these noises proceeded, was now a necessity'. The third sound is 'a very soft gurgle or rattle', which makes a dog in the house begin to whine –

One logical thought alone was able to enter her flurried brain. The little dog that began the whining must have heard the other two sounds even better than herself. He had taken no notice of them, but he had taken notice of the third. The third, then, was an unusual sound.

We learn afterwards that Miss Aldclyffe's father, like Keats's beadsman, has died in the night, and that the third sound, unusual enough to make the dog bark, was his death-rattle. In her naïve way the heroine parodies the elimination and deduction technique of a detective mystery, a Sherlock Holmes whose observations are as much more sensuous than his as they are inconclusive. Like Anne Seaway's, when she is observing Manston at the climax of the book, 'the whole surface of her body became attentive'. It is a method perfectly suited to the idea of *sequence as form,* which makes the book, and it is echoed by the most masterly sequence in it – the burning down of the Three Tranters Inn – in which the smouldering centre of a heap of couch grass becomes itself both villain and detective, the stealthy deductive experimenter creeping closer and closer to its target: for 'Nature does few things directly'.

The chronicle of events brings us into an intimacy both with the things in themselves and the recording consciousness, with the external sounds and with Cytherea listening to them as she lies in bed. As so often in early Hardy we are reminded of Virginia Woolf; not by the way he is writing and how he is concentrating, but by the sequential flow in which a consciousness is domesticated for us out of the impressions it is recording.

The feel of life, in the continuity of impressions showering down on the prose surface, is of course done with abandonment by her, an abandonment which demonstrates itself as a sort of brilliant helplessness. Hardy's leisurely concentration, like the unhurried working tempo of a professional craftsman, is a very different thing; yet the effect it produces is not so dissimilar. *Desperate Remedies* combines in a simpler way than the later novels the vulnerability of a tentatively methodical style with Hardy's strange gift of *reluctance,* the impression of which greatly increases the reader's curiosity. It seems to produce at moments what amounts to an *undertext,* a meditative contemplation, on Hardy's part, on the events of the night: Cytherea in bed, the relation with each other and to her of the components of the estate, the big house, the dilapidated older manor converted into cottages, the lake and water-wheel, the inn left derelict by loss of traffic from the highroad to the railway, the big bustling kitchen which acts as a convergence – below the loftier social convolutions of the plot – for local gossip.

The emergence of these things has a truer sort of helplessness than that cultivated by the style of Virginia Woolf, but one tending in the same direction of veracity: here as much subdued as in her world it is insisted on. Hardy's reluctance seems to extend back the area the reader desires to pry into – an investigation independent of the author, even though it seems to bring us into more intimate contact with him.

Our sense of an undertext is often most marked in Hardy when the plot is most emphatically at work on the surface. Thus the effect is not that of an interlude, a 'scene on its own', but of the author becoming absorbed in the objects which the plot makes use of as it passes. The road on which the story of *The Woodlanders* is launched and carried forward is at first a still centre on its own, engrossing Hardy's attention for this reason. There is the same feeling of private concentration during the sustained narrative sequence of Mrs Yeobright's pilgrimage to her son's house in *The Return of the Native,* which ends in her death. She sees a man advancing before her 'like a moving handpost', and she can only keep up with him because he pauses for a while at every clump of brambles. When she reaches these in her turn she finds 'half a dozen long limp brambles' cut from the bush and laid out straight beside the path.

This tableau seems to absorb Hardy so much that it is no surprise when she realises that the man is her son Clym, out furze-cutting. The intimate relation in an unexpected setting reminds us of the beginning of *Desperate Remedies,* of Cytherea's father and the dark figures on the tower-top, moving 'with a soft, spirit-like silentness'. But the strange effect of unfamiliarity – any mother's ignorance of her son's activities, or a daughter's of her father's past and present consciousness – is less striking than the more private vision of something much simpler, more primeval: the oddity of one human being seen by another. Such a perception is exactly what Virginia Woolf gives us and her heroine, when Mrs Dalloway sees, after a party, an old woman in the lighted window of a neighbouring house:

It was fascinating to watch her, moving about, that old lady, crossing the room, coming to the window. Could she see her? It was fascinating, with people still laughing and shouting in the drawing-room, to watch that old woman, quite quietly, going to bed alone.

Virginia Woolf is trying hard, and succeeding, in making us realise something that Hardy contemplates privately, on his own. But both writers are doing the same thing, a thing uniquely difficult, demanding the same quality of transmitted perception. It would indeed be possible to see *Mrs Dalloway* and some of Virginia Woolf's other novels as methodical explorations of these moments implicit in the Hardyan under-text. *Mrs Dalloway* contains a sentence that seems unconsciously to echo Hardy and follow on from him –

This late age of the world's experience had bred in them all, all men and women, a well of tears.

It is difficult to study Hardy closely without being constantly reminded of this unexpected disciple.

Of course not all his detachments are like this: some are gratuitous in an inert and ordinary way, like the detailed description of Mrs Swancourt and her jewels in *A Pair of Blue Eyes*. Precision here is idle rather than intent, and Mrs Swancourt remains wholly vague as a character, presumably because the form of that novel is determined not by an exactness of such moments and sequences, giving their life to the persons they encounter, but by a place, or rather a single *view* of coast and hinterland, with Elfride as its tutelary spirit. There is for instance a pure *Desperate Remedies* moment when Knight, investigating the collapsed church tower in the dark, feels under his hand an indefinable substance, which prolonged palpatory interrogation, of an extremely Hardy-like kind, reveals eventually to be a woman's hair. This promising event is also irrelevant in the novel's context.

A discussion of the nature of form in the novels would conclude that it is apt to be strongly influenced, if not actually determined, by Hardy's relation to the heroine. We have seen how effectually he enters Bathsheba's consciousness in her time of greatest tribulation, but neither with her nor with any other heroine does he presume to *reproduce* the nature of such a consciousness in the manner that Joyce and Virginia Woolf and later novelists have attempted, to the point where it has become a cliché or a mere convenience. Imitative form with Hardy is a much more subtle affair, interrelated as it is with his own consciousness transposed into locality and experience that was or might have been his own. He is not aware of the process as a technique, a deliberate method which exploitation is liable to render facile.

An Indiscretion in the Life of an Heiress inherited from *The Poor Man and The Lady* the most obviously autobiographical of Hardy's imaginings: that of a young man of humble origins, though with some better class-connections too, in love with a daughter of the manor in the same locality. Hardy must often have mused on this possibility in his own case, and its probable sequel were it really to happen. In *A Pair of Blue Eyes* he repeats, with variations, the same theme; his young hero Stephen being the son of a stonemason in the village of which the heroine's father is rector. The most telling item in the chapter of misfortune which separates the young lovers is the rector's discovery that the personable young architect is the son of a working-man in the parish. Hardy's understanding of class matters, and his sense of how he can use them in fiction, is already fully developed: the romance is developed in alliance with, but also in separation from, his knowledge of how matters really stand. Though Stephen's father is prosperous enough to 'buy him up', as the impoverished rector himself admits, the rector has the freedom and latitude which his class position confers on him – he can improve his position by a rich marriage. His attitude to Elfride's romance is brilliantly done; there is a deadly reasonableness about his point that in 'this county – which is the world to us – you would always be known as the wife of Jack Smith the mason's son, and not under any circumstances as the wife of a London professional man'. Hardy himself must often have had cause to consider, and with a certain grim satisfaction, that the village of his own upbringing lay many miles away from St Juliot.

Elfride's innocence is all the more attractive because it is not congenital; it means only that she has met nobody and that she has formed no standards. This too connects her with place. Twice during the book the sea itself is described as 'floundering':

The sea, though comparatively placid, could as usual be heard from this point along the whole distance between promontories to the right and left, floundering and entangling itself among the insulated stacks of rock.

It is an inimitable Hardy epithet, unexpectedly connecting the natural element with the girl who rides beside it. Elfride does indeed flounder, because she has no alotted place in society and no conditioned instinct about what to expect from it. It must have been precisely this that attracted Hardy in Emma.

And Emma soon acquired the gentilities that she came to feel went with her station, which it became clear was not her husband's. When she married at thirty-five she must still have had the floundering innocence of Elfride at eighteen, but it could hardly last. Hardy remarked late in life that Elfride had much of Emma in her. He did not report on how Emma must have become embittered by the sight of her husband famous and sought after in circles whose distinction and self-confidence made them contemptuous of mere gentility. As a 'lady', advertising her own refinement in contrast to her husband's lack of it, she would have been a tiresome bore to the distinguished and fashionable who accepted Hardy completely, and were as at home with him as he soon became at ease with them. It was the kind of irony which Hardy appreciated, but which he could scarcely make use of. By the time he had been beneath that particular harrow he was not disposed, one imagines, to 'notice' it as he did other things.

Elfride is certainly noticed, exactly and beautifully so, and with no trace of the sentiment which might be thought almost irremovable from a heroine in her literary tradition of innocence, pathos and betrayal. She bursts out to her father – 'He is my own Stephen, he is!' – but her deeper impression is is then recorded in one of Hardy's most laborious but uncannily effective literary allusions – 'of all the miseries attaching to miserable love, the worst is the misery of thinking that the passion which is the cause of them all may cease'. An adaptation of the tag from Boethius, Dante and Tennyson, that the worst affliction is to recall a happier time, means in Elfride's case the awareness that first love will not last. The reason is again the novel's form. 'I don't like it here – nor myself – nor you!' she cries in panic on Paddington station, after their abortive elopement. Away from her place she loses all the emotion connected with it. 'Every woman who makes a particular impression on a man is usually recalled in his mind's eye as she appeared in one particular scene . . . her special form of mani-festation throughout the pages of his memory'. Hardy's comment on Elfride determines the outcome, for both Stephen and Knight, in their different ways, can see her only as an emanation of the place. In poems as well as the *Life* Hardy implies that he should never have taken his wife away from Cornwall.

Elfride's helplessness is determined by the place she lives in and the being it has given her, and is paralleled by Knight's equally determined misogny:

Lifelong constraint towards women, which he had attributed to accident, was not chance after all, but the natural results of instinctive acts so minute as to be indiscernible by himself.

Hardy's determinism is a much quieter affair than Dickens's, quieter and more deadly, but as penetrating; and more subtle in the early than the later novels, where it has taken on something of the public status which it acquired in fiction in the late 1880s and 1890s. Hardy contrives to make out of it not the drama of self-realisation, but its intimate surface and texture. We can feel what those 'minute' things were, for Knight, though they have none of the vigorous emphasis that shows how Pip and David Copperfield have become what they are.

The most obviously poetic of the novels is in this discreet sense the most determined, appropriately enough when we think of its landscape: the sea eating away at the cliffs, and the fossil trilobite's eye which regards the suspended Knight. Its characters, too, have an appropriate passivity. In the novel that followed, *Far from the Madding Crowd,* they are all in their varying kinds strong and active, and yet the determined 'results of instinctive acts' are as subtle and as marked. There is no Gabriel Oak in the earlier novel, and yet in a sense there is a Troy, a Boldwood, and a Bathsheba. The triangle which is so strikingly presented in the second novel, and done in formal terms of rustic and Homeric hyperbole, is more obscured in the misty sea monochromes of its predecessor. But the greater emphasis, strength and variety of the latter has no less delicacy. Both stories show how it is determined that each person shall be unable to give what the loved one needs, and should require what he or she cannot have. Troy was not lying when he claimed Fanny Robin as his true love; her total devotion was what he needed, beyond his urge to show off. Bathsheba, who rejected Oak because of his fidelity, comes hopelessly to realise the cell of obligation to which Boldwood's far more powerful

obsession has condemned her: had the fate that eliminated her
husband also not disposed of Boldwood she would have had to
marry him. Elfride can physically rescue Knight, taking off her
underclothes to do so – a striking indication of her involuntary
readiness to rescue him in a sexual sense! But when he is safe and
in her embrace he does not even kiss her – a point emphasised – out of motives of delicacy. The irony of his physical rescue
is that his psychological condition cannot be helped by her. His
passion for 'untried lips', and his instant rejection of her when he
has the excuse, shows the real situation. Both Knight and
Stephen want to be in love with Elfride but not to be loved by
her. She is only really needed by the motherless Luxellian girls,
who recognise her capacity to love, and so by their father who
marries her. Not surprising that the novel was the favourite of
Coventry Patmore, who always had it read to him when
recovering from indisposition. A connoisseur of erotic sacrifice
and selfishness, the shrewd egoist of *The Angel in the House* must
have recognised what went on in the novel and relished it.

Did Hardy realise too? The question is hardly relevant to the
peculiar qualities of his art of fiction at this stage, but the novel is
certainly full of prescience and omen. It is generally agreed that
Knight has something of Hardy's friend Moule in him, and this
is probably true as regards Knight's mode of life and relation to
Stephen, much as Neigh, in *The Hand of Ethelberta,* carried a
good deal in physique and manner of the new acquaintance
Leslie Stephen. But much more clearly, and in keeping with the
formal lodgement of the novel in this for him new and intensely
romantic place, both men are personae of Hardy's own
self-awareness of the nature of himself in love: as a young
hopeful, and as a mature bachelor (he was thirty at the time of
his first Cornish visit). While Elfride is rescuing, and failing to
rescue, Knight, Stephen is just offshore in the little steamer, seen
by her through Knight's telescope and forgotten in the crisis of
the hour; and by a shift in fictional perspective he will presently
appear himself as the voyeur, watching from a leafy valley
inshore where first an animated white dot, and then a
slower-paced dark one, descend in succession the headland from
the adventure on the cliff without a name.

He does not know what the separated human dots signify, as he will not understand the novel's wider situation. Egbert Mayne, of *An Indiscretion,* has a more detached view of his situation, which – oddly enough – probably reflects the much greater degree of fantasy in that *nouvelle* and its original, *The Poor Man.* Geraldine Allenville is almost certainly a fantasy portrait, whereas Elfride has something of a real person and a completeness of real place behind her; yet in terms of class at least Geraldine is as sharply and effectively realised. Although so young she has 'insensibly acquired the tongue' of 'people of culture and experience' in the circles she moves in, and the most telling aspect of the tale is its periodic and painful reminder to the young lovers that the intimacy of their talk can be disturbed at any moment by misunderstanding: when Mayne says it takes two hours to get somewhere, she assumes he must mean driving, while he means on foot:

The remarks had been simple and trivial, but they brought a similar thought into the minds of both of them. On her part it spread a sudden gloom over her face, and it made him feel dead at heart. It was that horrid thought of their differing habits and of those contrasting positions which could not be reconciled . . . Thus they mutually oppressed each other even while they loved.

There is a sharp contrast in the *Indiscretion* between the fantasy in its idea and the shrewdness in its working out. The death of Geraldine, of some convenient congenital seizure, brought on by the terror of meeting her father after her marriage to Mayne, is necessary because of that shrewdness: the most sentimental reader must have got the point that such a marriage could hardly do. Elfride's death is unnecessary except to give some extra life to the past behaviour of her two suitors: it is a part of the sombreness which attaches – as well as its charm – to the sea-place which is her setting and to which death brings her back. Both stories show the nature of the heroine determining its form, in the sense in which I have used the term about these novels. And this concept of form is illuminating when we turn to the two most obvious hybrids, *The Hand of Ethelberta* and *A Laodicean.*

The continuity in form between *A Pair of Blue Eyes* and *Far from the Madding Crowd* is great enough to overset the distinctions that Hardy made between the kinds of his fiction when he prepared the complete Wessex edition in 1912. The former novel is categorised under 'Romances and Fantasies' and the latter under the premier class – 'Novels of Character and Environment'. *Desperate Remedies* is classed with *The Hand of Ethelberta* and *A Laodicean* as the three 'Novels of Ingenuity'. A more empirically justifiable category, including all but these last two, would be 'Heroines as fictional forms', or something of the sort. It would not be definitive – nothing in Hardy ever is – but it would suggest both the ways in which the novels determine themselves, and how these two evade such a determination. Hardy has two bogus heroines – Fancy Day of *Under the Greenwood Tree* and Anne Garland of *The Trumpet Major* – and two who fail more interestingly to be realised as heroines – Ethelberta, and Paula Power of *A Laodicean*. In the case of the first two the forms have been predetermined: the pastoral and the historical have been set up as forms conventional and second-hand in themselves before the heroines have been tailored to fit them; and from this dead touch – so alien to Hardy's kinds of involuntary experiment in form – the two novels do not recover.

Fancy Day and Anne Garland are genre heroines *tout simple*, and their remarkable lack of existence – remarkable in the light of Hardy's success, sometimes against all odds, in putting it into his other girls – shows how little he is a genre novelist. His feeling for the past, like his feeling for the country, is too much a part of him to be used so methodically, and it is a typically Hardyan paradox that what in another novelist – George Eliot most obviously – would be a 'loving' treatment – a rural painting in the Dutch school, and a careful historical reconstruction with muslins and parasols, loyalties and royalties, all in period – has the effect of alienating, both from the author and ourselves, the heroine who should be the centre piece of the display. There is little of that diversity and separation in tone and texture, all the unbothered unevenness, which brings us into intimacy with author and heroine. The form is too smooth, unified, and coherent, except when it seems to turn on the girls at the end as if in cynicism or even reproach. Indeed the endings of both novels show us a great deal about the importance of such endings in these forms of Hardy. The Russian formalist, Victor Shklovsky, wrote at large on Tolstoy's endings, as a particularly significant aspect of his structure, and Hardy's seem to me equally revealing, so much so that a consideration of them would not be a digression, the more since endings, like heroines, are so much a part of his characteristics of form.

VI

Desperate Remedies ENDS WITH A REPETITION, THE
first in the book. What had proceeded in terms almost of a
parody of sequence (the most memorable is Manston taking the
corpse of his wife to furtive interment, followed by no less than
three watchers, each unbeknown to the others) repeats its
happiest motif, a kiss in a boat, and so concludes. It breaks, at the
beginning of its last chapter, into the historic present, which also
emphasises the end of a sequence; and the repetition severs also
our intimacy with Cytherea, which took the form of her
reactions and responses shown to us one after the other. The two
other novels in which form, under this definition, is as
unobtrusive as successful – *Far from the Madding Crowd* and *The
Return of the Native* – end with a similar sort of appropriateness.
Oak and Bathsheba are properly diminished into marriage – Oak's simple pleasure in twice referring to 'my wife' is
sardonically noted by Jan Coggan – and Joseph Poorgrass has
his concluding comment on this decline from the pattern of
heroic 'absoluteness':

I were once or twice upon saying today with holy Hosea, in my
scripture manner, which is my second nature, 'Ephraim is joined to
idols: let him alone'. But since 'tis as 'tis, why, it might have been
worse, and I feel my thanks accordingly.

Joseph makes a good chorus on the grand formal values of
passion, obsession, and fidelity, because he knows nothing of
them.

The ending of *The Return of the Native* more than makes up
for any failing in Venn; for Venn himself, or rather Charley's
report of him at the wedding dance ('He has knocked his head
against the beam in gieing a skip as he passed under' . . .) is the

principal means of reversing the estrangement and solitude which have made up the form of the novel. Only Clym is left alone –

'. . . they are all holding up their glasses and drinking somebody's health.'
'I wonder if it is mine?'
'No, 'tis Mr and Mrs Venn's'.

He is deprived of both wife and mother; the failure of his relations with both merging significantly into one when he reflects about his mother that 'he should have heeded her for Eustacia's sake even more than for his own'. But this is not the end, for Clym too will join in the general process of uniting, in the sun on Rainbarrows, and through the unlikely medium of his own sermonising. It is Hardy the unperturbed sermonist taking farewell both of theme and form, with his two references to Solomon's mother, who had not crowned Clym 'in the day of his espousals', and in whose memory he gives out the text of his first sermon . . . 'and the King said unto her, Ask on my mother: for I will not say thee nay'. (Most of us today miss the allusion; the fact that Solomon not only did say nay, but ordered his brother's slaying, on behalf of whom his mother Bathsheba was petitioning her son.) But Clym had 'found his vocation' and 'every where he was kindly received' . . .

"O, 'tis the nightingale", murmured she, and thought of a secret she would never tell'. Some say that this ending to the story of Fancy Day, with its suggestion of the less idyllic aspects of marriage, and of the author's less than wholly enchanted view of the heroine herself, makes an effective counter to the sweets of rustic pastoral. But does it not rather confirm these things, altogether too fluently and decoratively? 'Murmured she' has a sort of built-in contempt, in the prose texture, a recognition of the nullity of the fiction; and this abandonment by the prose itself of its areas of sensitivity, exploration and unexpectedness is as unusual in Hardy as it is common at such moments in some other writers. Though Hardy himself may profess no regard for his fictions, he is in general belied by his own style and its natural intricacies. Here his lack of interest really is endorsed by the words he uses: the vacancy of Fancy as a heroine, despite the emotional flurry of the Vicar's offer and her short-lived acceptance – here referred to – remains not only unfilled but rendered the more perfectly void. If Hardy's best endings reveal a form by subtle contradiction or escape from it, this merely shows that the convention is to remain elementary and unchallenged.

The case of *The Trumpet-Major* is different, and much more interesting. John Loveday, the trumpet-major, is summoned for foreign service: Anne has at length accepted his sailor brother Bob. Hardy has made no attempt to enter Anne's feelings but has merely used them for the more or less effective little minuet of the story – she is not alive for him, and so not for us either. But at the end the bogus historical tableau is scattered by Hardy's real sense of war, of death, and of the past. 'John marches into the night' is the heading of the last short chapter, and it induces a different sort of sensation from any the novel has previously given us. Hardy is sniffing a different air altogether, and this is perhaps apparent in the abruptness with which he arranges the close, telling us five paragraphs from the end that John and four of the companions-in-arms who wished Anne goodnight, 'were dead men within the few following years, and their bones left to moulder in the land of their campaigns'. The end has suddenly the fervency and the lack of consciousness that might be in one of the poems, and there is no sense of let-down in the last sentence, as John, 'backed by the black night' turns away with a farewell smile, 'and went off to blow his trumpet until silenced for ever upon one of the bloody battle-fields of Spain'.

Hardy forgets the minuet and its patterns at one other point, when he imagines the *Victory* going down channel off Portland Bill. The *Victory* is emphatically not a historical property: she is a physical object in her own right, and her sudden appearance as such blows away all the business about Captain Hardy, and Anne's lover Bob 'in his snow-white trousers and jacket of navy blue', even the account of battle at Trafalgar afterwards by the returned sailor Cornick. In all such matters, including the proverbial unreliableness of Jack ashore, Hardy sticks doggedly to the clichés of literary situation, as if it were the sort of contemporary comedy at the Budmouth theatre in which his actress Matilda might be playing a part. The hint of his usual kinds of reality appear chiefly in the references to class and station: the chance of Bob becoming an officer, the status of the trumpet-major, an NCO, in the limbo of an army with no immediate occupation. Perhaps Hardy's subterraneous wish to be in kinship with his famous namesake, the Captain, induced a kind of embarrassment which made him keep that side of things in the safety of literary commonplace, while his hidden sympathy extended to a real kinship with the soldier and his unrecorded destiny to come? However that may be, there is nowhere a greater disregard for a heroine, a more uncompromising allotment of her to a lay role.

But what did a big ship of war look like, under sail? Not like the prints and engravings after which most of the book seems copied:

The great silent ship, with her population of bluejackets, marines, officers, captain, and the admiral who was not to return alive, passed like a phanton the meridian of the Bill. Sometimes her aspect was that of a large white bat, sometimes that of a grey one. In the course of time the watching girl saw that the ship had passed her nearest point; the breadth of her sails diminished by foreshortening, till she assumed the form of an egg on end . . .

The *Victory* was fast dropping away. She was on the horizon, and soon appeared hull down. That seemed to be like the beginning of a greater end than her present vanishing . . . The vessel was now exactly end on and stood out in the direction of the Start, her width having contracted to the proportion of a feather . . . She was now no more than a dead fly's wing on a sheet of spider's web; and even this fragment diminished. Anne could hardly bear to see the end, and yet she resolved not to flinch. The admiral's flag sank beneath the watery line, and in a minute the very truck of the last topmast stole away. The *Victory* was gone.

Bats, eggs, feathers and flies' wings are the similes Hardy's intentness seizes on, to express the physical apparition. His dimension is in general that of a whole country, not a 'sight' or a view, and when he does such a sight here, its reality shows up the rest of the historical reconstruction. This is not far from Wardour Street, a particularly degenerate genre in which Hardy does as well as can be, but does not really transform into something new and strange, as he does the almost equally conventional novel of mystery and suspense. Nor can he reanimate the simplicity of Scott, or of Pushkin, who followed Scott in making a heroine's meeting with the sovereign an occasion of true drama.

We may feel that Hardy was aware of all this and allowed its frustrations to appear in his ending, when John Loveday can abandon his cardboard role of the faithful man; and his brother Bob, the hero of Trafalgar and the engrosser (by Hardy's not unsardonic preference we may feel) of the book's local colour, is revealed as more insensitive even than his role required, just as brother John is in the end more truly heroic. That final fleeting and terrible image of the Peninsular War, that goes with him, redeems the whole debased picturesque image of Bob and Anne and Weymouth and King George, even of the report of Trafalgar itself.

Hardy's patriotism was as real as his sense of the past, and both are simple and native to the world of his poetry, but oddly enough he found no correlative for either in a complete novel. The good details and the telling comments – like the sergeants at the miller's party showing no interest in military matters, as the civilians discussed them, but only in the raising of chickens and pigs and bees – these things could be in verse; they show us how different is the 'poetry' in the novels from that of our concept of form in them. And the heroine here is outside the form, instead of being virtually coincident with it: when things are seen thus, she is forgotten.

The opposite happens to Ethelberta; she is not outside but too much inside, losing her identity wholly to her author instead of being the centre of his attention. The successful heroines are the result of a delicate equipoise between identification with, and looking at: they are 'standing in the quarry', but they are also diffused into Hardy's sense of life, for them and for himself, or for the two as one. Ethelberta is too wholly his creature, as she is too vivaciously a creation. Hardy was in the full flow of invention, and determined not to go on writing about sheep-shearing and dipping (as he tells us he felt expected to) but to launch out in a new field. And an ambitious one: nothing less than society as a cross-section, the levels being potentially interchangeable, an idea visibly realised in the remarkable scene in which the servants have a sort of private ball in a London mansion, above the rooms in which a grand dinner is going on. The scene is typically 'well-found' in physical terms, for we learn that the double floor is so solidly constructed that it prevents any sound coming through, a point of social significance as well as one that would fascinate an architect. And no country scene is better visualised, or contains more of the oddity of selfhood this artist's eye brings out, than the urban one on the parapet of the heroine's house where she and her sister gossip desultorily in the dawn and watch the 'swarthy columns of smoke' begin to soar up in the fashionable terraces around as the kitchen-maids light the fires.

The two are part of the extensive family of a butler, and as a result of the plot contrivance they live in an 'upstairs downstairs' world, familiar equally with both though at home in neither. But the insecurity and ultimately the insubstantiality of the book does not come – as has often been said – from Hardy's lack of certainties and 'feel' about these urban and intersocial worlds, but from his inability to frame and present his heroine, as an external portrait, in the first place. The reason is plain. Hardy is here, in fantasy and in projection, completely his own heroine. It is the most singular of his identifications, for as a man who would rather be silent than speak, an observer and not an actor, he projects an extraordinary daydream of *performance,* substituting for his own talent for writing the brilliance of an entertainer, and the daring wit and poise of a society beauty. Nor was that all. As a man whose relations with the world of responsibilities, however shrewd, were passive and unauthoritative, he becomes in the book the arbiter and goddess of a large family, all of whom look to Ethelberta for guidance and support in the shifts of their strange social situation.

We may guess that Hardy's mother was an image not too remote here – indeed Robert Gittings goes so far as to see a pun in the title itself, for her maiden name was Hand. Possibly one's mother defies imaginative embodiment in the form of a novel's heroine? However that may be, there is no doubt that the ghostliness of Ethelberta, who is more like a Meredith heroine than a Hardy one, dissolves also what might otherwise have been an effective and original Hardy 'form'. Like *The Trumpet-Major*, though for very different reasons, the novel is equally a matter of scenes and pictures, although these often carry a real novelty of intellectual and social meaning. Ethelberta running to watch the pursuit of a duck by a duck-hawk in the marshes near Anglebury; she and her sister making a surreptitious nocturnal visit to the sinister and houseless estate of Neigh, where broken-down horses are fed to the local pack; the servants' mock ball; Lord Mountclere's instant ordering of the destruction of a grove of beech-trees, which shelters his Purbeck estate from the sea winds, because Ethelberta frivolously observes that she prefers a blue nick in the hillside to a green one – all these are not only telling in terms of a novel about society but are Hardyan actualities as well. Ethelberta's brothers, Dan and Sol, in Rouen; their account of how they made their carpet-bag, and their interest in the physique of a French hotel ('What a rum staircase – the treads all in little blocks, and painted chocolate, as I'm alive!') are details seen not only by Hardy's eye at its best, but with the humour at which he excels.

And yet Ethelberta remains too much an idea and a daydream – the family support, 'the prime ruler of the courses of them all' – to engage our interests as Hardy's real heroines can. Hardy is too dispassionate about her, and in a curious way too much in practical earnest about what she might represent for him, if he had been in the position of bringing up his own family in the social scale and being responsible for what ensued. Ethelberta's fate and fortune, her success in the social gambling stakes, is turned at the end into an enigmatic image of a woman who has become unknowable through her triumph. He has been too close to Ethelberta for her to be a proper heroine, but after her marriage to Lord Mountclere she is too far away to be imagined either by him or by us. Hardy seems to be wryly envisaging the possible effects on himself of his own social and literary success. We hear of her only through the reactions of the family she has made and kept together, and these are by no means entirely grateful or flattering.

With whatever degree of consciousness, probably not much, Hardy reversed the form of the previous novel when he decided to write one of a wholly different kind. Bathsheba has her heroic absoluteness; she is naturally virginal, but when she falls she does so in a big way; her emotions take complete control. Ethelberta, with her staunch Saxon nomenclature (perhaps her ancestors did come over with those Sleswig pirates) has no time for that sort of thing. Her one idea is to achieve success with security, and since she cannot do this through her 'art' she must do it through a rich marriage. If the form of *Far from the Madding Crowd* depends on absolutes, the 'upstairs downstairs' one of *Ethelberta* suggests their absence in this sort of world – primitive rural forces and feelings have no place. D. H. Lawrence hailed Ethelberta as Hardy's realisation of the woman who saw that 'love' was no good, that it got in the way of the kind of self-fulfilling arrangement that his own Birkin was to have with Ursula. We can be sure that Hardy had no such feelings himself: what he admires about Ethelberta is her enterprise and self-sacrifice, for the paradox of her betwixt and betweenness is that she does not act on her own, but as the leader of this nomadic and decentred tribe.

But, much more important, Hardy could not portray love without its involuntariness, which is its danger and likely disaster. His sense of the thing is unmistakable, and Bathsheba's situation is exactly the one he can enter into, as he can enter into the fate that caused Elfride to meet Knight and Stephen. But fate has no part in the form of Ethelberta, and a heroine who is not fated cannot in Hardy be one with any real substance. The social comedy of her achievements is so well done as to make up for it – he gets as much humour out of the Chickerel family's righteous alarm for her virtue, and Sol's zealous playing of the faithful brother's conventional role, as if – which is not far from the case – they are so cut off from their roots that they must react as the literary commonplace of the time dictated they should. They know about bold bad baronets from the music hall and the circulating library. The converse of this unusual use of convention are the comic actualities of unexpected relation, at their best when Sol and Mountclere's brother, bizarrely united in their desire to stop the marriage, arrive at the local at two in the morning and try to get something to eat –

'There's but little in house', said the sleepy woman from her bedroom.

'There's pig' fry, a side of bacon, a conger eel, and pickled onions'.
'Conger eel?' said Sol to Mountclere.
'No, thank you'.

The comma shows a perfect ear for the tone of the nobleman's resignation. Hardy gives to the literary business of inns and pursuits a literalness as complete as he managed for the mystery in *Desperate Remedies*.

And yet, as the exchange suggests, the effect is wholly offhand – Hardy does not expect the praise accorded to 'pure literature'. He is the only nineteenth-century novelist who in such a context hits off a Shakespearian felicity without giving the smallest impression that he is doing anything really 'worthwhile'. His lightness of touch never seems deliberately light, not self-regarding, like that of Dickens and Thackeray, when it changes into another key. The end of *Ethelberta* breaks off comedy for a note of melancholy. Ethelberta has disappeared into her new role as 'old man's darling', which she prosecutes with competence and vigour. She appears now only in the report of her relatives, and Hardy gives the impression that she has lost both worlds, both the 'upstairs' and the 'downstairs', and is sustained only by her own will; and into this impression he puts his own kind of intimacy, as if he knew well himself how such a state of affairs might come about.

One thing which seems to me certain is that *Ethelberta* is *not* a failure: and that it does not show, as most Hardy critics assume, that he had no sense of how to handle a social and metropolitan theme. Rather he had too much sense of it. *Ethelberta*, like *Hamlet*, is an imaginative impression of 'court life', about which the novelist is too intrigued to be sure-footed. Yet except for Shakespeare himself no English writer is more naturally a courtier than Hardy. Their attraction towards places where the role is played is a matter of feeling as well as imagination; and they have the art of pleasing both the self-appointed great, and those great by nature, without forfeiting an essential detachment and an inner amusement. His social success meant a great deal to Hardy, not least because it confirmed him as an 'intrinsicalist', one who naturally understood and responded to the nature and psychology of worldly success. It is common enough now for novelists to lament their lost social origins and announce their disenchantment with the new world they have entered. Hardy's reticence conveys that he must have known the experience in some form. We learn that Ethelberta is occupying herself with an epic poem, a sort of paradigm of wasted artifice after the vigour and excitement of her early enterprises.

She is the only woman in the novels to exercise coolly something like freedom of choice, which the form makes an ironic perquisite of these between two worlds. She rejects Neigh and Ladywell, the dilettante and the conscious gentleman, and she also rejects Christopher, the poor musician who is kin to all the other novels' refined and youthful heroes, because the picture of poverty in a little music shop repels her. Hardy does not give the impression that a temperament capable of choosing is a privilege likely to make its owner happy. It implies rather a renunciation, and it is appropriate that on the last page Ethelberta will hand over heroine status to her sister Picotee, who longs to marry Christopher. Will her family be pleased? he asks, and Picottee utters without irony the novel's last words, more fervent than any preceding ones. 'Berta will, I know'.

The quality of instinctive performance which fuels the energy of *Far from the Madding Crowd* – we remember how pitifully this instinctual force is distorted from its proper shape in the love-lorn Boldwood – is transformed in Ethelberta into the force of the will, directed to comparatively sophisticated intellectual and social ends. Although Hardy is careful to deprecate it later as a frivolous work, the will involved is clearly his own in a serious sense, as are the ends to which it is applied. At this stage of his life Hardy was 'on the make', in so far as such a phrase could ever be used about him, more than he ever succeeded in being before, or needed to be again. The rewards and drawbacks of the process are faithfully reflected in the novel. In *A Laodicean* we have an equally faithful reflection, it seems to me, of a state of mind very much more congenial to and customary with him, that of 'lukewarmness' and the lack of thrusting intellectual vitality. How can one, in the creative imagination, grasp and interpret the present and its signifi-

cances, when one is so passively committed to the past, the
suggestiveness of whose happenings is precisely that they are
finished with and make no demands? Conversely, how can one
take seriously such questions as paedo-baptism and the fervent
doctrines of religious revival, fascinating as they are to the
student of fonts and architecture and the uses of biblical texts?
This peculiar combination in the hero of Laodiceanism, with the
enthusiasm of a dilettante, is reproved by the old baptist minister
as insincerity, but it is of course nothing of the kind – it is a state
of mind in a sense peculiar to Hardy, and as such fictionalised
inimitably by him in the form of the novel, somewhat as he
embodies such states of mind in the fictions of his poems.

The novel itself 'gives up', like the state of mind of which it is
the embodiment. And the hero and heroine, Somerset and
Paula Power, remain suitably unrealised and negative figures,
who are none the less remarkably alive in terms of the novel's
negative form. Their attraction for each other is peculiarly
apposite, because – like Ethelberta – each is in a quite elementary sense a figment of Hardy's self-awareness: the one placed
more or less in his own circumstances as an architect of
thoughtful and susceptible habit, the other an attractive girl,
even though not quite 'a Hebe' or 'an Aphrodite', who has
brains and an ancient estate without claims to distinction of
birth. Typically, Hardy spends quite a while establishing his
hero Somerset's provenance, which like his own is eclipsed but
not without interest to a connoisseur of genealogy; while that of
Paula should offer the *tabula rasa* on which the new age is
writing its vigorous achievements.

In practice, which is the powerful charm in the novel's
background, the situation is at once more tepid and more
complex. Being a woman, Paula has no way of exploiting her
situation other than through marriage, and she is drawn to De
Stancy, the handsome soldier whose family long owned the
castle her parvenu father has bought. The fictive notion, with
the sort of schematic significance it has in *The Golden Bowl* or in
Howards End, is that her new money and new attitudes should be
united with his ancient house and lineage. This has some sort of
appeal for her, but, she being a Laodicean, not very much.
However blurred and indecisive is the handling of this side of

things, it is also shrewd; Hardy seems to sympathise with the idea of a fine girl in a challenging situation, to which she makes no adequately stylish response. Her dilemma is to prefer inertia to decision, her position being felt with some subtlety; for she must choose the servitude which suits her from a position of freedom which does not. And yet freedom at least allows her to go on being 'luke-warm'.

Ethelberta's servitude was that of dominance, first of her own family and then of the old nobleman her husband. Not unlike Shaw in *Candida,* Hardy is looking at the idea that being a 'new woman' does not help with the old problem of what bondage to commit oneself to. But he does not do so with confidence or with clarity. It is often said that in both *Ethelberta* and *A Laodicean* he finds an original and promising subject, and then muffs it, makes a mess of it; not only through lack of nerve and verve in intellectual execution, but from not possessing the sort of flexible and adroit instinct about money, position, class, their relation with each other, which Meredith or Forster or Proust could all in their ways command. But the two novels are more like plants than computers; tentative, putting out shoots insensibly and irregularly, some of which die back. Both remain inveterately physical, significantly even more so than the other novels, as if intellectual possibilities could not survive the mere coming-together of people in places, and what results from it. Both are permeated with the kind of aimlessness – triviality even – when they might be concerned to reveal about the society they deal with.

The usual pattern of such novels, we feel, is to achieve emancipation from that society by what is revealed in them; and it is here the two fail to conform. Hardy is as physically taken over by what he is writing about as when he is in Weatherbury. *Ethelberta,* the 'comedy in chapters', is a kind of social diary, a Bayswater *Dynasts* in which generalship and endeavour are of a piece with the fatuity implicit in such a campaign. The substance of the text is not disassociated from this. In *A Laodicean* it is equally of a piece with inertia, with enterprises not maintained.

Of course this does not make the two novels masterpieces, or anything like it, but it does show us something about Hardy's originality, and the odd and fascinating ways it works in an inauspicious cóntext. The two pieces of fiction are more characteristic, more concentratedly Hardyan, than the two last great, and also more dynamically doctrinaire, novels. In them the physical intimacy with the form is hardly in evidence. Considered as subjects, *Tess* and *Jude* – and what they are significant of – are abstracted from the unconscious physical being of the author, as they are from any sense of his tentative mental process. It could be relevant here that Henry James, who sincerely disliked *Tess,* may have done so in part because he felt such an abstraction about it; and in the span of his creative life he might be said to have moved in the opposite direction from Hardy. He begins with the representative and collected, the comparatively Olympian style of *The Europeans* and *The Portrait of a Lady*; and he ends in the thick dense intimacy of the last novels, which, whatever their greater degree of success as works of art, have more in common with early than with late Hardy. James's principle of 'saturation' is a feature of *Ethelberta* and *A Laodicean,* although in a confused involuntary way which James would hardly have appreciated.

He was especially indignant at the presentation of sex in *Tess,* the presence of which the reviewers professed to be shocked by, but which in James's view was not properly established at all in terms of art. It is not easy to be sure about this, but if James had in mind the kinds of suggestion he was to succeed so well in making in his later fiction – in *The Golden Bowl* and *The Wings of the Dove* – he might well have failed to find them accomplished in *Tess*. He had postulated the *idea* of sex attraction in, say, Caspar Goodwood of *The Portrait of A Lady,* but he had failed there to make it more than schematic; and it is arguable that Hardy mounts a comparable kind of schematic display in *Tess* and *Jude.*

But in the earlier novels the saturation in sex and its social preoccupations is complete. In *A Pair of Blue Eyes* the correlative of the social fatuity in *Ethelberta,* and of the languor in *A Laodicean,* is clumsiness – a lack of ordinary competence and instinct for give and take – which in the erotic atmosphere of the setting takes the form of naïve egotism on the males' part, and on Elfride's of blundering self-immolation. The tendency of the novel is to render in its own workmanship the same kind of suggestiveness. It is perhaps not so remarkable that Proust not only admired it deeply but announced it was the novel of all others he would like to have written; he saw how closely and poetically the novelist's technique was subdued to what it worked in. It was very well for him to announce and to demonstrate in his novel the primacy of egoism in love, in every relation and especially that of Albertine and Marcel. He must have recognised how Hardy, in such an exchange as the following, had saturated his creation in the same awareness:

'Do you love me deeply, deeply?'
'No!' she said in a fluster.
At this point-blank denial Stephen turned away his face decisively, and preserved an ominous silence; the only objects of interest on earth for him being apparently the three or four-score sea-birds circling in the air afar off.
'I didn't mean to stop you quite', she faltered with some alarm; and seeing that he still remained silent she added more anxiously, 'If you say that again perhaps, I will not be quite – quite so obstinate – if – if you don't like me to be.
'O my Elfride!' he exclaimed, and kissed her.
It was Elfride's first kiss. And so awkward and unused was she; full of striving – no relenting. There was none of those apparent struggles to get out of the trap which only result in getting further in: no final attitude of receptivity: no easy close of shoulder to shoulder, hand upon hand, face upon face, and, in spite of coyness, the lips in the right place at the supreme moment. That graceful though apparently accidental falling into position, which many have noticed as precipi-tating the end and making sweethearts the sweeter, was not here. Why? Because experience was absent. A woman must have had many kisses before she kisses well.
In fact, the art of tendering feminine lips for these amatory salutes follows the principles laid down in treatises on legerdemain for performing the trick called Forcing a Card. The card is to be shifted nimbly, withdrawn, edged under, and withal not to be offered till the moment the unsuspecting person's hand reaches the pack; this forcing to be done so modestly and yet so coaxingly that the person trifled with imagines he is really choosing what is in fact thrust into his hand.
Well, there were no such facilities now . . .

The facilities are lacking to other things than the kiss. The seemingly knowing account of the feat of legerdemain becomes in fact a part of the artlessness of Elfride herself; its knowingness as much a part of the 'charm' as her 'awkwardness'.

The saturation is less effective, and less naturally dramatic, in *Ethelberta* and *A Laodicean*, because Hardy is so much identified with both heroines.

'I would give a good deal to possess real logical dogmatism'.
'So would I'.

Paula's remark and Somerset's reply are fused together in the general thesis and atmosphere of the novel, as is his 'solution' of the modern dilemma in his plans for the remodelling of de Stancy castle, as a new dwelling with an ancient castle attached. And at the end both characters merge in Paula's quotation from Matthew Arnold about the 'modern spirit', which at its best is represented by 'imaginative reason'. Nothing could show more clearly the gap between Hardy and Arnold than the former's use of that respected phrase at the end of the novel, where its Victorian attempt to satisfy by definition and hopeful intention falls hopelessly wide of the inert physicality of the book, its true Laodiceanism, and what Barbara Hardy has well called its 'uncontrolled fascinations'.* In failing to give intellectual grip and satisfaction to his theme Hardy shows how little this matters in his case, and for the form of his novel as it emerges under his imaginative process. Where George Eliot sought thoroughly to 'incarnate' her ideas in flesh-and-blood characters, Hardy here appears to do the opposite: and yet these flimsy, idea-uttering persons leave around them a greater sense of the Novel's proper saturation in physical necessity and contingency than do her careful incarnations. By invoking ideas Hardy seems both to give them their freedom (as Arnold cannot be said to do) and also to find one of the most cogent ways of revealing in art their limitations in the face of physical being.

The remark that forms the book's last sentence shows this, leaving in a sort of limbo of actuality, as it does, both 'the modern spirit' and the attempt at mediaevalism –

* Introduction to new edition, London, 1973.

. . . and we'll build a new house beside the ruin, and show the modern spirit for evermore. . . . But, George, I wish – ' And Paula repressed a sigh.

'Well?'

'I wish my castle wasn't burnt; and I wish you were a de Stancy!'

She loves him, but –. Barbara Hardy detects a schematic pattern in the fact that the hero is 'eclectic', i.e. he has a man's privilege to accept several conflicting ways and ideas, while female 'Laodiceanism' strays passively and illogically between one and the other. I doubt the distinction is really there, except in Hardy's most conditioned taking for granted of masculine and feminine characteristics; for the form of the novel as a whole suggests that 'provisional necessity' of not bothering too much, just as Hardy gives the impression of not bothering too much at the end of so many of his poems – not bothering, that is, about the 'thought', and its possible rigours and distinctions. In both poems and fiction the form has the capability of its own physical rather than mental fulfilment.

It would be absurd to claim that our apprehension of this form is a sign of the success or the stature of the work in terms of Hardy's whole achievement, but it does tell us much about the idiosyncratic nature of that achievement. Particularly about the growing tendency of the themes to overlay in some degree or other, the poetic texture of the work. This is particularly true of *Two on a Tower,* about which Hardy wrote in 1895, thirteen years after it came out:

This slightly built romance was the outcome of a wish to set the emotional history of two infinitesimal lives against the stupendous background of the stellar universe, and to impart to readers the sentiment that of these contrasting magnitudes the smaller might be the greater to them as men.

Hardy is accepting in his own way his role as novelist of significances, and the Tennysonian splendour of the contrast must have inspired his original idea. But the real texture of the novel is not much concerned either with Pascal's 'infinite spaces', or with Gide's bald retort that it was precisely them and their 'eternal silence' that did *not* terrify him. As Hardy's rather blurred and characteristically backward-facing sentence of 1895 indicates, it is the observatory and not the stars that give the novel its significance. The strange oddity of the Tuscan shaft rising above the pine-trees, whose branches rub and discolour it in a gloomy darkness for half its height: the equal oddity of the relation between its two occupants. It is not the greatness of human emotion, in terms of the universal scale, which the novel fashions into shape, but rather its peculiarity, agitated in a shadow like the squirrel-runs down the tree-bark, and the 'exuviae of reptiles' that lie on the pine needles above the bones of paleolithic man.

The first half of *Two on a Tower* is marvellous – humorous and haunting – Hardy never ever wrote anything better. Romance combines with the originality of his peculiar literalness to the maximum effect. (Bending over the sleeping young astronomer the heroine cuts off one of his curls – 'or rather crooks – for they hardly reached a curl – into which each lock of his hair chose to twist itself for the last inch of its length'. A moment of *Märchen*, like that in *The Return of the Native*, when Thomasin's little figure, in best blue dress, is seen setting off across the heath to get married.) Standing in the middle of a vast ploughed field, the tower and its conical plantation are completely solitary, 'probably visited less frequently than a rock would have been visted in a lake of equal extent'. Its owner is like an enchanted princess, dying of ennui in her domain, and prevented for many months by the sodden ploughland even from visiting her tower, an object of languid curiosity, and accessible at last when the weather grows fine. 'She had heard that from the summit of the pillar four counties could be seen. Whatever pleasurable effect was to be derived from looking into four counties she resolved to enjoy today'. She finds there the young astronomer Swithin St Cleeve, whose mother was a farmer's daughter and his father the local curate, embittered into retirement by the ostracism attendant on this social *mésalliance*. The young man has effectively taken over the place for his observations. She emphasises that it is *her* property, and so in an important sense it remains, its domination of place and aspect entirely eclipsing the heavens which are his dominion, as her personality is much more strongly felt and exhibited than his. It is in this way that the book becomes a part of its subject, like the others we have been discussing. Swithin the scientist is an imperfectly realised human being in the book, because by tacit admission an elementary one.

The ending may seem at first glance the most perfunctory and even flippant of any that Hardy wrote. As so often occurs, the complications that separate the lovers and nullify their apparent marriage are the thinnest of fictional covers for the reality of their situation – fervency, devotion and subterfuge on her part, readiness to be loved when away from his telescope on his – which determines the issue. Finding herself pregnant by Swithin, after he has set off for his observations at the Cape, Viviette is compelled to accept the offer of marriage of the Bishop of Melchester. She bears her child, seemingly by the Bishop, who dies after a few years. Swithin returns, and meets her and her child on the tower top. He sees the change to age in her, and she sees he sees it:

'I shall be glad to know through your grandmother how you are getting on,' she said meekly. 'But now I would much rather that we part. Yes; do not question me. I would rather that we part. Good-bye.'

Hardly knowing what he did he touched her hand, and obeyed. He was a scientist, and took words literally. There is something in the inexorably simple logic of such men which partakes of the cruelty of the natural laws that are their study. He entered the tower-steps, and mechanically descended; and it was not till he got half-way down that he thought she could not mean what she had said.

Her delight when he returns to embrace her and say they must marry is fatal:

Sudden joy after despair had touched an over-strained heart too smartly. Viviette was dead. The Bishop was avenged.

The terse sentences are the culmination of the meeting in the book between what is human and what is scientific, between the tower with its trees, rabbits and stones on which 'here and there shade-loving insects had engraved on the mortar patterns of no human style or meaning; but curious and suggestive' – and the starry heavens. It is Hardy's most symbolic use of form, his most humorous, and also – to judge from the 1895 Preface – his most conscious. But though so much simplified and unified in terms of symbolism, it shows no less than the other examples of form their close correspondence between the feel of a subject and its equivalent in a literary manner.

The Bishop has been avenged: not only on Viviette, but on science and its representative. Characteristically Hardy professed puzzlement at the reviewers who took him to task for crude satire. 'It is sufficient to draw attention', he says in the later Preface, 'as I did at the time, to the fact that the Bishop is every inch a gentleman'. Tongue in cheek of course, but the Bishop *is* a gentleman in the sense that the ancient concept lives as naturally and traditionally by revenge as by religion, neither of which makes sense in terms of science. The mannerism of the book puts him in the same natural and human order of things as its broad sexual comedy, Chaucerian or Shakespearian, which Hardy referred to in his letter to Gosse at the time of the novel's first reception. 'I conclude we are never again to be allowed to laugh and to say with Launce – 'it is a wise father that knows his own child'. The flippancy of the final sentence brings the respectable modern Bishop into grotesque proximity with his unregenerate forebears in the church – men of strong appetites and emotions that were open to the world. And it is this humanity, involuntarily reincarnated in the Bishop, which is in bizarre opposition to science and astronomy and its devotees.

For although Swithin may appear as well-intentioned and devoted a lover as he is a youthful and handsome one, there is a nullity in him, a void like that in the galaxy itself, revealed by contrast with Hardy's treatment of the warmly sensible and susceptible Viviette, and by his much more conventional handling of the young man's lover-like qualities. Swithin's position is not very different from that of Will Strong and Egbert Mayne, those two lovers of socially superior ladies; and shows the same continuing theme of Hardy's imagination, only now it is done with a humour a little too conscious at times, as Hardy's letter to Gosse suggests. This is as broad in relation to Swithin's sudden realisation of what the rustics are saying about his chances with Viviette, 'He's planned, cut out, and finished for the delight of 'ooman', as it is to the trick played on the Bishop. But it is much more wry and subtle about Swithin's psychology as a scientist, 'There was a certain scientific practicality even in his love-making', in deciding to end the distraction to his work by getting her to marry him. The inference is that, to the scientific mind, love is a time-consumer which can be cured by marriage.

Two on a Tower is the most elaborate version of Hardy's favourite theme: an incongruous love-situation in a peculiar setting. But – appropriately to its form – it has less personality in it than the others. Swithin has the absence of sensibility, of revealed inner life, which is congenital in Henchard or Troy, and which in him is the result of a fanatical application to his beloved science. (The novel makes its indirect comment on the idea fashionable in our time that science and art share a common inspiration, and their practitioners a similar sensibility.) Viviette is blighted by this student of the Milky Way, the sign showing itself in her 'masses of hair . . . becoming touched here and there by a faint grey haze, like the Via Lactea in a midnight sky'. And in an abrupt and equivocal concluding turn life avenges itself upon science, by dying under its hand.

As we should expect, these meanings are subdued in both the eroticism and the romance of the story, and its local habitation, the atmosphere of desire and tenderness in that odd setting where 'the fir-trees rubbed and prodded the base of the tower, and the wind roared around and shook it'. This is as moving and incongruous as the life of earth with which the stars have nothing to do, although the fair stories and fabliaux, romances and Chaucerian tales which – as Hardy hints – are combined in the novel's substance, assumed they did. The love of Viviette for her youthful astronomer and her pride in his talent – 'that charity which . . . seeketh not her own' – is as warmly and as movingly endorsed as is Tess's love, which does not alter 'when it alteration finds'. But we may none the less feel that both Hardy's strength and weakness are intimate here with the difference that always exists, in one of his love relations, between the social and geographical setting and the moral one. It is the former which fascinates him. Even though the moral emotion is not weakened thereby, it remains separate. Grace

Fitzpiers of *The Woodlanders* goes out into her father's garden to gather parsley, like the maid in Shakespeare, and so is reunited with her husband. Rustic humour, tragic chivalry, and the plain need to rub along together somehow, are assembled, not fused together, at the end of *The Woodlanders,* as they were for other purposes in *Two on a Tower.*

VII

NOWHERE DOES HARDY'S ART ACHIEVE A MORE INSPIRED use of this style of separation than in the passages of *Tess* which relate to the disaster which occurs when Tess, on the first evening of her marriage, tells Angel about her past. The moral point that Hardy seeks to make is both conscious and cogent, much more emphatically so than those brought up in parallel to form and action in the earlier novels. It is of course – as Tess puts it when she ecstatically begins her own confession after Angel has made his – 'because 'tis just the same', i.e. that derelictions in this field should be judged in either sex by the same light and with the same charity. But in everything that follows this humane and enlightened ideal is set aside – not contradicted – by the power and conviction of the narrational texture, and in the minds and bodies of the participants themselves.

The episode, and its significant kinds of over-emphasis in direct suggestion, begins at the moment when news is brought of Tess's two former colleagues, Retty and Marian, one of whom has on this momentous day been found drunk, while the other has tried to drown herself. The rich absentness of the narrative hardens into its conscientiousness of cause and effect: they were innocent girls, Tess is not, and 'the incident turned the scale for her'. The numbness of Tess at the news decides Angel to embark 'abruptly' on the mutual 'telling of faults'; and it is clear that in the circumstances he regards this as an act of wooing, to stimulate new vitality and with it his own self-importance. 'For me', he says, referring to their undertaking over this, 'it was no light promise'. His tone escapes pomposity – Hardy is too intent at this point to indulge in any of the mockery of Angel that Viviette's Bishop had come in for – but the 'seriousness' which gives poor Tess such hopes is unconsciously assumed to increase his fascinations. 'It can hardly

be more serious, dearest', catches the exact note of self-congra-
tulation in remorse which an adventure with a prostitute might,
in that day and age, prompt in recital; yet there is a certain
poignancy in the fact that Clare's confidence in how she will
take it, is a compliment to Tess.

The scene that follows has much of the force of a scene in
Tolstoy – Karenin's meeting with the baby daughter Anna has
had by Vronsky, or the meeting in gaol between the Prince and
Maslova in *Resurrection* – where physical truth seems also to put
moral purpose in the shade. No obvious point about the 'double
standard' involved can overcome the actuality of the difference,
as Hardy presents it, between the girl whose 'image' is
everything in terms of her sex, and the man who has freedom
from it. It could almost be said that Hardy makes the moral
point only to have it recoil upon him, and to be revealed as a
hopeful abstraction, when compared with physical and instinctual responses. In such a case no irony is needed, and the passage
at the beginning of Chapter 39, after Tess has completed her tale
and Angel begins to be aware of it, is the most graphic
realisation in Hardy's writings, of that commonplace which Dr
Johnson referred to: that a man would be as happy in the arms of
a chambermaid as of a duchess if it were not for the imagination.

It is imagination which determines the direction and force of
erotic feeling, and Angel is much in the position of Bathsheba
after she has become entangled with Troy in the fir thicket and
heard in the plumy darkness his gallant words, and stood
stock-still while his sword shone around her. Or of Viviette
when she sees Swithin in her tower, all his attention concentrated in the telescope. His erotic image of Tess is fixed and
overmastering; and it also represents, which is perhaps unfair on
Angel as a character, the culmination of Hardy's own locality-
centred daydreams on a womanly image. The image of Tess, as
he once let fall – her 'standing in the quarry' aspect – was a
waitress seen briefly in a Weymouth teashop. But a great deal
more important was her evolution from the girl of the manor in
previous novels. Tess, for Hardy, was an apotheosis of having it
both ways. She was an ideal of the peasant girl, the sort of girl
who in his earlier novels would have been regarded sympatheti-
cally but without personal sentiment, but who has now become

the kind of *princesse lointaine* whom the girl in the grand house once represented. His first conception of Tess stopped there, but the ingenuity of reverie then provided her with an under-image of the distinction – even the hauteur – possessed by his early aristocratic heroines. 'My Tess' became both the girl of his youthful dreams and of his adult sense of a lost and unregarded past, of a time when, emotionally speaking, he was 'looking away'.

This explains what is perhaps the greatest drawback of Tess in terms of Hardy's most characteristic feel of things: the complication of her appeal. In his poetry this is no problem, for an image out of the past can be fixed there to 'shake this fragile form at eve / with throbbings of noontide'. But over the extended period of a novel such a degree of evident retrospection does not suit with Hardy's instinctive binding together of form and matter. Tess is in general described in a manner other than what she is, or appears to be. There are great moments both with Alec (her ride in the gig) and with Angel, as in this scene after the wedding, when the two seem merged as in earlier novels; but the extended idyll of the days together at Talbothays, for all its richness and specificity, shows how much Hardy formerly depended for erotic spell-binding on more immediate and ingeniously engineered events. Such events – Bathsheba's ride, the sword display, the tower, the adventure on the cliff without a name – establish more than anything else the individuality of the heroine involved. Form, and his instinct for it, depends greatly upon such a localisation of the feminine principle.

In *Tess* all this is reversed, and the change shows Hardy's powers of innovation. In general he clung to the unusual, because it gave life to the serial and to suspense, and because what he called 'uncommon events' were most congenial to his imagination. They are allied with, even identical with, the sense of a place that also determines individuality. The idea of Tess makes a break with these familiarities. Its success is immense, as all readers have recognised, but it is won at a cost. Tess is never continuous with her destiny, neither her sexual one nor with the contrived events which leads her to the gallows. Hardy cannot hold her steadily either before himself or before us, and yet even this 'weightlessness' is made into a sort of virtue. For naturally enough he is not really using a new method, but combining the old one with new kinds of form and treatment which are incongruous with and separate from it. Separation is again a key, but now its equanimity is lost: Hardy's apprehensions of Tess *do* seem uneasily aware of each other, and of their relational liabilities.

Tess descends yawning to the dairy, the red interior of her mouth like a snake's. Tess stands under the holly on the rainy evening when she and Angel have come to deliver the churns at the railway halt – 'like a friendly leopard at pause'. When Alec at 'The Slopes' insists on finding her a specially fine strawberry of the 'British Queen' variety, she parts her lips 'in a slight distress' to take it in. These are like the glimpses of Hardy's poems, and also of such moments as Bathsheba's unorthodox mode of riding under the thickets near Norcombe Hill. But the space between these glimpses is not that of an earlier equanimity, but a more ominous kind of effectiveness which seems to mortify even the best moments. It is as if, looking years later through an album and finding a snap of the girl taking the strawberry in her mouth, we did not say, as the feeling of the thing seems to require, 'I wonder what happened to that girl?' but – 'that is the girl to whom the awful thing happened'. For Hardy is using his device of the glimpse, speculative of past and future, in the context of a fiction in which past and future seem too emphatically predetermined.

Such a fragility and discontinuity in so important a conception as Tess turned out to be was no doubt one of the reasons for the irritation of Henry James, for whom a novel could not succeed if such a thing were not 'ideally *done*'. Tess is an ideal, but she is not *done*, not, at least, with the attention and exigence that James would demand. 'I really think I could answer a stiff examination on that lady' was his reply to a criticism of Mrs Brookenham, of *The Awkward Age*. Hardy would fail on Tess, would not even know an exam was on. The saturation of his earlier novels was never 'doing' in the Jamesian sense, or the George Eliot sense, and in *Tess* it has been entirely abandoned.

Yet this abandonment may itself constitute the novel's inner formality and mainspring. It is the lack of placing, of fixity, in

Tess which constitutes her power and attraction, both for us and for the characters she comes in contact with. She appears different to Angel, who has been loving 'another woman in your shape', because in terms of form she really is different. It is this reality, again, which swamps the moral idea that her 'offence' and his are the same; for what is certain both to the reader and to Clare is that she *is not* the same woman – to Clare because of the difference between the fact of her past and his image of it; and to the reader because she is isolated at every moment in the visionary, as in the compulsion of plot. The relation of the two is odd – not equable indifference, as in other Hardy contexts but an air of guarded and formal non-introduction, like that between the country girl, and the county girl who is also, in the insistence of Hardy's vision, present in her, as a spectral other self.

Deliberate policy, even ideology, enters here of course. Hardy frequently asserted his own refined and perceptive version of the idea that 'the Colonel's lady and Judy O'Grady are sisters under the skin'; and he makes it completely convincing in many different contexts, like that of Ethelberta and her father, or Giles Winterborne, or even young Charley in *The Return of the Native*. It goes with his sharp eye for class distinction, and his curious imaginative sympathy with it. In the *Life* he tells how a *grande dame* recited to him the whole of the *Elegy* in Stoke Poges churchyard, a feat of total recall he could not have managed himself, but which put him instantly in mind of the similar complacency with which a lumpish village girl who had the same gift would recite collects to him as a child. But the case of Tess, with her refinement and her simplicity, her humility and hauteur, is emphatically not a case of observation and perception. We note that Retty Priddle, though descended from Paridells as Tess is from d'Urbervilles, is not thereby endowed with inherited attributes of distinction in the way that Tess is alleged to be.

In terms of form, then, Tess is a triumph of *non-realisation*, and it is this which makes her so totally different from the earlier heroines, even though, in successive detail, she is composed of the same elements as they are. The climax of the triumph, which vindicates this idea of form at the same time as it strikes the decisive blow in the plot, is Angel's discovery that she is not the same person as the one he has been infatuated with. He is, of course, absolutely right. And the manner in which he sustains the blow subtly underwrites the nature of Tess as a changed, or rather as a specifically indeterminate, being. For it emphasises in the most physical way possible his own continuity, in an ordinary humdrum way, and as the character we know:

Clare performed the irrelevant act of stirring the fire; the intelligence had not even yet got to the bottom of him. After stirring the embers he rose to his feet; all the force of her disclosure had imparted itself now. His face had withered. In the strenuousness of his concentration he treadled fitfully on the floor. He could not, by any contrivance, think closely enough; that was the meaning of his vague movement. When he spoke it was in the most inadequate, commonplace voice of the many varied tones she had heard from him.

Clare's consciousness is seen as a progress which has now become as laborious and impeded as possible, but which is none the less bound to go on. That inadequate commonplace voice which is unfamiliar to Tess is quite natural to the reader, for it suggests both the plodding of ordinary sequent consciousness and the weaknesses in Clare which the reader, but not Tess, is already well aware of. 'He tried desperately to advance among the new conditions in which he stood', and his impulse is to get up and walk. *Clare is experiencing as a personal drama the sense of Tess which for the reader is a sense of the book's form;* and conversely she is brought up against the limitatiions which make him, beside her, a very ordinary sort of literary conception.

He sees her discontinuity as something almost repellent – 'her cheek was flaccid, and her mouth had almost the aspect of a little round hole' – and in the physical oppression of the scene the magical Tess, the 'visionary essence of woman' who produced a love 'imaginative and ethereal', and in Clare 'a fastidious emotion which could jealously guard the loved one against his very self' – all are reduced to sorry actuality; and Tess herself to a pathos of the commonplace which seems connected less with her confession than with the general nature of disillusionment:

'O Tess, forgiveness does not apply to the case! You were one person; now you are another. My God – how can forgiveness meet such a grotesque – prestidigitation as that!'

He paused, contemplating this definition;

Becoming aware of the change in her own image she gives way to a self-pity all the more pathetic for being so commonplace. It is typical of Hardy to have so involved himself and us in Tess's discontinuity that we do not dissociate ourselves from Clare's separation from her: the form involves us in it. Moreover the tendency of the scene is to emphasise with a greater realism than at any time before how necessarily primitive Tess is, as simple and elementary a human being as Marian or Retty Priddle, from whom the previous vision of Hardy, as of Angel Clare, effortlessly separated her. At that time she *was* different; now her being seems as crude in its animal vulnerability as theirs.

In this again there is nothing as theoretical as Hardy's thesis that the milkmaid and the *grande dame* are the same in basic instinct and behaviour. He makes, indeed, an artifice out of something quite different: that she can have the tone of either from moment to moment. A striking instance is after the demise of the baby Sorrow, when she asks the parson to give him Christian burial, as if he had been properly baptised; and with 'the natural feelings of a tradesman' whose customers are botching the job themselves, he is disposed to say her own performance of the rite means nothing, but then, relenting, finds himself trapped in Tess's logic. Her query – 'another matter – why?' – has the imperiousness of the lady of the manor, but there is an immediate acoustic return to the note of the haggler's daughter when she bursts out with 'I'll never come to your church no more'.

Tess is not the first of Hardy's characters to slip inconspicuously between one kind of social stance and another, a process very different from Dickens's frankly fairy-tale convention in the matter, and made possible by the sober accuracy with which Hardy – from personal observation – can enter on the inside at several social levels, whereas both Dickens and Meredith clung to their status as fairy princes who had entered into their rightful inheritance among the gentry. Hardy's note in the *Life* on the pleasure of watching, in a grand London drawing-room, the tea poured out by the gentle and kindly Winifred Herbert, who used to tell him about her forthcoming marriage – always referring to her fiancé as 'he' – and who wondered if he would give her name to one of his characters, shows the kind of metamorphosis that took place in his imagination of Tess. To find so sympathetic and unassuming a person in this aristocratic family must have been as enchanting an experience for Hardy as it was for Angel Clare to find a Tess among the milkmaids.

Tess's confession to Clare is an acute form of the disillusion that follows enchantment. Tess as wife would in any case be due for the reaction that marriage always brings in Hardy; and stripped of her other quasi-aristocratic persona she becomes all peasant, wearisome precisely in the degree that she is dumb and pitiful. Years later Hardy answered a query about Tess – admittedly with a touch of that exasperation such intrusions always aroused in him – by saying that of course Clare would quickly have tired of her, because the disparity between them, in terms of class and outlook, was too great. There is more than a hint of this in the novel itself, for misfortune in Hardy, like the sudden death of the young heiress in *An Indiscretion,* is often a symptom of – or a substitute for – the less visible unsuitability which weighs life down, but can have no place in the conventions of melodrama.

Plot both abets and destroys romance, but form more surely undermines it. Tess is born discontinuous because Hardy makes it so. Neither Clare nor the author can face the idea of a placid domestic Tess, however much her pathos and their feeling tries to protest that there could and should have been one. In her unadjustable fate it is right that romance should have almost the last word. Their only consummation is in the strange idyll in the shut-up country mansion after Alec's death, where the sight of Tess's smart dress and silk stockings beside the bed persuades the old housekeeper, who plays the inadvertent role of voyeur, that this is no vulgar trespass but 'a genteel elopement'.

Poems are in the background of the scene after Tess's confession: the one Hardy wrote, probably years before, about the couple he saw on Tooting Common, wandering one behind the other through the rainy evening; and one that sounds like an experience of his own, of the pair silently irked by each other's presence in a holiday room 'when the rain came down'. These, like the night walk of Clare with Tess behind him, are piercing scenes: dangerously so. They are apprehensions of the nature of life, forcing itself into the individual consciousness. Clare, on his walk, must have apprehended how wrong he was about country matters. Tess is not 'pure'; but he can hardly have failed to grasp from this, and the reader senses it, that what he asks of life, and more particularly of Dorset cottage life, is something wholly unrealistic. We are here on the verge of things that threaten the serious artifice of the book, and Hardy hastens to transform the atmosphere with the aid of the famous sleep-walking scene.

It is an instance of our major point: that the separate ingredients of the narrative in *Tess* are not equally indifferent to each other, as in previous fictions, but uneasily aware of each other's presence and effect. Formerly such episodes were, so to speak, quite natural: here the gothicism seems a let-out, a deliberate relaxing of the tension; and Tess's reflections, as Clare carries her, fall in so patly with the plot as to give no sense of any of the separate selves of her in which the novel's form establishes itself.

Indeed it might seem, at this point, as if the successive personae of Tess were beginning to operate against each other. Both the gothic and the exemplary – Tess among the dying pheasants, the appearance of Alec at the fire with his pitch-fork – display crudity, as in mutual emulation. I have the same sensation near the end of *Jude the Obscure,* when the gaiety on the river and Arabella's new flirtation are contrasted with Jude's solitary death-bed. But the later novel operates under laws that set it as far apart from *Tess* as from the earlier novels. In *Tess* the crudity of texture at this point no longer matches form to feeling, in the old way. The 'poetry' of Tess herself has its light put out by her confession, for the novel as well as for Clare. She has lost the power to enchant; her 'face is made bare', as in the verse of Swinburne which Hardy suddenly inserts; she becomes 'as a tale that is told'. Our sympathy increases, but so does the alienation of Tess in her various forms; and as the story declines and straightens so does the sense of her as a 'soul at large'. Only on her solitary journeys, pausing by the warmed bricks of a cottage chimney and hearing the clink of supper within, or in her night walk through Nuttlebury where the inn sign creaks in response to her footsteps, does she seem again a part of Hardy's consciousness, and so our own.

Her unique attraction puts Angel in the same boat with Alec d'Urberville, and it is by the truest propriety of irony that when she loses her uniqueness in Clare's eyes, becoming one of deceived and deceiving womankind, she possesses it again for Alec. Instead of clinging to him originally and asking to be married, as he had anticipated, she had gone away; and when she meets him again it is her disinterested contempt that offers the strongest sexual attraction. The carving-knife, completing the process which a blow from a heavy farm-glove had begun, ensures also that Alec's enthusiasm has no time to tire. The scenes with Alec are tableaux; The Slopes, with its allegoric name, being meticulously real in terms of the detail of a Pre-Raphaelite painting. Alec, with his cigar and tent on the lawn, resembles both a bad wizard in country folklore and a moustachioed impresario; and this kind of touch sets the scene, down to the shape of Tess's mouth as she whistles to the pet bullfinches, and the white spots they make on the covers as they fly about the room.

A different, though equally attentive, style of approach to Tess comes out in the account of her drive by Alec to Trantridge, when he tries to numb her into docility by his reckless display down hills with the gig, like a modern young man in a sports car. Her spirited behaviour, during this admirable *tableau mouvant,* is reminiscent of an earlier heroine, the tough and level-headed young Marjorie of *The Romantic Adventures of A Milkmaid.* Tess as captive maid among parvenu luxuries, and Tess as smartly outwitting the cad in the gig, are both exteriorisations which seem aware of themselves as such, aware that they do not represent her 'essence' or 'soul at large'. So that these scenes form a significant exception to that stylistic coincidence (Elfride is a clumsy girl clumsily presented) which is so characteristic of Hardy, and emerges with such power in the scene after Tess's confession, where the words seem to lose interest in a being whose potential to the imagination is already fulfilled.

That being said, the sexual background of her relations with Clare and d'Urberville has a sureness of understanding which every reader recognises, and which makes the strongest contribution to the sense and humanity in the novel that underlie the author's more purely subjective preoccupations. Critics have attempted to suggest that her real appetite and affiliation are with Alec, as they also assert that Jude's are with Arabella. In both cases a sex dogma is vulgarised from D. H. Lawrence, and imposed upon a situation to which it has not the smallest relevance. In fact Hardy conveys with a total delicacy and accuracy the repulsion this unawakened girl feels for the sexuality of Alec, and the corresponding discovery of feeling aroused by Clare's considerate adoration, which has 'light rather than heat'. Tess, whose indifference so much excited Alec, is herself sexually aroused by the to her novel and enchanting sexual gentility of Angel Clare.

Anomalies do of course exist here, as throughout the whole spectrum of the heroine's presentation. Not the least of the admirable things about Hardy's imagination of Tess is its avoidance of the vulgarism of the 'natural woman'. This looks forward to the sureness of understanding in Lawrence's most successful heroines; and Lawrence recognised as much in his own personal view of Tess. Her sense of herself, her own 'precious life', is repelled by Alec; and Hardy perfectly understands and shows us why she stayed with him, and why she leaves him. Readers who have maintained that she is attracted to him despite herself, and remains so notwithstanding her adoration for the superior being of Clare, are merely imposing on her their conception of a 'vital' woman. Tolstoy, characteristically, had such a conception, and imposed it upon Natasha Rostova and Anna Karenina; but he chose his male protagonists so carefully, and with such authority of observation, that we hardly notice the fact. Natasha is ready to elope with Anatole because Prince Andrew is away and 'she must have a man'; but in the context this is not because she is a woman who, as Tolstoy put it in his notes, 'needs a husband, even two', but because she is Natasha. Similarly, in terms of Hardy's art,

Tess has no sexual feeling that is separable from her own 'precious life'.

None the less an anomaly exists. Tess's loathing of Alec and love for Clare are part of herself, her dignity and individuality. Her experiences alienate her, and it is this which Hardy wishes most strongly to convey. It is, as we shall see, the key to his own peculiar apprehension of her. But he muddles this by presenting her at moments as a child of nature who has done nothing contrary to nature's law. If the pregnant Tess, stealing out in the evening among the rabbits and the birds, really felt her state to be as natural as theirs, she would not be the 'pure woman' whom Hardy wished faithfully to present. He implies that the cruelty of human law and custom, as much as the malignity of chance, have prevented Tess from being her right and natural self. But, as he shows elsewhere, nature and custom are equally cruel, and get along pretty well together on that basis. Car Darch, Tess's antagonist on the Chaseborough walk which ends in the seduction, or Jude's wife Arabella, have indeed the simple instincts of nature, and are as insensitive and as callous. Arabella, who treats the pig as a fox might a rabbit, would have no trouble with what Hardy calls 'an arbitrary law of society, that had no foundation in nature': her eminently natural self makes her easily able to accommodate any social arrangement.

In an introduction to *Tess* which includes some acute criticism of Hardy, P. N. Furbank none the less takes for granted that she is the 'culminating triumph' and 'embodiment of the Wessex landscape' – 'an integral part of the scene' in Hardy's words – and like Nature in his poem *The Milkmaid*:

> Of whose life, sentiment,
> And essence, very part itself is she.

She is certainly milkmaid personified when it suits Hardy to present her in that light. And this is the paradox, above all, that makes her insubstantial and discontinuous. For she is also one of those about whom he made an entry in his diary on 13 February 1887:

You may regard a throng of people as containing a certain small minority who have sensitive souls; these, and the aspects of these, being what is worth observing. So you divide them into the mentally unquickened, mechanical, soulless; and the living, throbbing, suffering vital . . .

The triumph involved in Tess's creation, a triumph whose limitations constitute the book's essential form, is the bringing together of such an objective and traditional idea of a milkmaid with the Hardyan intimacy of a 'sensitive soul'. In *The Mayor of Casterbridge* the 'man of character' and the sensitive soul – that of Elizabeth-Jane and her author – are poles apart. Henchard is capable of suffering to be sure, but who in the novels is not? Troy, and even Alec d'Urberville, have that potential. The real distinction is between the inner consciousness of things and the external demeanour of life – the consciousness of natural objects, meetings and events, the Wessex and Casterbridge life of Boldwood and Henchard. We have seen how Hardy brought together the inner life and the outer man in Gabriel Oak, with very limited success, and how the implication of their co-existence in Diggory Venn is better not examined at all. It may be significant that Giles Winterborne, although a sensitive soul, is treated none the less from the outside, his goodness and decency of feeling being all the more soundly established in consequence.

It is equally significant that Clym, or Wildeve, or Fitzpiers, though possessing in abundance that *erreur d'âme* of Montaigne, as much exploited by Hardy as by Proust – that tendency 'to care for the remote, to dislike the near' which, Hardy tells us, 'is the true mark of the man of sentiment' – are never let into the private arcanum of true sensitivity. They are not passive; all are deluded by action, or the desire for it, and although Clym worships his native heath he is in fact as vainly enamoured of the far as are Eustacia and Wildeve. True sensitivity, wholly familiar with the author's own, is in Hardy's fiction the prerogative of women; and when, well after the first conception of Tess (or Sue, or Rose Mary, as she variously started life as) had come to him, he hit on the idea of creating by division Durbeyfield and d'Urberville, he found the ideal formal method of combining his own consciousness with that of an observed Wessex inhabitant.

To the rigorous theorist and technician, like James, such a combination could only be cheating. No doubt it struck George Moore in the same way. Neither was interested in Hardy's poetry, the root of his art or his simple subjectivity: to them what mattered was the art of seeming objective in relation to a *conscience*. It seems to me almost certain that in *Esther Waters*, published three years after *Tess*, George Moore was fashioning a criticism of her, and a protest against her success as a story of stark pathos, a humble life trapped and destroyed by circumstance. If so, such a mode of reply would be in the tradition of the novel at an earlier date: *Shamela* and *Joseph Andrews* succeeding *Pamela*, and the stationmaster's daughter, of Pushkin's story, constituting a criticism of Karamzin's pathetic tale, *Poor Liza*; Dostoevsky's poor clerk, Devushkin, of Gogol's Akaky in *The Overcoat*.

The interest for us is the way Moore seems deliberately to concentrate on what is glossed over in *Tess*. Like his predecessors he determined to show a truer pathos, a more comprehensive reality. And in his drab and creepy way he pursues with an effective logic what must have seemed to him facile about *Tess*. Esther has an illegitimate child, but it does not, like Sorrow, conveniently die. She struggles to maintain it on a servant's wages, finding she can just manage in a situation bringing in eighteen pounds a year, but not if she can only get sixteen, the usual sum for a kitchen-maid. The role of religion is made far more specific. A superior young man, an ardent Plymouth brother from the sect in which Esther has been brought up, wishes to marry her, and she decides to accept. At that moment the child's father, now a successful bookie and pub keeper, reappears in her life. She despises him, but he is anxious to marry her; he wants domesticity and his child, to whom he brings presents. Esther is exasperated but helpless; her own exclusive love for the boy, and all her sacrifice, are as nothing beside this new and exciting parent.

This, one feels, is a real trap, and as such it makes the stages of Tess's return to Alec look like the outcome of clumsy contrivance. Esther feels compelled to marry the child's father, and in spite of their subsequent misfortunes and his death the marriage turns out well. Moore has been to school with the

French realists, and his novel seems to insist that a tale of this type requires not only prosaic plausibility but a fidelity to the wear and tear of time. Like James, Moore was clearly irritated by what they considered to be Hardy's attempt to combine melodrama with naturalism. If a story of this type is really to move us it must not make use of the kind of contrivance which came so naturally to Hardy but which, in a story with the pretensions of *Tess,* could easily be made to seem like evasions and escape routes leading to sentimentality.

It could be said that Moore's demonstration of what it really means to be trapped by life is both more cogent than Hardy's and less unrelenting. He probes at Hardy's weakest spot: the attribution to Tess of every sort of life-affirming characteristic, together with the care that these should never be shown soberly and specifically in action. There *is* something theatrical, in a damaging sense, about Tess's 'abundance', of which Hardy necessarily remains the voyeur rather the chronicler in action. Probably the most damaging thing that Moore's treatment of the theme reveals about Tess is the area in which Hardy seems to be trying too hard. Not laying it on too thick: that suits both method and forms, and we are well accustomed to it. It is not the misfortunes of her heroine that may seem to go against the grain, but rather the excess of feeling willed into her image. Hardy, who always seems to keep something back, to have an unconscious reserve, here seems to write with positive abandonment.

It is this abandonment on which the sobriety of Moore could be said to make its comment, not because Moore is here the more refined artist – he is so obviously inferior to Hardy – but because the life of Hardy's own prose seems for once to over-emphasise its own nature. The idyll with Clare, Tess's comments on her mother and sisters, her feeling about the stars, and for the wounded pheasants, all tend to exaggerate her being and give it an unnatural uniformity of tone. It shows us how little Hardy's prose is in general concerned to maintain a tone, or needs to. Such an overall pressure of enthusiasm on Tess transforms even such things as the Norman coffin and the altar at Stonehenge, which would normally have their own kind of equable and separate life as properties, into manifestations of

personal devotion by Hardy, culminating in his feeling for the
scaffold, and the figure upon it.

I bring up *Esther Waters* only to point out not where Hardy is
unlike Moore, but where he is unlike Hardy. In spite of all the
other aspects of discontinuity in Tess she is ultimately and
absolutely a visionary figure; and nowhere else in Hardy does a
vision dominate so completely, and at such length. Does it for
this reason represent the crown of his work? I cannot really
think so. Hardy is too convincing an exponent of 'neutral-tinted
haps', however the texture of his fiction may colour them, to
sustain in his art so continuously fervent an image. It is a part of
his modesty that he is never afraid to invoke the grandest of
literary parallels – Clym toils in discovery like Oedipus; Bathsheba at the crisis of her marriage utters a cry recalling that of
Christ from the cross – but these have not the pretension of rival
comparisons, any more than the iconographic touches in a
painting. That is true even of Henchard going away to die on
Egdon Heath, a Lear outcast. Such references are like those of
the author and his characters to events in the Bible, they impose
no burden of significance on themselves or the reader.

Indeed they seem to be almost involuntary associations by
Hardy of literature with place. The great Heath, or 'He'th',
which Hardy had wandered on as a child, must have seemed
Lear's place as soon as he read the play, and in typical fashion he
converts association into historical fact, identifying Lear with
the Wessex king Ine, records of whom existed in place names of
the neighbourhood. It was almost inevitable, therefore, that
Mrs Yeobright, in her travail on the heath after failing to meet
her son, should become a female Lear, her fool the country
child, Johnny Nunsuch, who observes and comments on the
signs of her exhaustion with the interested detachment common
to his elders. Once the place has made the connection the rest
follows with the dream-like inevitability of a mumming play,
seeming as time-honoured as it is unemphatic. Winter storm
becomes an oppressive summer's day, 'mine enemy's dog' a cat
(we have met the real one asleep on the bare gravel of the path,
as on one such a day 'beds, rugs and carpets were unendurable')
and the water her small fool brings from the shrunken pond is

too nauseous to drink. The cup does not pass from her, and the adder's bite is not so sharp as her sense of having a thankless child.

There is certainly no 'refurbishing' quality in this memorable scene: the objects of the heath are in their natural and proper relation to literary and scriptural analogues; from the moment when Wildeve, with an echo of Iago and Faustus, comments on the sweet sleep which the weary Clym is enjoying, sleep which Wildeve has not known 'since I was a boy'. But the most fitting thing of all is Hardy's relation to Mrs Yeobright, which is as neutral and external as to Henchard. Her author regards her with an impersonal friendliness which seems the normal relation for dwellers hereabouts.

But there is no such inevitability in the analogies which attend his imagination of Tess. When he brooded on her, and on her fate, and what she meant to him, he certainly thought of Cordelia. And here the reference is distinctly inapposite. The compact and prosaic function of Shakespeare's heroine, her reserve and her unavailability (so different from the officious presence in the old *Leir* play) is not one with which to risk any comparison. Little as we see of her it is enough to reveal the limitations in Hardy's presentment of Tess, of whom we see a great deal. The play is not concerned with Cordelia's domestic relations with her husband, the King of France, but if speculations about it occur to us they in no way disturb the image of Cordelia that we actually have. This is not the case with Tess, whom the novel cannot but make us imagine in situations – her home, her early and later domestic relations with Alec – where Hardy's jealous vision very obviously does not want to follow her. Esther Waters is haunted by the man who seduced her, as Tess is haunted by Alec, but for Esther the actualities of paternal and maternal feeling are far more important – more fateful indeed – than Tess's seduction by Alec and romance with Angel can be represented as being. Hardy has to leave out too much. So does the Shakespearian drama, but the hard simplicities taken for granted in Cordelia make it in a sense more effectively a fiction than the drama of Tess.

For the visionary side of Hardy never really settles down with the fictive. His Shakespearian qualities are his comedy, and his equanimity, and these are of no use to him in the problem set by Tess. Hardy can only solve it, and characteristically he does so, by carrying to an extreme the process of separation. His objectivity about Tess does not recognise his intensely subjective feel for her.

Thus, on the one hand, he answers the query about her and Clare with a 'Do you not see that under any circumstances they were doomed to unhappiness?' – and in his essay 'Candour in English fiction', written in 1890, affects despair about the pharisaism which prevented him from going into the full detail of Tess's life:

If the true artist ever weeps it probably is then, when he discovers the fearful price that has to pay for the privilege of writing in the English language, no less a price than the complete extinction, in the mind of every mature and penetrating reader, of sympathetic belief in his personages.

The whole business of bowdlerisation in the *Graphic* had indeed been ludicrous, but would he really have wanted to make Tess more believable by means of the sort of explicitness the conventions compelled him to leave out? For, on the other hand, his feeling about his heroine is one of such possessive intensity that he could not have described her either living with Alec, or married in the ordinary sense to Clare. Of course convention stops him at the bedroom door, but in the case of Bathsheba or Grace, still more Arabella or Sue, all is made quite clear. With Tess it is a different matter. Her life with Alec at 'The Herons' is blocked off, a nameless activity in which her physical body is no longer herself – neither for her nor, it seems, for Hardy – and her marriage can only be consummated in a doomed idyll, out of the world and with no future. Hardy's possessiveness can let her be seduced, and hanged. But though he insists on the passion of her sexuality, as in the embrace she gives Angel in the milk-cart to show how much she loves him, it is protested too much to carry conviction. Henry James may have sensed this when he called it a fraud; and it may certainly strike us that Hardy had put so much of himself into Tess that he could not 'do' this side of her with his usual lack of effort. It has to be supplied with deliberation.

So it might seem. And this element of deliberation summons up the nineteenth-century heroine who, for me, has most in common with Tess, or rather with the way in which she is created. Madame Bovary may seem about as unlike Tess as any woman could be, but in formal terms they have a great deal in common. Both are closely identified with their authors, and yet presented with an appearance of objectivity. It is often said of Flaubert – he said it himself – that life only acquires meaning in art; and Lawrence speaks of his turning aside from life as if from a leprous corpse. That is not said of Hardy, whatever the views on his pessimism. Yet we should remember that the Flaubert who vomited his dinner, after describing how Emma poisoned herself, was as close to the life he had created as Hardy was to Tess.

The realistic study of *moeurs de province* is incongruously related to the English tragic idyll, because in both cases the process of distancing turns out to be one of identification. Tess and Emma are officially, and apparently, shaped by their society, and how it determines their lives, like other notable heroines of the century; but what really matters about both is their isolation. They are not a part of the worlds they have to live in. Both exist to embody, as they superlatively do, their creators' sense that consciousness cannot be at home in the conditions of existence. The meagreness of Emma Bovary's consciousness, the 'meanness' of which Henry James complained, is the equivalent of Flaubert's ennui, his gloomy despair about his art, the very virtues which by making him a dedicated artist prevented him from living.

Tess too, like the 'Journeying Boy', is an image of this sense of isolation. Neither Tess nor Emma are conscious of the gulf that separates them from those who feel at home in life, but to embody such a consciousness is none the less their form and function. And, in imagining these, both writers are romantics, in the orthodox old-fashioned sense. Shelley's poetry had been the most heart-felt in Hardy's adolescence. 'We look before and after / And pine for what is not – and –

> The desire of the moth for the star
> Of the night for the morrow

must have seemed immediately true to experience as he found it. As much a necessity for Flaubert was his escape into the exotic, and his creation of Emma is not a revenge upon the real but a rescue from the imagined horror of her circumstances, the conversion of her into a figure as remote from Tostes and Rouen as is the Carthaginian princess Salammbo. What seems meticulous sociological placing is also romantic longing.

Figures like Hölderlin and Lenz, those tormented romantics of a century earlier, had embodied in themselves the kind of alienation which Flaubert and Hardy were able to elaborate and objectify through the great medium of the nineteenth-century novel. Tess and Emma are in a particularly lucid sense descended from those original 'blank misgivings', however fully their authors have placed them in the novelist's world of things and facts, relations and developments. Of the two Hardy is the freer and more flexible, if only because he was not concerned – whatever the deliberation that went into *Tess* – to make so uniform and consistent a work of art as Madame Bovary. That kind of formal principle which moves in a mysterious way in *Tess,* as I believe it does in all Hardy's novels, means that she is discontinuous with herself in a way that Emma Bovary could never be.

But this is not a crucial difference, otherwise I should not be labouring the comparison. It would be absurd to compare any other novel of Hardy with one of Flaubert's, but I am certain that we can have more sense, and a deeper one, of Tess, if we consider her in the same context of creation as her French sister. Of course Hardy's intention was certainly very different. In the poem, *On An Invitation to the United States,* he describes himself as the chronicler of an ancient country

> Enchased and lettered as a tomb,
> And scored with prints of perished hands . . .

His role is to 'trace' such lives, past or present, – 'and their experience count as mine' – and this is indeed what novels as well as poems incomparably do. But in fact he does not in general 'merge' with his the routine experience of his characters; he lets the two lie side by side while experience is noted between them; such as the noise of rain falling on different arable crops; the way night meets a cottager 'flatly on the threshold'; the sound of wind in different trees. But with Tess it is very definitely Hardy's experience that makes her and counts for hers, the experience of the mature as of the youthful author. Like Flaubert, Hardy creates his heroine in order both to disown the world, and to rejoin it by being at one with its victim, the heroine.

Hardy may lack Flaubert's method, but here at least he has all his earnestness. *Tess* makes us aware how much the 'tracing' process of the previous novels, for all its craft and its density, depends on a certain perfunctory air, a seeming lack of involvement amounting to indifference, like that of the mummers in *The Return of the Native* perpetuating their art. It is somewhat ironical that the kind of intentness and impassiveness so natural to Hardy in most contexts (the *Victory* passing Portland would be a good instance) is cultivated with such care by Flaubert, as a self-conscious and meticulous impersonality. That is of course not a bit the tone of *Tess,* in which earnestness goes with enthusiasm, even with the abandonment I spoke of. For the first time Hardy seems to throw all his weight into the scale, a process less effective in securing our instant conviction than when he hardly seems to try.

Tess's religion and home background is a case in point. It could be taken for granted, established with the oblique and absent touch. But Hardy's identification is so close that he seems determined to deny it by over-emphasis on her objective status. After Troy has shown her the sword exercise and kissed her, Bathsheba's religious upbringing makes her feel suddenly overwhelmed with guilt, and with a shock the reader is recalled to an awareness of the times she lived in and how they have formed her. But because Hardy demonstrates them so conscientiously, Tess's religious impulses and beliefs are curiously unconvincing. The reader's impression is that she feels as he does, and for the same reasons; and all his efforts do not tell us different. As little taken for granted, and with the same consequences, is her sense of the hills round her home, and that home itself:

Part of her body and life it ever seemed to be; the slope of its dormers, the finish of its gables, the broken courses of brick which topped the chimney, all had something in common with her personal character.

Why? The assertion is quite unlike Hardy's usual sense of things. His architect's eye is on those broken brick courses, but the factitiousness of their identity with Tess is revealed in the falsely fervent cadence of the reversed opening 'it ever seemed to be'. The belonging together of person and place in the novels is more accurately assumed in something that suggests its opposite: the more integral people are with places, the more idiosyncratic and individualised they appear. There would be no need to make the claim for Liddy Smallbury or Marty South that is made here for Tess. It is one indication of the novel's influence by outside ideas on the relation of the individual to environment. But – more important – by placing her so emphatically here in terms of her dwelling, Hardy gives away more than ever how close she is to him, as Emma in her provincial ménage is to Flaubert.

Yet the changes between his instinctive seizure of Tess (her mouth in a yawn) and these laboured displays of being objective, save her from that consistency in alienation which is the fate of Emma Bovary. Both authors seek intimacy by evading it. This attitude is quite different from the one we find in novels earlier in the century – such as George Sand's *Valentine,* or Hans Andersen's *Improvisatoren* – in which a simple change of sex or role is used to compound the intimate identification of author with hero. Both Flaubert and Hardy do things on the grand scale. Certainly the alternations between one kind of Tess and another do not weaken the novel's powers but augment them: its power, above all, to move us.

How effective, for instance, that Tess – like 'the Darling' in Chekhov's story – comes to identify so much with Clare that she confounds Alec with bits of logic picked up from him. Still more so is the switch from Tess as a part of her home-scene to a figure from outside it. It is the first Tess who helps her mother to get her tipsy father home from Rolliver's.

The two women valiantly disguised these forced excursions and countermarches as well as they could from Durbeyfield their cause, and from Abraham, and from themselves.

It is the second who, before going off to work at The Slopes, submits to her mother's ministrations to enhance her beauty – 'saying serenely – "Do what you like with me, mother"'. This latter Tess is not in any sense incredible, but her indifference here to the normal care and preoccupation of a young girl is discreetly stylised to the extent of her seeming hardly to belong at all to the world she moves in.

And this of course is the point. She does not. Yet at other times she no less incontrovertibly does, whether she is helping her mother to get her father home, or travelling with her small brother Abraham to get the beehives to Casterbridge by morning. In a sense both Hardy and Flaubert have heroines who are as much male fantasies as, say, Dickens's Little Dorrit, exercising the strong hold that they do over their authors' imagination. It is after all a type that belongs to the great age of the novel. But while a conventional male fantasy is apt to fit snugly, as Little Dorrit or as Agnes do, into the male conception of an ideally ordered world, Emma Bovary and Tess make a more subtle appeal to such a fantasy by being quite unfitted – deep down – for any of its standard requirements.

Thanks to Hardy's method Tess seems to *try* to fit into life, to try to be 'normal'. The pathos and the pity are in her failure; for the accidents which befall her really seem to arise from her inability to be like other people, and to be the natural consequence of it. That may seem a defect – would she not be more appealing if completely the victim of accident? But a more random victim, otherwise adapted to life, would not attract so many of them. And Hardy here is skilled at giving her the worst of both worlds – the pathos of a common victim, and the pity for a rare and unusual one. As the former, she sings her 'foolish little songs', in the allotment, with hardly a hope that Clare will now ever hear them. As the latter she is a traveller by night, walking the odd twenty miles from Stoke Barehills back to Marlott, aware of the sleepers in the cottages she goes by, and their rhythm of repose and labour, in which she is haplessly involved, yet cut off from. The journey by night is Hardy's most moving image, and the one that comes closest to combining an objective idea of Tess with his own imagination of her.

The novel's form is Tess's own discontinuity, a stylisation (however inapposite the term may be to Hardy's fiction) of the more natural hiatus between plot and person, description and emotion, which the earlier novels take for granted. Its emphasis is never more apparent than in the final confrontation of Tess and Clare in the Sandbourne lodgings '. . . he could not get on. Speech was as inexpressive as silence. But he had a vague consciousness of one thing, though it was not clear to him till later; that his original Tess had spiritually ceased to recognise the body before him as hers . . .' It is the climax of that sort of biological drama whose third act, so to speak, was his recognition that Tess was a different person from the girl he had fallen for. And just as Clare overcomes his physical sense of Tess's difference in their last time together, so Hardy seems to establish in the end the oneness of Tess, although all appearances are against it, although she is seen in such different ways both by others and herself.

He was immensely sensitive to the ways in which a woman does not possess herself but is possessed by others, and the method turns this to account. His physical awareness of things was as strong as his sense of disquiet, amounting to incredulity, at the thought of the world they existed in. The image for such a paradox is a feminine one; Tess is the most striking embodiment in literature of the woman realised both as object and as consciousness, to herself and others. It is this which makes nonsense of Virginia Woolf's criticism – surprising from so sympathetic a reader and disciple of Hardy – that behind the living creation of Tess we see his mechanistic view of things. Virginia Woolf takes the famous passage when Tess and her small brother are journeying under the stars together, before the horse Prince is killed by the oncoming mail-van. What makes the passage memorable is our sudden sense that Tess is not what she seems, that she is not an objective portrait of a rustic girl.

And the comedy in the exchange – for it seems to me decidedly a humorous one – is little Abraham's amazement and fascination at the reply she gives, a recognition that his sister is not as other people are; the same recognition that the receptive reader will have to make. The stars are like apples on their stubbard-tree, Tess tells him – 'most of them splendid and sound – a few blighted':

> 'Which do we live on – a splendid one or a blighted one?'
> 'A blighted one'.
> 'Tis very unlucky that we didn't pitch on a sound one, when there were so many more of 'em!'
> 'Yes'.
> 'Is it like that *really*, Tess?', said Abraham, turning to her much impressed, on reconsideration of this rare information.

Virginia Woolf observed, fairly enough it seems to me, that Meredith's characters seem to say: 'Since our author apparently brought us into the world to express his own views of it, we would rather lie down and die' – which they then proceed to do. She implies that Tess is similarly in jeopardy. But just the opposite is the case. Tess gets up and lives because Hardy puts his words into her mouth, as she does when he involuntarily sees her leading her own 'precious life'. The fancy about the stars is not Hardy's. It belongs to Tess.

VIII

IF TESS IS IN ITS WAY THE FORMAL CULMINATION OF methods always congenial to Hardy's fiction – the natural uses of inconsistency and separation – *Jude the Obscure* is a departure in an entirely new direction. Clare is a figure who looks forward to the next novel, but he is undeveloped and overshadowed by Tess, such overshadowings constituting, as not infrequently in Hardy, some of his best effects. Clare's is essentially a social predicament, and one on which Hardy must in his time have meditated a good deal. His problem is the opposite of that of Hardy's early heroes: he is studying to marry not above him but below. His chief impulse is to do something different from his family, but he is not fundamentally less conventional than they. Clym Yeobright is a forerunner, and Hardy is intimate with the motives of both. As Maggie Tulliver and Dorothea represent George Eliot's sense of a feminine destiny not unlike her own, but devoid of her special talents and vocation, so Clym and Clare are explorations of that state of not fitting in, with which Hardy was socially familiar. Neither has obvious talents – there is no reason to suppose that Clare would be any better as a farmer than Clym as a school-teacher – and it is effective and ominous that Clare's teasing of his brothers, settled in the grooves of church and college, is not endorsed with much conviction by the author.

The moving felicity of the passage in which Tess and Abraham travel through the dark together comes from the imaginative force with which Hardy identifies with *both* as children – 'wisps of humanity', isolated in the dark like the Journeying Boy – and childishly speculating 'more for the pleasure of utterance than audition', about the nature of their world and its predicament in the universe. In no novel does Hardy identify so closely and so fervently with himself as the child who did not want to grow up, and for whom arrival in the world was 'an ordeal of degrading personal compulsion', as Tess feels it in the midst of her family. The Durbeyfields are the children of the novel, and the helplessness and vulnerability of their class in face of chance and accident, are identified with the helplessness of childhood. Tess's isolation makes her in a sense a child twice over, in relation to the world at large and to her own family. The middle, and the *parvenu,* classes of the novel are as it were its adults, in relation to social custom, religion, and sex. The reverence in which Clare is held at Talbothays, not excessive at the time for a gentleman and a parson's son, gives him – as the text implies without sarcasm – a sense of the advantages of belonging where he does. On the farm he can be both democrat and demigod. And this 'adult' side of the novel presents his ensuing predicament in subtly social terms. The blow of finding Tess not as he thinks not only brings out the class-conditioning in him, as the text makes quite explicit, but also something which parodies the rigid certainties of his evangelical parents.

Poor Tess inadvertently visits on her lover the worst kind of social insult, for her confession is also a parody: that of the revealed trick played on an equal, who has been deceived into marriage and so caught. She consigns Clare to the status, always risible in rustic eyes, of an outwitted yokel; and the need to get over what 'nine-tenths of the world views as a joke', for him blends intolerably with the common view of marriage as a settling down and rubbing along somehow. There is not much doubt that Hardy knew that he – and most of his male readers – would have behaved in a similar situation much as Clare does; and this gives unerring verisimilitude to the story on its adult and domestic level.

And makes all the more poignant the fact that Clare at the end is reunited with Tess in a hopeless, childish bond, shorn of adult jealousies and calculations. Like truant children they camp in an empty house; Tess, sleeping at Stonehenge, seems 'a lesser creature than a woman'; her sister Liza Lu is consigned to Clare at the last as a perpetual child companion with whom to walk hand in hand. The climax of this most intense and unforced vision of the book is Clare's sudden conversion to the state of

innocence without hope, when he sees Tess at the Sandbourne
lodgings:

They stood fixed, their baffled hearts looking out of their eyes with a
joylessness pitiful to see. Both seemed to implore something to shelter
them from reality.

It is a moment which parallels the grief of Tess and Abraham
after the horse Prince is killed, the boy sleeping soundly through
the accident. When he is roused and told of it – 'all the furrows
of fifty years were extemporised on his young face'. It is the
moment when Hardy's intent but relaxed language produces
the telling word, Abraham's features putting on a performance
which has an authority they are not conscious of, and which
knows that the world of casual disaster has no interest in them.
'In silence they waited through an interval which seemed
endless'.

In talking of 'forms' in the novels I am not suggesting a
deliberate attempt on Hardy's part to 'artificialise' his stories,
more than by the simplest and most time-honoured devices of
plot and coincidence. 'Form' is the atmosphere of the text in a
dominant but imponderable sense, connected with contrivance
but not determined by it. Or not necessarily so. Hardy may well
have set out deliberately to reverse his previous romance
conventions in *The Hand of Ethelberta,* giving us, instead of
characters in the country who act under the spell of emotion, a
girl in town who most decidedly does not. Toughness shapes
the form instead of helplessness, resource rather than passivity.
In *Two on a Tower* ennui verges on indifference, the indifference
of the stars invisibly in league with what we intuit to be the
author's indifference to his story. Swithin nearly dies of
pneumonia brought on by lying out in the rain, in the apathy
caused by his great astronomical discovery having been just
anticipated by someone else. But, observes the author, taking a
leaf for the moment out of Fielding or Thackeray, he would not
be likely to die at this early point of the tale, and of course he
does not; he recovers quickly at the prospect of watching a
comet which has just appeared in the skies. At the end of *Evgeny*

Onegin Pushkin notifies us that his hero, though unable to get over his feeling for the heroine, did not become a poet and did not die. Pushkin's disclaimer is more compatible than Hardy's with our sense of the exploratory feeling, and freedom, in his novel. The same kind of formalised playfulness on Hardy's part is bound to seem a little unwieldy; and, besides he has accustomed us (no mean feat) to assuming that although the universe is hostile or at best indifferent to human beings, he as their historian and recorder feels a plain pity on their behalf.

But in these last two novels we have a glimpse of a Hardy being more specifically sardonic about such plain feeling in fiction, and showing it in the interest of a deliberative though tentative fictional tone. Hardy has none of the adroitness of the artificially formalising novelist, nor his lightness of touch, and when he uses such a tone on a weighty scale, as he does in *The Well-Beloved,* and in *Jude the Obscure,* the reader's teeth can be set on edge. Something seemingly unnatural is about, which can still disturb us, as it disturbed his original audience. The use of a persona, of whatever kind, is always inimical to the texture of Hardy's prose, as is shown by *A Group of Noble Dames* and other stories; and some kind of persona – perhaps an exaggeratedly Hardyan one – seems mixed into the narration of the last two novels. As in the stories, it is its systematic quality which is upsetting: its appearances in relation to Ethelberta, or Swithin St Cleeve, are merely piquant.

There is no better proof of the powerful virtues of Hardy's own presence than the kind of eclipse which overshadows his text when the tone becomes for some reason too consistent. One must repeat that his presence is the reverse of a *persona:* he is a landscape of kinds of mutually oblivious intentness, constituting his intellectual being, his *animula.* Form, of his own peculiar kind, is the product of this composite awareness. But in the last two novels he seems to investigate, although still through the natural craftiness of his fiction, his increasingly unified self-consciousness as 'a young man of sixty'. He says of his ageing hero Pierston, of *The Well-Beloved,* that 'he was subject to gigantic fantasies still'. It is these that are stylised in that novel, and also, in ways not so wholly dissimilar, in *Jude.* It is typical of Hardy that he can put so much more simple and whole-hearted feeling into

Marty South or Winterborne, Troy or Eustacia, than into the feelings and experiences of somebody who might – despite all a novel's adjustments – be assumed to be at least in part himself.

No one would think he was Tess, and he could refer to 'my Tess' without any constriction of self-consciousness. But he was sensitively scornful of the suggestion that Jude was in any sense himself when young, or even modelled from any of his experiences; and he was quick to refer him to the baker's boy whom he used to see reading on his rounds, and whom he subsequently 'lost sight of'. To a friend he writes of Jude with dismissive objectivity as 'my poor puppet'. Yet the young Jude who in fits of depression covers his face with his straw hat and watches the light glinting through it *is* the young Hardy for that moment, as the *Life,* indicates; and Pierston of *The Well-Beloved* is, in however ironically stylised and simplified a guise, his mature self.

Transposition into Tess, into Tess as a vulnerable child, is an act of sympathy and imagination. And Tess remains the vulnerable child throughout, whereas we 'lose' Jude, as it were, when he grows up. This is partly because he is in a state of delusion. Hardy's early critics guessed, surely rightly, that visits to Ibsen's plays may have fallen in with his mood at this time and helped to suggest new lines of approach, and Ibsen's irony would be a dangerous model. After *Tess* he could be said to be more and more preoccupied in his fiction with dissimulation, and with illusion as its ironical companion, a process which culminates in the *Life* itself, a work which for all its appearance of simplicity and serenity, possesses not only the kinds of disingenuousness which are the converse of Hardy's fund of those qualities, but could almost be said to parody the concealments of the stock Edwardian life of 'great author', as *The Well-Beloved* had parodied the emotional being of a self-made artist and sculptor.

Dissimulation is not on the face of it the *mot juste* for the method of *Jude,* which is as stark and straightforward as anything by Hardy – more so, and more deliberately so – with none of the emotional collusion that gives its being to *Tess.* Yet it is a very ambitious novel, in which Hardy seems deliberately to have set out to turn separation into what he calls 'contrasts'. These were to be the hallmark of a novel of really large scope and authority, as the two letters to Gosse, quoted in the *Life,* make clear:

Of course the book is all contrasts – or was meant to be in its original conception. Alas, what a miserable accomplishment it is, when I compare it with what I meant to make it! – e.g. Sue and her heathen gods set against Jude's reading the Greek testament; Christminster academical, Christminster in the slums; Jude the saint, Jude the sinner; Sue the pagan, Sue the saint; marriage, no marriage; etc, etc.

Like most things Hardy wrote about his own work this is more odd than illuminating, contriving to seem disingenuous even though it is quite clear. The main contrast – familiar enough to us – was mentioned in the previous letter:

The 'grimy' features of the story go to show the contrast between the ideal life a man wished to lead, and the squalid real life he was fated to lead. The throwing of the pizzle, at the supreme moment of his young dream, is to sharply initiate this contrast. But I must have lamentably failed, as I feel I have, if this requires explanation and is not self-evident.

That contrast – indicated by the missile, the pig's pizzle, that Arabella flings invitingly at Jude – is our old friend the Shelleyan one. It is the same as the idea of Tess, in Hardy's imagination, and the Tess who is condemned to live in the actual world. That contrast was latent and invisible, the unrecognised 'form' of the book which gives it its inner being. But here all is out in the open, made objective, and Hardy expresses surprise that it is not self-evident. He certainly tried to make it so, for the schoolmaster Phillotson says that Jude and Sue remind him of Laon and Cythna, the ethereal lovers of *The Revolt of Islam.*

The letters to Gosse are of particular interest – Hardy's most specific and detailed declaration of intent in a work of fiction – and they show why *Jude* is so different from its predecessors, from *Tess* even especially so. Hardy is reported as saying that he would have tried to make *Tess* a really good book, if he had known what a stir it was going to cause. Those efforts might have been rather similar to those he refers to in the Gosse letters. Instead of following his instinct, in which *Tess* grew into a unique composite figure, giving its form to the novel and embodying all that untroubled variety of method in which his fiction had grown up, he might have tried to be equally explicit in presentation, as he presents Jude and Sue. *Jude the Obscure* has no form, in the sense I have been using the term, because the appearance of such a form in the realisation of the novel is not compatible with the mechanical intentions about 'contrast' in Hardy's 'original conception'.

Perhaps he realised this. At any rate the comments he makes about the novel give the impression of a smokescreen behind which he can, once again, withdraw. Here is the element of dissimulation: for an extremely ambitious work is shrugged away as a failure, 'a miserable accomplishment' which has 'lamentably failed' to be what the author intended; but – *tant pis* – it was only a novel, and the author was foolish to suppose anything better might have come of it or been understood from it. Already in the preface, after the usual irks of periodical publication, Hardy had begun the disclaiming process, stating that 'like former productions of this pen' the novel was 'simply an endeavour to give shape and coherence to a series of seemings, or personal impressions, the question of their consistency or their discordance, being not of the first moment'. All these 'contrasts', then, are something in which their author has little confidence – or else he is ensuring himself against the possible response of his readers? It is certainly significant that the most challenging of all his novels, and the one in which he most presumes on his now very considerable literary status, is also the most openly protected by his instinct to disappear into the Gogolian 'nothing in particular'. This diffidence – the uncertainty that in *A Laodicean* comes out in the form and pressure of the story itself – is just as marked in *Jude*: but in *Jude* it has become externalised. The novel itself tries not to show it.

Hardy had always had the instinct to withdraw from a previous mode; it is an aspect of his diffidence, and of his reluctance to be identified with what he had done. There was the change from *Far from the Madding Crowd* to *Ethelberta,* the wish to escape from being an 'authority' on Wessex and its

people and write a smart book about town. The change from
Tess to *Jude* is much more of an undercover affair, and all the
more positive for that reason. It would hardly be too much to
say that *Jude* and *The Well-Beloved* are a sort of repudiation
of – even a sardonic commentary on – the consciousness that
produced *Tess*. To the extent that *Tess* was an unbalanced
novel, carrying to an extreme his own peculiar kind of romantic
fervour and identification, Hardy might well have wanted to
get away from it and from the kind of popularity it achieved.

Tess was a climax of the sort of romantic powers on which all
the novels depend, and the poems too, the power of falling in
love in words, of rendering the experience of

– where you saw her
Standing in the quarry!

This was the immediacy that grasped and conveyed Cytherea
and Elfride, Bathsheba and Eustacia; and not the girls only but
the personality of Winterborne or Henchard or Troy. That
instant and unselfconscious romantic authority is supremely
Hardy's, to an extent greater than any other novelist, for it fuses
the power of the novelist with that of the supreme poet, and
appears more involuntary than anything even at a great
novelist's command. In *Tess* it seems no longer involuntary, and
the swiftness and certainty operates in flashes, filled out with too
conscious a labour of love. The harmony of separates which
makes up the mode of Hardy's fiction, depend on an oblivious
intentness. *Tess* may be too much, and by intention, the figure
who ends *The Chosen*:

A various womanhood in blend –
Not one, but all combined.

Earlier heroines have not only complete individuality, but the
kinds of seclusion, of privateness, that goes with the vision.
Hardy's powers, as I have tried to analyse them, depend on a
natural and equable relation between romantic identification
and dissillusion, the synthesis being a relapse upon the humdrum, the 'neutral-tinted hap'. It is the pattern of engrossment

and disappointment, its harmony depending on the three elements not seeming in collusion or mutual awareness.

The extreme to which Hardy carries identification with Tess may account for the absence of any such thing in Jude. The harmony that is still natural to the poems has vanished in Hardy's last novel. In *The Journeying Boy,* as in the *Lines to an Unborn Pauper Child,* there is the identification which seems to come so easily and simply, but it is absent in the account of Little Father Time. Having been so close to Tess, and to Clare, as images of childhood, he externalises the real children of *Jude* to the point of making them puppets. Even the barmaid at the Christminster pub, 'with the bearing of a person condemned to live among animals of an inferior species', may appear as a comment on the isolated being of Tess, and the fervour with which it had been imagined.

Nothing could be less suited to Hardy's genius than this new approach. *Mut verloren – alles verloren –* when he gives up the romantic vision he gives up everything. There is a finality about *Jude* and *The Well-Beloved,* an air of no further place to go. Nothing so portentous as despair is involved, for what is lost is not something personal but that intangible quality of form which in the past had united novelist to poet. The scene and atmosphere of *Neutral Tones,* for example, could be from *Jude:* but its *feel* as a poem is utterly different, for Hardy is as much identified there with his vision of the two lovers as in *Jude* he is – by deliberate policy? – alienated from it. Nor has this anything to do with the seizure of place – the new method never alienates us from that – but there is no longer the sense of historical and personal intersection – 'and their experience make my own' – which is so intimate in Hardy's romanticism, from the train in the cutting of *Desperate Remedies* to the nocturnal journeys of Tess. When Viviette Constantine sees the tower, an unvisited island across the expanse of ploughed field, we feel all the subdued and powerful presence of Hardy's romantic identification. The huge expanse of plough in which Jude is put to bird-scaring is equally memorable, but it has no comparable inner meaning, and the familiarity of what Hardy *says* about it only serves to emphasise this:

The fresh harrow-lines seemed to stretch like the channellings in a piece of new corduroy, lending a meanly utilitarian air to the expanse, taking away its gradations, and depriving it of all history beyond that of the few recent months, though to every clod and stone there really attached associations enough and to spare – echoes of songs from ancient harvest-days, of spoken words, and of sturdy deeds. Every inch of ground had been the site, first or last, of energy, gaiety, horse-play, bickering, weariness. Groups of gleaners had squatted in the sun on every square yard. Love-matches that had populated the adjoining hamlet had been made up there between reaping and carrying. Under the hedge which divided the field from a distant plantation girls had given themselves to lovers who would not turn their heads to look at them by the next harvest; and in that ancient cornfield many a man had made love-promises to a woman at whose voice he had trembled by the next seed-time after fulfilling them in the church adjoining. But this neither Jude nor the rooks around him considered. For them it was a lonely place, possessing, in the one view, only the quality of a work-ground, and in the other that of a granary good to feed in.

The tone of that is not so different from the tone of many similar things in *Tess,* but there it served to accentuate the distance between the heroine herself and her surroundings. Hardy's closeness to her made him cut off from them: in *Jude* he cuts himself off from place and person alike.

He himself had absconded from the prose world into poetry, and prose is made to register the fact. If he is able to shrug off the scope and ambition of his last novel, it may be because he can and will repeat them, on an even bigger scale and in poetry. *The Dynasts* has none of the alienation of *Jude,* though it has an even greater deliberateness of intention. But it is clear that in it Hardy felt perfectly free and himself, and free to *be* himself, as he had been in the diary entry which had probably suggested to him the site of Jude's crow-scaring:

October. At Great Fawley, Berks. Entered a ploughed vale which might be called the Valley of Brown Melancholy. The silence is remarkable . . . Though I am alive with the living I can only see the dead here, and am scarcely conscious of the happy children at play.

The naturalness of that is like both earlier novels, and poems, the melancholy of the scene (the enormous valley field still looks the same at that time of year) stimulating the romance of identity which is absent in the set piece in *Jude,* and giving the note the *feel* of Hardy in his writing, a tone too absorbed and too intimate to be 'melancholy', and which does not have the dismissive fluency of that passage from *Jude.*

Hardy seizes people as he does landscapes. 'The Valley of Brown Melancholy' gives the *Hardyness* of the great field in a way that the big account in *Jude* does not, impressive as the latter undoubtedly is. (There is a curious parallel with the 'multi-breasted' image, which has lost its satisfaction, so to speak, when it is used in *Tess,* where it was inserted at a late revision of the manuscript, as what seems a piece of bleakly mechanical ornamentation.) He discusses Troy, or Wildeve, after they have appeared before us; but the talk seems an extension of the way they have been seen, with all its involuntary authority trans-posed into tentativeness. The comment on Wildeve that ends a chapter – 'He might have been called the Rousseau of Egdon' – is not an open attempt to 'place' Wildeve, but a suggestion that increases intimacy. The perversity of Wildeve, in 'caring for the remote, disliking the near' is proffered to us as if to see what we think of it in the light of the visual impression, of him and of Egdon.

This confidence of poetry and tentativeness of prose, work-ing together, is absent from the situation of Jude and Sue. Hardy told Gosse that 'Sue is a type of woman which has always had an attraction for me, but the difficulty of drawing the type has kept me from attempting it till now'. Had he ever *seen* her though? One may feel that to be attracted by a type is not the premise of Hardyan creation: that the poet-voyeur is not so much interested in what he sees as absorbed by it, in a way into which he draws the reader; and the very consistency with which Sue is exhibited tends to alienate both author and reader from her. That expressive or imitative form which can be so subtle – in the case of Elfride for instance – is not present in the delineation of Sue. Hardy has no ear here, either, for the sound and characteristic of peoples' speech. To say that Sue and Jude talk like an Ibsen translation would be an insult to Archer: in fact they talk as Hardy often writes in his didactic expositions and essays. It means as I have said, that we 'lose' Jude early on, and Sue is never anything else but lost to us, in this sense.

We might indeed feel, I suppose, that the consistency and the abstraction which frame the presentment of Sue are the marks of what she is indeed like, her lacking in the physical, her pseudo-spirituality. Yet even these things are not in themselves very convincing. And the failure shows how much the life in his people must depend on alteration of form and viewpoint, in which the analytical is only intermittently and musingly present. It actually appears to strengthen our intimacy with Troy for him to turn into a stock theatrical type for the gulling of Boldwood, after the elopement with Bathsheba; or with Grace Melbury when she proclaims – 'Wives all, let's enter together' – conducting into her bedroom the two women who have had relations with her husband; most of all, perhaps, in the difference between the Marty South seen in the lighted window splitting gads, and the Marty who whispers her thoughts to Winterborne over his grave. These differences reflect in some measure our intimacy with the differences in Hardy himself – in approaching him at such points we also approach the individuality of the characters, with whom he is not necessarily 'concerned'.

With Sue he is much concerned, and the odd result is to remove Hardy from us as much as Sue herself: in no novel – except *The Well-Beloved* – are the habits and familiarities of his presence less evident. And this may be because a real muddle is going on, of a very Hardyan kind, but which the character and scope of this novel cannot turn to its advantage as the earlier ones can, as even *Tess* can. Its source is not only in the degree of objectivity which Hardy seems to be seeking to put into the novel, but in the element of repudiation of a previous mode. Sue and Jude are a 'study', as Tess is not. But what in? It seems clear that Hardy was first concerned with Jude's education, which remains the most successful 'straight' element in the novel as well as the most effective and influential – Hardy was proud it came to be said that Ruskin College might be called the college of Jude the Obscure. But as he informed *Harper's*, where serialisation was to take place, 'the development of the story was carrying him into unexpected fields', in which it is clear that he was formulating those 'contrasts' of which he wrote to Gosse.

It is these which are hardly likely to give 'shape and coherence to a series of seemings'. Yet their scope *could* be impressive. A man's ideal for himself in life, and what circumstances force him into – this might surely make a natural pair with his ideal of a sexual relation, and what in fact occurs. Hardy's skill and ingenuity in plotting determine what I have called the unanticipated and unperturbed form of each novel, but the prior organisation of theme is a different matter. And how will an ideal of education relate to an ideal of sex?

In fact it does not. The earlier title of the novel, under which the first instalment appeared in *Harper's*, was *The Simpletons*, changed in the second to *Hearts Insurgent*, with the explanation given that a novel by Charles Reade called *The Simpleton* had already been serialised in the magazine. Neither is reassuring. *The Simpletons* suggests that romance has left the author to become situated in his characters, where it will be appropriately studied. It also suggests that Jude's romance about learning, embodied in Christminster and the mystic vocables of the Greek testament, is as much doomed by the universal unfitness of things as is an ideal romantic relation.

In *Tess* it did not matter whether life or 'the system' was to blame: Tess was at once the symbol of consciousness imprisoned in life and the justification for living. To imagine Tess, to write a poem, to see, to read and to dream, are immanent throughout that novel as the romance that makes life possible for Hardy. It is there in the 'valley of brown melancholy', as when he sees the girl standing in the quarry. *Jude* destroys that immanent and secret mode of life-enhancement by looking at it objectively and finding it dust and ashes. Consciousness is not only imprisoned in life and in the system, but its only refuge – the spring of romantic feeling and passionate interest – is choked up with disillusion.

No wonder the method here negates the secret of Hardy's other novels, even parodies it, as does Little Father Time's outlook on things:

The boy seemed to have begun with the generals of life, and never to have concerned himself with the particulars. To him the houses, the willows, the obscure fields beyond, were apparently regarded not as brick residences, pollards, meadows; but as human dwellings in the abstract, vegetation, and the wide dark world.

Hardy's engrossment, and ours, is in the particular: the general is a kind of insult to it, as the conditions of the world are to consciousness. Father Time turns Hardy's own creative being inside out, and we might note how wholly different is his view of the matter from that of Tess and Abraham talking in the waggon together. A grosser parody, and much in keeping with Hardy's sense of humour, is the episode of the pig's pizzle. One could hardly find anything more 'particular', on the face of it; yet it is obviously flung at us, as at Jude, as the most meaningful *abstract* proof of the conditions of life.

'That's all the facts when you come to brass tacks' – is an attitude quite peculiarly unsuited to his creative temper. To secure the proper contrast between flesh and spirit Arabella has to be 'a complete and substantial female animal – no more, no less'. Troy was no doubt a fine example of a male animal, and his desire to make love to Bathsheba no less elementary than hers to be loved, but Hardy's inner sense of things knew too that this is not the way the run of humanity sees things or feels them. In making his 'contrast' he is too concerned to make a point from outside, as if he had himself become a wholly articulate Tess, a being not made for the conditions of life.

'I would give a good deal to possess real logical dogmatism' said Paula to Somerset in *A Laodicean*. 'So would I', he replied. So no doubt would Hardy: we know the quotation well by now. It unites the hero and heroine of *A Laodicean,* not in love exactly, but in a convincing kind of intimacy, more convincing than that of Jude and Sue. The whole feel of the earlier novel, its very lukewarmness, has acted to bring its protagonists naturally together, while the intensity of Hardy's interest in Jude and Sue keeps them apart. It is the most striking instance of how little intensity suits Hardy's process, and how incongruous it is with the fact – a natural and proper one to that process – that he does not really know what he thinks of the relation of the pair and their significance as types in an evolving culture. The letters to

Gosse imply as much; but the form of the novel itself will not
admit it, and neither will the authorial presence. *The Laodicean*
seems determined to exhibit here the conviction of Ibsen or
Zola.

And Sue and Jude let him down, naturally enough. Although
he may wish to present them as 'the Simpletons', with all the
unavoidable kinds of patronage the title suggests – and what is
suggested could hardly be more different in its tone as a title
than 'The Woodlanders' – they do not meet the specification.
Sue's inability to commit herself is an intimate part of Hardy's
own outlook on life, so much so that it cannot be satisfactorily
externalised in this treatment. 'The difficulty of drawing the
type', as he put it to Gosse, was of objectifying a range of inner
feeling which had no trouble in slipping into his earlier
creations, both male and female, but which was now to be
examined as a social phenomenon. Impossible to imagine Hardy
commenting on any previous character as he does on Sue: 'her
sexual instinct . . . healthy as far as it goes, but unusually weak
and fastidious'. The judiciousness is strangely unnatural, as if
Hardy had just learnt to talk like that (perhaps from Gosse and
Ibsen) and it was no doubt this unnaturalness which discon-
certed his admirers and contributed to the frenzy of repulsion
felt by the worthy Bishop How (author of 'For all the saints
who from their labours rest').

The suggestion that Hardy makes – even perhaps wanted to
make – that he was 'coming clean' at last, turns out to be a new
version of his old mixtures and separations of plainness and
reticence. The central issue is his fascination with the psychology of marriage, in its quotidian sexual manifestation, and it
was in this context that he had his first warning when *Far from
the Madding Crowd* was coming out as a serial. Leslie Stephen
had a complaint from a lady correspondent – who like most of
Mudie's ladies, one imagines, had more perception than
propriety of mind – about Jan Coggan's account of Bathsheba's
father: a man who could only tolerate what by implication are
the sexual routines of marriage by pretending he was not
married; calling his wife by her maiden name and asking her to
take off her wedding ring. This 'most ungodly remedy', as
Joseph Poorgrass calls it, becomes a bitter matter in *Jude*. 'It

keeps his passion as hot at the end as at the beginning', as Hardy
said in his letter to Gosse, 'and helps to break his heart'. Sue,
repelled by the notion of marriage as a state of 'being licenced to
be loved on the premises', 'feels at liberty' (says Hardy) 'to yield
herself as seldom as she chooses'. To Jude, who was reduced to
sated indifference by marriage to Arabella, this is far from
agreeable; and Sue's unexpected fertility does not aid matters.
Hardy points out that they occupy separate rooms 'except
towards the end', that is, after the children's death, when they
move into Christminster lodgings in Beersheba near St Silas's
church. The significance of this change seems evident: what
they have gone through has reduced them to marriage in the
ordinary sense; the excitements and frustrations of their
'companionship' seem utterly irrelevant. And there is a further
significance. Now that she is in this state, Sue might as well be
back with Phillotson.

   Her feeling for Jude, and his for her, was indeed a matter of
the kind of life they were living; and living together reduces all
things, sooner or later, to the marriage state. The haunting
thing about *Jude* as a novel is its power of conveying the
actualities of the daily grind – train travel, domestic proximity
and intercourse, the local pub – in a fashion unswervingly
stating how grim they are, to men who are 'not at ease'. The sex
relation, and its sure stripping-away of all the romantic roles and
fantasies with which it is surrounded, becomes as grimy an
aspect of the unfitness of things as any other. This image of the
daily grind is as strong as it is idiosyncratic – stronger surely
than any image in the limbo of Gissing.

   The fact that it is Hardy's own exclusive vision of things
reminds us how little the world of his earlier novels appears to
belong to him in this way, but he is sole proprietor of the
sombreness of *Jude,* as he was of the romance of *Tess.* It is
probably this which determines the nature of the *Jude* world,
rather than any impression we may have of Hardy 'coming
clean'. He takes Sue into his awareness not as he had taken Tess,
yet giving the same impression of female feelings imagined by a
man. Eustacia and Bathsheba, by contrast, are naturally outside
this area of Hardy's curiosity and concern: thus they appear
completely as themselves.

He knew instinctively there that women are romantic about love and its object: about sex not at all. This is the opposite of the typically masculine preoccupation, and we may feel that Sue's attitude to sex is imagined by a man rather than felt by a woman. However repelled, she would have a more down-to-earth indifference, such as is felt by Anna Karenina at her husband's marital routines, and this Hardy's solicitude could not accept. On the other hand he has an admirable sense of Jude's and Sue's self-deceptions, although he has all the sympathy for them that he also has for the modesty and goodness of Phillotson, with his delusion that Sue and her cousin resemble the Shelleyan hero and heroine, Laon and Cythna.

Hardy kept his irony well submerged here, though he was no doubt very conscious of it. For Laon and Cythna are ideal lovers in the specifically sexual sense, 'the solace of all sorrow':

> – as might befall
> Two disunited spirits when they leap
> In union from this earth's obscure and fading sleep.
>
> Was it one moment that confounded thus
>   All thought, all sense, all feeling into one
> Unutterable power which shielded us
>   Even from our own cold looks, when we had gone
> Into a wide and wild oblivion
> Of tumult and of tenderness? . . .

The poetry is remarkably explicit. But it also conveys, as no prose description of a sexual encounter could do, a feverish rapture of freedom in the ideal experience. In the inspiration of Shelley's account this is wholly authentic, as Hardy must have felt. But of course such rapture cannot be licensed for daily repetition, a point to which Shelley's own life and love affairs bear sufficient witness. 'The dreariest and the longest journey' is made 'with one chained friend, perhaps a jealous foe' – with whom such an experience can be only a memory. Eustacia 'longed for the abstraction called passionate love', and when she and Clym are first married they live in Shelleyan style:

They were like those double stars which revolve round and round each other, and from a distance appear to be one. The absolute solitude in which they lived intensified their reciprocal thoughts; yet some might have said that it had the disadvantage of consuming their mutual affections at a fearfully prodigal rate.

Yet the experience itself is no illusion, as Shelley's poetry triumphantly declares, and as Hardy endorses with those two characteristically Shelleyan metaphors. And Shelley, too, can suggest the nemesis of such emotion as shrewdly as Hardy, as in that comment on the 'power which shielded us / Even from our own cold looks . . .' Eyes being what they are, their most loving interchange is circumspect compared to the lovers' blindness in sexual joy. Shelley's perception (for it is that) might be contrasted with Donne's ('And now good morrow to our waking soules, / Which watch not one another out of fear;') of the rediscovery of love at the daily human level.

Hardy's echoes of Shelley are comparatively rare, considering how fond he was of the poetry when young, and it may be that the references in *Jude,* to Laon and Cythna are followed by others, not long after, in the poem at the turn of the century on *The Darkling Thrush.* Both novel and poem contain a subdued and melancholy reference to Shelleyan idealism, about sexual relations, and – in the poem – on Shelley's vision of the poet in the call to 'unawaken'd earth'. Contemplating the winter coppice, Hardy sees the tangled bine-stems as strings of broken lyres, where Shelley had cried: 'Make me thy lyre, even as the forest is'. The poet's lyre is broken, and only the bird is left in the 'fervourless' time to break unexpectedly into song. The idealist and prophet resigns his role. In *Jude* the fervency and hope represented by an outlawed love is situated well outside the author, and is set by him, in one of those preordained contrasts, not only against the machinery of society but that of the universe itself. All fervency is 'as a tale that is told' – the phrase in which Arabella's publican lover is described as wearying at last of her charms and her induced dimple. All is on the side of disillusion. And it is here that the temper of the book eclipses a main object of its planned 'contrasts'. Society, it turns out, can contrive no penalty for the idealists to be compared with the damage they inflict on each other: indeed it might be said that the conventional social contract would have made things easier for them, not harder. The tendency to dwell upon the unfitness and hypocrisy of the marriage bond is thus pushed aside by the stronger tendency to reveal the grim actualities of a free and emancipated sexual relation.

Wistfully generous, Phillotson compares Sue and her lover to Laon and Cythna, but Cythna would not have demurred, as Sue does, if she heard that Laon had booked a room for them together, even though it is at the Temperance hotel in Reading. Sue not only objects, requiring separate accommodation at the George, but has a fit of jealousy when she finds that Arabella and Jude have shared a room there, and torments him by saying that otherwise she might have gone with him to the Temperance hotel – 'for I was beginning to think I did belong to you'. (It is typical both of her masochism and her wish to tease to use the word 'belong', which Hardy himself is oddly fond of in the context of sexual relations.) Even less typical of Cythna that Sue should only bring herself to become Jude's mistress when she feels threatened by the reappearance of Arabella. An unromantic instinct to be on the same footing as the 'other woman' is increased by Arabella's uncomfortable perceptiveness. It is a matter of prestige, of the most conventional sort; and it says much for Hardy's powers of feeling and communicating sympathy that Sue is never more sympathetic to us than at such a moment, when there is no suggestion of any 'contrast' between lofty ideal and lower instinct.

It is not easy to say if Hardy intended to reveal the unfitnesses of a Shelleyan contract so clearly. Certainly his 'simpletons' never become 'Conformers' – the title he gave to a poem:

> Yes; we'll wed, my little fay,
> And you shall write you mine,
> And in a villa chastely gray
> We'll house, and sleep, and dine . . .

> When we abide alone,
> No leapings each to each,
> But syllables in frigid tone
>   Of household speech.

Their words are seen as 'frigid' in the same sense, perhaps, in which the ordinary looks of Shelley's lovers are 'cold' when they are not in a blindness of ecstasy. Hardy is certainly perversely interested in imagining the behaviour that has kept Jude's 'passion as hot at the end as at the beginning'. But to do so is, for him, to reveal the stations of something worse than the dreariest of marital journeys, and with as much shrewdness as compassion. It is only after the death of the children, when they are united in the most pitiably domestic of shared suffering, that the lovers share a bed, as Hardy is at pains to discreetly advise us, and it is this which Sue leaves to lie on the floor of St Silas's church. If the death of the children is a routine contrivance by Hardy, to maintain his puppets in the condition which so much preoccupies him, he also shows us without emphasis or effort such unschematised facts as Sue's love for and pleasure in her children and step-child, and a grief as absolute as Niobe's when they are buried. Revealed in the same way is Jude's all too commonplace thoughtlessness as a partner – his determination to watch the Encaenia procession, without seeking quarters for Sue and the children, helps to bring about the disaster. One wonders whether Hardy knew about and thought of the deaths of the Shelleys' two children in Italy.

The rigidity of the contrast pattern is happily violated in other ways. It is touching that Jude should come to see in the pillows of their nuptial bed an ideal as seductive as Christminster's lights on the horizon had been, and as doomed in attainment. When Sue leaves him he removes one of the pair of pillows, saying 'Then let the veil of our temple be rent in two from this hour'. Under the eyes of Mrs Edlin Sue tears up the pretty nightdress she had once bought 'to please Jude' – 'the tears resounding through the house like a screech-owl'. The imagined sound, summing up the tension and intensity in Sue, is almost physically painful to the reader, reminding us of all Hardy's literalness (Eustacia rocking in her misery under her umbrella on Rainbarrow, and crouching as if something underground was drawing her in) which is here impressed not on large emotions like grief, jealousy, or rage, but on the nerve of sexual impulse and response. No wonder the Bishop was distracted.

In fact – and it is another blow for 'contrast' – Jude's court-
ship of Arabella is more essentially Shelleyan than his relation
with Sue. The pizzle may come as a slap on the ear from brute
fact, but it is a fact seen 'with his intellectual eye' –

just for a short fleeting while, as by the light of a falling lamp one
might momentarily see an inscription on a wall before being
enshrouded in darkness. And then this passing discriminative power
was withdrawn, and Jude was lost to all conditions of things in the
advent of a fresh and wild pleasure . . .

As the metaphor takes charge it is Arabella, not Sue, who
arouses the passions suited to Shelleyan lovers, however rapidly
these may be disillusioned or sated. Even the pig-killing has a
kind of terrible intimacy about it, as if the two were joined like
the Macbeths in an involuntary bond, a sacrifice to human
appetite, and need. 'That's it; now he'll go', said she. 'Artful
creatures, – they always keep back a drop like that as long as
they can.' The comment makes us shudder, because its
cameraderie is so unquestioning. Hardy catches to a hair the
essence of Arabella, itself compounded of 'artfulness' almost as
unconscious as that of the unfortunate pig. When Jude, at the
agricultural show, murmurs 'Happy?' to Sue, he thinks their
relationship wonderful, and perhaps Hardy does too. 'She
clasped his arm and they went along silently, as true comrades
ofttimes do.' The expression of that last sentence involuntarily
suggests what is unreal in the relation of the pair: indeed its
curious coyness 'ofttimes' takes us back to those simply
imitative forms of an earlier period, when different kinds of
experience were not meaningfully contrasted with each other,
but remained naturally collateral.

This is what is really the matter with Sue: she develops no
natural form. And the reason, ultimately, is a straightforward
one. It is hinted by Havelock Ellis, in his article on Hardy's
novels in the *Westminster Review* in 1883, ten years and more
before *Jude* was written. It is the most searching and sensitive
essay ever written on Hardy, the more so because it neither
praises the novels in the conventional way, nor makes what had
come to be the equally conventional attack on their vices. As
one might expect, Ellis is interested in the more intimate places

of the Hardyan psychology, though he probes them with delicacy and tact. He points out that all women in his novels must be weak, even when weakness is an aspect of their strength, as with Bathsheba. They are incapable of moral firmness or ascendancy – the natural birthright of George Eliot's women: if they possessed it they could not attract Hardy, or be seen by him and identified with as they are. Naturally Ellis does not speculate on the reasons for this, though as a doctor and psychologist in training he is clearly thinking about it.

Sue is an Elfride, with all the 'irresolution' of her predecessor, distorted out of its natural form by the ideas and tendencies of the time that Hardy seeks to impose. The more he emancipates her, and the more she seeks herself to be a sexless comrade, the more 'feminine' she actually becomes. Hardy could not deal with her or look at her otherwise; his own nature required women to be as unlike men as possible. It is the premise of their romance and their 'otherness', as it is also, for him, a premise of form in the novel. The comparison here is with George Eliot or with D. H. Lawrence, whose genius is to see the sexes in the same moral, and in the same physical, context. It is a necessity for Hardy's imaginative life, as it is for Tolstoy's, to keep things apart.

The fate of Sue and Jude is to try to be the same: and the whole formal world of Hardy protests it. 'True comrades ofttimes . . .' Sue and Jude are no more able to get along than Jude and Arabella; indeed the really painful thing is that they are less able: they cannot separate because they are not separate. Such a relation is bound to be factitious in Hardy, as the phrase remorselessly indicates. Where feeling is concerned, Hardy's true style can only concentrate on difference. Winterborne can never love Marty South, who is as close to him as the trees.

The last sentence of all of the novel strikes a false note which is in a sense appropriate, and sounds two ways. Arabella dismisses Mrs Edlin's report that Sue 'said she had found peace' in returning to Phillotson. Arabella declares that Sue has never found peace since she left Jude's arms, 'and never will again till she's as he is now'. Arabella and Mrs Edlin are left to dispose of the casualties of the ideal, and their comments have something of the authority of a chorus. It is one of Hardy's typically resonant conclusions, and yet it is off-key – perhaps deliberately so?

Is Hardy allowing deathless love its head at last? Surely no: Arabella is getting it wrong, and it is right that she should. It is her kind of sentiment. For all her shrewdness earlier on, when she spotted the absence of a sexual relation between the lovers, she has no way of understanding Sue. The ending shows only her own crude self-assurance, elevated by having 'the last word', and in a very different sense to that in which Marty South had it at the end of *The Woodlanders*. Sue had no peace with Jude, nor he with her; they will get it only because death brings peace to all. For poor Jude, Sue never loses her romantic 'otherness'. His last journey to her, which breaks his heart and hastens his death, is – as Hardy on the evidence of his letter to Gosse must have intended – the last effort of an unsatisfied passion. It only distracts her. Returning to Oxford and Arabella, Jude takes his own farewell of what has been his own equally chimerical sense of Oxford's glamour, as they creep through the streets on the way home. Hardy has no trouble in implying here something familiar from the Wessex context: that the ordained inhabitants of this place take it for granted, as countrymen do the country, or sheep the field.

Yet although Jude's romantic passion for Oxford shows the place as indifferent to him, the novel shows how well he is fitted to Oxford. One of the most moving things in it is Jude's reflections near his end, which are uttered to Arabella and not to Sue, and which, in a horribly touching way, are uttered in the humorous and indifferent manner which the novel cannot help but show to be appropriate to the married state. Jude observes that he could be a good teacher:

I could accumulate ideas and impart them to others. I wonder if the founders had such as I in their minds – a fellow good for nothing else but that particular thing . . .?

They certainly had. It had been so in the past, and would again be in the future, as Jude envisages. And this is much more to the point than talk about 'the grind of stern reality'. It is appropriate enough that Jude and Sue should converse in such a way, but it brings out the 'contrasts' too mechanically, unless we feel – which is not improbable – that the demonstration of this speech is an obscure article in Hardy's humour, and that it shows how his 'simpletons' would converse about the world and its ways.

What cannot be intended is the false causal link between society as preventing Jude from taking his place at Oxford, and society as destroying the ideal comradely relation between Jude and Sue. E. M. Forster remarks that 'the flaw running through Hardy's novels' is that 'he has emphasised causality more than his medium permits'. It would be fairer to say that his medium almost always escapes from the consequences of such an intention, even in *Jude the Obscure,* where 'crass causality' is schematised so obviously, and the romantic ideal so mercilessly externalised.

The route of escape, it seems to me, is the deep simplicity with which Hardy used his own experience: that with his mother in *The Return of the Native,* with his wife in *Jude the Obscure.* And in *The Well-Beloved* he could be said to parody, virtually, this kind of experience, turning his perennial daydream of women into a deliberately ironical and externalised plot, which – like most of Hardy's plots – has still something vulnerable and intimately moving on its inside. Sue is usually connected with the 'new woman', or with his experiences of cousin Tryphena, and of Florence Henniker. But the deeper connection may be with Emma Hardy herself, and she may even have felt it: her special animus against *Jude* is well attested, and usually put down to its 'irreligious' tendency.

This aspect of things comes out most clearly, and in a sense appropriately, in those same rambling reflections of Jude at the end, to Mrs Edlin this time, not Arabella:

. . . For Sue and me when we were at our own best, long ago – when our minds were clear and our love of truth fearless – the time was not ripe for us! Our ideas were fifty years too soon to be any good to us. And so the resistance they met with brought reaction in her, and recklessness and ruin on me!

He asks Mrs Edlin if he is boring her, and she replies 'Not at all, my dear boy. I could hearken to 'ee all day'. But the significant 'contrast' has already slipped out, a few sentences back in Jude's meditation:

Strange difference of sex, that time and circumstance, which enlarge the views of most men, narrow the views of women almost invariably.

This may be a commonplace, but it is also extremely shrewd, too shrewd in its context here for Jude. It ignores his claim that the love-relation with Sue was fated by coming before its time, before society would recognise its beauty and enlightenment. It conjures into the objective presentation of these two 'simpletons' in a hidebound society the real interior of Hardy's own experience of marriage. And in *The Well-Beloved* there is an almost exactly parallel observation, not of course about any of the successive Avices who make up the phantom of the Unattainable, but about the widowed society lady, Nichola Pine-Avon, who would like to have married the hero but who has settled instead for his friend Somers, a landscape painter:

Mrs Somers – once the intellectual, emancipated Mrs Pine-Avon – had now retrograded to the petty and timid mental position of her mother and grandmother, giving sharp, strict regard to the current literature and art that reached the innocent presence of her long perspective of girls, with the view of hiding every skull and skeleton of life from their dear eyes. She was another illustration of the rule that succeeding generations of women are seldom marked by cumulative progress, their advance as girls being lost in their recession a matrons; so that they move up and down the stream of intellectual development like flotsam in a tidal estuary. And this perhaps not by reason of their faults as individuals, but of their misfortune as child-rearers.

Both in Jude's ramblings and these remarks on Mrs Somers's progress into matronhood, an attack on the conventions of the age in regard to women merges into a general observation about them. The anomaly may blur Mill's arguments about the position of women but it also humanises them in the way fiction can. The biological role is seen as inhibiting intellectual development, so that any advance is followed by a corresponding withdrawal, an assumption being that in generations of male development there may occur a steady 'melioristic' advance towards enlightenment. Jude himself is an instance. But deprived of the natural retrenchment involved in bringing up a family (the kind that Natasha and Princess Mary exhibit so shamelessly in *War and Peace*) Sue seeks it in the church, and in a superstitiously rigorous concept of marriage. Had the children lived she might have brought them up to conform, as Mrs Somers was doing, and above all to be – as became Mary Shelley's devout wish for hers – 'the same as other people'.

Or she might not. Hardy is incapable of extrapolating so magisterially as Tolstoy from his own experience; besides, his own experience may not have entirely borne out the truth of the generalisation. Childless Emma Hardy may have withdrawn into reaction on matters of religion and class, but perhaps because of her less than happy marriage she had a lively interest in female emancipation and went to London, as her husband recorded, to take part in Suffragette marches. That image of the tidal estuary, with the aspirations of the sex moving up and down it like flotsam, is full of Hardyan 'sub-humour', and like all such humour in him it finds a natural companion in another image of a different kind – Pierston's for the successive incarnations of the Well-Beloved:

Each mournful emptied shape stands ever after like the nest of some beautiful bird from which the inhabitant has departed and left it to fill with snow.

In such phrases, and their application both to Hardy and to the characters he creates in his last two novels, there is his own 'grim friendliness', of the kind that Mrs Yeobright and Wildeve come to feel for one another in *The Return of the Native*. It is a phrase that defines something in the form of these novels. Arabella would be its most obvious recipient, and it is directed by the author against what has become by now his own persona, an individual 'too grievously far, chronologically, in advance of the person he felt himself to be'. It is the person who perceives and describes, with the same kind of friendliness, that 'the seeking of the Well-Beloved was of the nature of a knife which could cut two ways', as Pierston finds when Avice the second reveals the same kind of temperament as his own – 'this obscure and almost illiterate girl engaged in the pursuit of the impossible ideal, just as he had himself been doing for the last twenty years'. The same kind of humour is allowed its head in *Jude* in the relations of Sue and Phillotson. 'What do I care about J. S. Mill!' moaned he. 'I only want to lead a quiet life'. It is an exclamation all the more telling because of Phillotson's qualities of domestic common sense as well as generosity. And as unShelleyan as the point that since a scandal at Sue's Teacher Training School concerning a girl who had claimed her lover was a relation, 'the management had been rough on cousins ever since'.

Although Hardy's humour has come out into the open in the last two novels it still conforms to that basic law of his imagination: the separation of one order of perception and comment from another. The comedy of the Well-Beloved in her successive embodiments does not affect the poetry of the Island, 'whence many a fine public building had sailed – including St Paul's Cathedral', nor the romance of those encounters which are – here almost literally – 'standing in the quarry'. But the ending, which as usual gives the clearest indication of the form the novel has taken, shows Hardy determined to coalesce his matter into a suitably climactic joke. In the serial version this took the form of the injured Pierston coming to his senses to find himself being nursed by Marcia, his wife, 'a parchment-coloured skull moving about the room', while a photograph of the last Avice looks down on him from the mantelpiece. 'The contrast . . . brought into his brain a sudden sense of the grotesqueness of things', and the novel closes with his 'irresistible fit of laughter' at 'this ending to my would-be romantic history'.

Revising the book for publication Hardy altered a good deal, and made the concluding jest more subtle though hardly less obvious. Respectably married to Marcia at the end not the beginning of the novel (her rheumatism makes it necessary for her to be wheeled to church in a chair), Pierston is liberated by 'the extinction of the Well-Beloved and other ideals', and engages in a programme to improve and modernise the old buildings and cottages on the Island. The eclipse of his imagination of the feminine also brings to an end his feeling for the past.

The comparative elaboration of such a 'joke' makes a painful contrast with the humour constantly implicit in Hardy's prose texture. Verse can structure such a joke with its own kind of adequacy – and, as we have seen, it is the strength of Hardy's verse to be quite content to be adequate in this way – but in prose they can seem very heavy indeed. This is the case at the end of *Jude,* where the dying man whispers quotations from the third chapter of the book of Job, to the accompaniment of 'Hurrahs' from the undergraduates' games outside, interpositions as contrived as those which Flaubert arranges at the Agricultural Show in *Madame Bovary*.This is admittedly followed by the most telling contrast in the novel, between death and life, Jude inconveniently dying at the moment when Arabella has been invited to go out and watch the procession of boats on the river. *Jude* might indeed be said to have an imitation ending, following on the climactic deliberation of the contrasts. It is Arabella's final pronouncement, which recalls Sue, and brings the trio together in one sentence; but its effectiveness in terms of form is to add a query to what has gone before, and set it against the determined span of the novel's plot. The question of Jude and Sue's relation is suddenly brought up once again in the guise of a settled valediction.

IX

THE SHORT FINAL CHAPTER OF *Tess* IS UNDOUBTEDLY the most moving of Hardy's endings. It is also the one which most clearly illustrates his 'separations', even though it has come to the point of making use of them, or so it might seem, instead of their being a natural product of his ways of undertaking fiction. *Jude* and *The Well-Beloved* end with a reiterated emphasis on the ironic; in *Tess* there seems used on a consciously spacious scale the collateral modes of perceiving and narrating that we take for granted in the earlier novels. The novel's constant preoccupation with Tess herself seems abruptly lifted, and we are in Wintoncester, that is, Winchester, where we have never been before in the Wessex novels and shall never go again. Hardy spends most of the two-page chapter showing us round –

The prospect from this summit was almost unlimited. In the valley beneath lay the city they had just left, its more prominent buildings showing as in an isometric drawing – among them the broad cathedral tower, with its Norman windows and immense length of aisle and nave, the spires of St Thomas's, the pinnacled tower of the College, and, more to the right, the tower and gables of the ancient hospice, where to this day the pilgrim may receive his dole of bread and ale. Behind the city swept the rotund upland of St Catherine's Hill; further off, landscape beyond landscape, till the horizon was lost in the radiance of the sun hanging above it.

The serene guide-book tone ('Where to this day the pilgrim . . .', etc) with its note both of contemplating and imparting knowledge, has already been suggested by a reference to the native of the town, whom familiarity has made indifferent to the spectacle –

From the western gate aforesaid the highway, as every Wintoncestrian knows, ascends a long and regular incline of the exact length of a measured mile, leaving the houses gradually behind.

The purpose of our visit is to witness an intersection, the most momentous in Hardy's works, between a time, place, and event. Angel Clare and Tess's sister, Liza Lu, are walking up the exact length of that measured mile, and they pause beside the first milestone as the clocks strike eight. The view they see is the panorama described to us, but their gaze is fixed on an 'ugly flat-topped octagonal tower' and the object that moves slowly up its tall staff 'a few minutes after the hour had struck', and becomes a black flag.

The famous final paragraph changes without modulation into a style that knows nothing of the beauties of Winchester. The sentence: 'And the D'Urberville knights and dames slept on in their tombs unknowing', does not refer us to picturesque antiquity but to the absence of what the novel had dwelt on so much: continuity between Tess and her ancestors. In place there are only the two speechless gazers, bent to the earth as if in prayer, but for once Hardy has no need to observe that they might be out of a canvas by Grünewald or Giotto. All is now directed to the novel's final purpose, in the original manuscript set out in a short preliminary paragraph to the chapter which balanced the concluding one, the two being equally in contrast with the guided tour of Winchester that goes between. The story of Tess was summed up in it as not an actual but a typical history, which requires complete sincerity in the telling, for the reason that the author, 'in glancing at the misfortunes of such people as have or could have lived, may acquire some art in shielding from like misfortunes those who have yet to be born'. The case is a typical one, taken by an artist whose greatest interest is in the actual – the real place and the recorded event – and who, moreover, has felt it his duty to 'above all things be sincere, however terrible sincerity may be'. He assumes too, as George Eliot or as Zola both might have done, that the novelist is engaged on an undertaking in social engineering.

Sincerity is apparent both in the paragraph itself and in the fact that it was dropped from the printed texts – Hardy would always on reflection have wanted to withdraw from the impulse to make such claims – but the triptych it makes with the concluding paragraph and the interlude between gives a sense, like no other of his endings, of the peculiar quality of naturalness in Hardy's form, its capacity to alternate between modes of concentration unmindful of each other, as the day's life beginning in Winchester, and her ancestors sleeping in their tombs, are alike unmindful of Tess.

Tess, as Hardy afterwards remarked to his publisher, proved 'a good milch cow'. Prudent as he was in money matters, it was clear by 1896 that he had enough capital to keep him going in comfort. Two years later he offered to pay for the cost of bringing out *Wessex Poems.* But in the sale of his last three novels he had been pertinacious about getting the maximum profit, even more so than previously; he was ready to go to great trouble to produce a suitable serial version. In her reviews of *Tess* and *Jude* Mrs Oliphant implied that 'hot and strong' subject matter was as much in the interests of money-making as the care taken about dual publication, a sneer that must have upset Hardy particularly, since it was as untrue that his subjects had been chosen with any eye for publicity as it was correct that he wanted to make all he could from his trade. In the past he had certainly studied the market and got up material for the current genres – novels of romance and mystery or society – and the decision to leave Sturminster Newton, where the happiest part of his married life was spent, for Surbiton, was prompted by advice that a professional novelist must be in touch with metropolitan activities.

But ironically enough the greatest success came when Hardy had stopped taking such conscientious measures to secure it. *Tess* was his own fantasy in a very particular sense, but any market researcher today could see it has exactly the right ingredients for popular success – a beautiful and persecuted heroine, the victim of social injustice, a hanging, and above all the romance of history brought up to date – any of us might be descended from D'Urbervilles, or their equivalent, which makes identification all the more seductive. Moreover, as in all the most successful best-sellers, Hardy was himself firmly in the grip of his own fantasy, which turned out to raise a fervent echo in so many other bosoms. But the last chapter in Tess's story returns to all the simplicity of an episode, even though it is one of a climactic kind. Her death is an event, in Hardy's special sense, where that of Jude is an aspect of his own obscure history. Though it is not a surprise and a turning away from the tone of the tale, as is the reported death of the Trumpet-Major, it too has more to do than any of the other novels with what will become in *The Dynasts* the whole method and object of the narrative.

The end of *The Trumpet-Major* is the most striking case of Hardy's skill at changing the genre, a different thing from the more instinctive separation of things and persons in the tale from each other. Parting the modes of treatment suited to sorts of characters can be like the 'You that way, we this way' at the end of a Shakespearian comedy. His own comments suggest that he took no pleasure in the process, protesting that a novel should conclude in the same key as its major theme, and yet he was certainly a good hand at it. *The Woodlanders* is eased to its end in a way that is no less masterly for being aptly contrived. Grace and her husband and father are metamorphosed into elements in a comedy that fits the traditional mould rather than a Hardyan matrix. Melbury protests that his daughter went out to pick parsley, and was not seen again till the search party found her reunited with her husband at the local hotel. Those members of the cast who are sent off in this fashion are unaware of the presence of Marty South, in the churchyard beside Winterborne's grave.

This contrast shows something of the calm and equable separations that end *Tess* – the tour of Winchester, the road that leaves it, the D'Urbervilles in their tombs. Like the end of *The Trumpet-Major* – 'John marches into the night' – an antithesis is made deliberatively. *Jude* makes one most of all. But *The Woodlanders* has the advantage of Hardy feeling he was spoiling the right ending, and this is a good sign. His deepest instincts as an artist are not concerned with getting it right on his own account. If he had left Grace on her own she would have joined the solitary Marty in an atmosphere too redolent of elegy. She would seem to be the same sort of person if she shared the same fate. As it is, Grace has put Winterborne behind her and settled for a life in the area of the less obvious unfitness of things, where resentments on both sides are condoned but barely overcome. The attitudes to life in which she and Marty diverge are implicit in the alteration of genre.

To put events and meetings at the service of a plot is natural enough, and is Hardy's staple method, but in the novels they detach themselves without effort or disturbance from the purposes for which the story uses them. *The Woodlanders* begins with a man making a stride from a wood on to a lonely road:

The physiognomy of a deserted highway expresses solitude to a degree that is not reached by mere dales or downs, and bespeaks a tomb-like stillness more emphatic than that of glades and pools. The contrast of what is with what might be, probably accounts for this. To step, for instance at the place under notice, from the edge of the plantation into the adjoining thoroughfare, and pause amid its emptiness for a moment, was to exchange by the act of a single stride the simple absence of human companionship for an incubus of the forlorn.

It is the openness of this event which appeals to the text, and which remains independent of our ensuing knowledge that the man is Barber Percomb, from Abbot's Cernel, and that he has lost his way on the journey to Little Hintock, to try to persuade Marty South to part with her hair. The situation remains while the barber dwindles into insignificance, becoming nothing more than 'the Sherton man' when Grace and Mrs Charmond, after losing themselves in the wood, happen on to the road at the same place at later stage of the book.

Even in *Tess* such meetings – not even excluding her final one with the hangman at Winchester – retain their independence in the text parallel to the articulations of the plot; but in the shorter stories, as also in *The Well-Beloved,* there is no scope for this independence. The encounters, formalised to an extremity deliberately grotesque (as in *Interlopers at The Knap)* become merely the victims of the tale. Novelists none of whose material is independent of them, like James, are also natural writers of nouvelles and short stories, but Hardy's instincts are for the novel in prose – the story only in verse.

The comparative triviality of the stories shows how form in the novels has to develop slowly, as an aspect of their natural separabilities and relaxations. Where there is no room for these the text seems brittle rather than unstable, its shrivelling away ominously imminent. Our disappointment is a different, more commonplace sensation. Many of the stories begin like novels, and the opening sentence of *Fellow-Townsmen* continues to haunt its methodical misadventures with a suggestion of encounters more proper to the setting, the narrow town of Port Bredy between its small steep green hills:

The shepherd on the east hill could shout out lambing intelligence to the shepherd on the west hill, over the intervening town chimneys, without great inconvenience to his voice, so nearly did the steep pastures encroach upon the burghers' backyards.

On The Western circuit has a casual but telling non-meeting towards its end. The lady who has written letters for her maid to the young barrister has herself fallen in love with him, and he with her. After the *dénouement,* when her maid marries the doomed young man, she returns home:

When at dusk she reached the Melchester station her husband was there to meet her, but in his perfunctoriness and her preoccupation they did not see each other, and she went out of the station alone.

This suggests a different dimension of action and time to that enclosed by the story. But in general time in these tales is not on Hardy's side, seeming as much at one with the plot as the encounters themselves. An extreme case is *The Waiting Supper,* where the wife and her lover wait for year after year, gradually reconciled in their apartness, while the absent husband who keeps them apart lies all the while drowned in the weir piles outside his wife's door, where he had fallen when returning to claim her.

Poems which make their point and fall flat, or retail an anecdote which interests Hardy more than ourselves, none the less retain the quality the stories lack. The distinction of non-effect, of a narrative indifferent to its audience, which is the trademark of both his verse and novels, is not something the

story form can allow. The short story is a self-conscious form by
nature: it has a strong element of self-regard, alike in emphasis,
timing and tone. And when these are arranged by Hardy the
tales take on the impersonality of journeyman work, emptied
alike of the separable aspects of narrative and of the 'animula'
whose presence goes with them. At best they have something of
the 'wan quietude' of the hero of *On The Western Circuit* when
he discovers that those lively sympathies in the letters he has
been receiving are the work of the married lady, and not of her
maid to whom he is engaged.

That story was written at about the same time that Hardy was
completing *Tess,* and its theme of 'ruination' – that of the
young man who finds himself yoked to some childishly good
but unsuitable young creature – relates to the novel's theme:

She did not know that before his eyes he beheld as it were a galley, in
which he the fastidious urban, was chained to work for the remainder
of his life, with her, the unlettered peasant, chained to his side.

Childishness here is not, as in *Tess,* the parting perquisite of
doomed lovers – parting being a theme as dependably erotic as
meeting – but a sign of the unmatchedness which makes for a
couple 'the dreariest and the longest journey'. Hardy's metaphor exaggerates that of Shelley's chain into its own kind of
grim literalness; the apparently open end of the story is grimly
determined by Hardy's metaphor. In their short span the stories
are jostled uncomfortably by all those unstable elements in the
prose which are so effective in the longer run. The story's
stability, and its 'moral', if it has one, are bound to seem
perverse.

That kind of simplicity which makes its blunt point about the
ill-matched marriage of *On The Western Circuit* does not accord
with Hardy's other kind of simplicity – the kind that muses
over an odd thought occurring to him whether in the garden or
at St Mark's or Warwick Castle:

'To think,' said Nicholas, when the remains had been decently
interred, and he was again sitting with Christine – though not beside
the waterfall – 'to think how we visited him! How we sat over him,
hours and hours, gazing at him, bewailing our fate, when all the time

he was ironically hissing at us from the spot, in an unknown tongue, that we could marry if we chose!'

But this, too, is not a kind we find in the novels, or if we do it is dwarfed by perspective, not obtrusive as here. On the other hand much is done in the stories by inference, and well done, even though it is at the cost to us of Hardy's company. Edith Harnham, employer of the little maid Anna in *On The Western Circuit,* is 'a woman whose deeper nature has never been stirred', the barrister 'an end of the age young man' – labels that echo the economy of the first sentence and do not need to be amplified:

The man who played the disturbing part in the two quiet lives hereafter depicted – no great man, in any sense, by the way – first had knowledge of them on an October evening, in the city of Melchester.

That 'no great man, in any sense' is in formal keeping with the scale (Henchard and Winterborne and even Troy *are* great men, in some sense). 'First had knowledge of them' suggests the two kinds involved – carnal knowledge of one, and an ironically more intimate knowledge, a marriage of true minds, through the letters written by the mistress and signed in the maid's name. The mistress longs for his child but it is the maid who will become pregnant. It is startling, rather than stimulating, to find so much concentration in a prose which normally gives itself and its meanings all the space they require.

With this goes here a withholding of the direct viewpoint. One might guess that the author of the story had read his Mill, and perhaps knew of Mill's argument with Comte on the nature of female intelligence, but no comment is made. And we always miss this author's comments, however we may disagree. It is the same in *A Changed Man.* When the hussar captain Maumbry elects to leave the service and become a clergyman he breaks the heart of his vivacious young wife. There is no comment on the fitness or otherwise of this, and on whether by joining 'the church militant' the captain is neglecting a duty promised nearer home. Again we are tantalised by a sudden breath of space in the story, when Hardy switches from the immediate human situation and follows for a brief moment the regiment now ordered away from the town and 'smalling towards the Mellstock ridge' on their way to the bustle of the capital, leaving the new curate and his wife in their mean Durnover lodging. 'Smalling' suggests the dimension of the story, and its attitude towards the inhabitants: an attitude formalised in the narrator, a semi-invalid with a turn for versing (he composes on the couple a Hardyan triolet) who sits in a high oriel window, having 'a raking view of the high street, west and east'. He can see a white ribbon of road that disappears over Grey's Bridge, 'a quarter of mile off', and is imagined in its many windings and undulations 'for one hundred and twenty miles until it comes to Hyde Park'.

An exception to the feel of competence, of a depressing kind, in the treatment and climax of the story (it is especially marked in *The Fiddler of the Reels)* is that other 'life's little irony' called *To Please His Wife.* The hard-natured wife Joanna, left husbandless and childless at the end by the obstinacy of her own will, is treated by Hardy with something of the same feeling he has for Henchard, the kind of character he makes us feel for all the more because he cannot feel with them, and does not try. The two best stories – *The Son's Veto* and *A Tragedy of Two Ambitions* – have this and something else beside: they use the hard rigidity of the story form to indicate the same characteristics in the world it reveals. With a simplicity appropriate to tone and scale, Hardy directs indignation against the church and its conditioned inflexibilities and hypocrisies, to which are especially vulnerable those vigorous aspirants of the lower class who use it as a career to rise by. Hardy must have had such feelings since his own youthful project of becoming a clergyman. In 1868 he combined them with his literary ambitions to concoct his denunciatory novel, causing Macmillan to observe of *The Poor Man and The Lady* that, 'unlike Thackeray', its author meant mischief. The stories refer to social tendencies in the church more evident in Hardy's youth than at the time they were written, but they are a far better vehicle than the novel to concentrate the author's feelings and produce the most effective tone.

A Changed Man is dated 1900. That bird's eye glimpse, and the space between viewpoint and protagonists, reminds us of *The*

Dynasts, where Hardy will be as exact in the record of geography and mileage in Spain or in Russia as he was in Wessex –

> Friedland to these adds its tale of victims, its midnight
>   marches and hot collisions,
> Its plunge, at his word, on the enemy hooped by the
>   bended river and famed Mill stream . . .

Separation here becomes for him a panoramic method and end in itself. In *The Well-Beloved* Pierston stands on the summit of the Isle of Slingers and hears 'the drub of Deadmans Bay', as a *Dynasts* poem calls it, the sound of the sea to the west pulsing on the shingle of the Chesil bank. It seems to summon a presence

– an imaginary shape or essence from the human multitude lying there below: those who had gone down in vessels of war, East Indiamen, barges, brigs, and ships of the Armada – select people, common, and debased, whose interests and hopes had been wide asunder as the poles, but who had rolled each other to oneness on that restless sea-bed. There could almost be felt the brush of their huge composite ghost as it ran a shapeless figure over the isle, shrieking for some good god who would disunite it again.

Hardy had never needed to disunite the elements of his imagination; but now, in a historical context, the conscious urge to do so, as a kind of emancipation from the trials of the novel form, must have appealed greatly. 'The brush of that huge composite ghost as it ran a shapeless figure over the isle' – the remarkable image contrasts vigorously with Hardy's anthropomorphic poems in which the separated dead rest comfortably and often articulately in their adjacent spaces. (We may remember the little spade-shaped wooden instrument he devised and carried for the purpose of scraping tomb-stones so that their inscriptions could be read.)

Returning the 'huge composite ghost' of history to its singularities, before its coming together, has always been in the background of Hardy's creation; but none of his works, before *The Dynasts,* seems specifically designed for the purpose. He might be said to have been working for years towards the method of *The Dynasts,* a capacious structure with its own logic in terms of purpose, and put together to effect in a deliberate manner what all the novels and poems indirectly achieve. That its form itself should be so obviously and naïvely composite is a contradiction which sinks it *as* a form. All the structure is on the outside, with none of the conventions of the novel to be observed. On the top of event Hardy has to supply his own meaningful emphases and repetitions. The Immanent Will is to be shown at large. But in fact it is this entity, with all its attendants and accessories, which seems itself carried powerlessly forward by Hardy's evocation of place and event, by the gaze of the voyeur of history. There is no odder kind of separation in Hardy than the enclosure of the metaphysical representatives in a sort of *VIP* lounge, from which they can watch, and we with them, the unfolding of events. To *see* everything as it was, when it happened, is a dream of Hardy's, now presented literally. We all share the same dream, and the simple formula satisfies it. In fact *The Dynasts* shows in diagrammatic form the constituents of Hardy's popularity: events and facts are there, together with speculations about the meaning of the whole which are both impressive and easy to take in. And the two are isolated from each other, so that each can be enjoyed and reflected on in a manner appropriate to its own nature.

In his journal Hardy recorded one of his visits to the Waterloo men at Chelsea hospital, on the sixtieth anniversary of the battle. An aged campaigner, John Bentley, took a fancy to his wife and told her a lot of things he remembered about it, but the one Hardy recorded in detail was his experience with a Brussels girl. She was much in love, and said she would hide him if he would desert, but though strongly tempted he declined. He wrote to her after the battle, as he had promised, and received an answer saying she would meet him in Paris on Christmas Day at three o'clock, but he never kept the appointment as his regiment was ordered away. The idea of this non-meeting made Hardy plan in the same month of 1875 a ballad on the Hundred Days, and then of the earlier campaigns, 'forming together an Iliad of Europe from 1789 to 1815'. The history, when he came to do it, was taken from books and memoirs: but as the novels transform clichés – even G. P. R. James's 'A solitary horseman might have been seen . . .' – into moments of sustained fact, so the historical cliché is given a habitation in the exact geography of the dumb-shows.

'At one time Bockhampton had a water-mill. Where was that mill, I wonder? It had a wood. Where was that wood?' Art, as Bacon noted, 'gives some show of satisfaction to the mind at those points where reason doth deny it', and it is this satisfaction that *The Dynasts* supplies. It is the most purely indulgent of Hardy's works because we can feel his own pleasure in answering these questions through the medium of his art, the kind of questions that he had asked not only of seventeenth-century Bockhampton with its records, but of Roman Caster-bridge:

Standing, for instance, on the elevated ground near where the South-Western station is at present, or at the top of Slyer's Lane, or at any other commanding point, we may ask what kind of object did Dorchester then form in the summer landscape as viewed from such a point; where stood the large buildings, where the small; how did the roofs group themselves, what were the gardens like, if any, what social character had the streets, what were the customary noises? . . .

Such unanswerable queries as these are turned by *The Dynasts* into descriptions.

The spirits are like an audience to tableaux imposed by place and action

taking the shape of a monotonic delivery of speeches, with dreamy conventional gestures, something in the manner traditionally maintained by the old Christmas mummers, the curiously hypnotising impressiveness of whose automatic style – that of persons who spoke by no will of their own – may be remembered by all who experienced it.

Hardy's remark in the preface shows how the impersonal forces of history have been converted into an impersonal idiom whose agents (as he says of the mummers in *The Return of the Native*) 'seem moved by an inner compulsion to say and do their allotted parts whether they will or no'. The effectiveness of this is that it not only gives the impression of history surveyed, but holds inevitabilities of comedy as well. The spirits have a homeliness and helplessness shared by actors at a mumming-show and those who watch them. They converse like an audience of rustics:

The season is far advanced towards winter. The point of observation is high amongst the clouds, which, opening and shutting fitfully to the wind, reveal the earth as a confused space merely.

SPIRIT OF THE PITIES
Where are we? And why are we where we are?

SHADE OF THE EARTH
Above a wild waste garden-plot of mine,
Nigh bare in this late age, and now grown chill,
Lithuania called by some . . .

It would be a mistake to suppose that Hardy was not aware of the humour. The world show is watched by his spirits with the absently critical gaze of villagers promoted to metaphysical status.

Hardy avoids in this way any pretension; he does not grasp or shape it all, like a nineteenth-century poet-dramatist, or Goethean sage. There is the usual gap between the apparent scope and impressiveness of the work and the actual pleasures of its inward texture – Sheridan's sedulous wit, Napoleon's meeting with Marie Louise outside Soissons, Wellington's efficiency – that of a capable country gentleman of few words – the desperation at Mack's headquarters, the note on the Dorset volunteers, called the 'Green Linnets' from their uniforms of red with green facings –

These historic facings, which, I believe, won for the local (old 39th) regiment, the nickname of 'Green Linnets' have been changed for no apparent reason. (They are now restored. – 1909)

History, in the form Hardy understands it, is now going on; as it was when the dullness of Pitt's speeches, as long now in the reading as then in the hearing, can still impose on the reader an attentive stillness, once to be marked in the House in which can be heard the rustling of the trees without, a horn from an early coach, and the voice of the watch crying the hour.

Hardy is at last able to give himself the pleasure of writing a novel with all the things he enjoyed putting in, and none of the ones he supposed a novel-reading audience expected. It goes forward across the familiar ground in a steady undeviating line like the road across Egdon – the chronology of *Desperate Remedies* in a historical setting. This is the secret of its convincingness as a vision of history. It does not arrange and analyse events, as a historical survey does, for like a novel of suspense it does not seem to know how it is going to end; and yet a novelist cannot help but gather his matter into a compact significance – in his choice of what to tell and the way he manipulates it – and this again is a long way off from *The Dynasts*.

The unusualness of the process, portentous as it might appear to be, until we are into it, lies in the way it escapes from the poet, too, no less than from the novelist and antiquarian. So perhaps does the modest but analogous mummers' play. But even this is avoided in the degree to which the play is a time-honoured business of traditional confrontations and formulae, whereas *The Dynasts* makes use of what seem unexpected contingencies, as it makes use of the sturdy flatness of formula at such a moment as the death of Nelson. These things are not joined together or made 'harmonious'; we drop from one to the other without difficulty and without any smoothing of the path. A miniature instance of Hardy's style as custodian of such things, rather than their interpreter or inventor, comes early in *Tess*; and, small as it is, it gives an insight into the way *The Dynasts* absorbs the reader into its workings. As he shows her round the property Alec D'Urberville gathers strawberries for Tess, and presently offers to her mouth 'a specially fine product of the "British Queen" variety'. In another novelist the strawberry's title, and Tess herself, would be placed in a significant apposition: indeed critics of Hardy who mention the incident invariably so place it themselves. What is memorable about the moment, though, is not any significance selected by art. The reluctance of Tess, and the resounding appellation of the strawberry, give the moment the absurdity of history, uncontrived by historian or narrator. There is nothing 'British' about Tess. It was a word Hardy disliked, and its insipid convenience, incarnated in the fruit, stands apart from the Englishness of Tess as historiography stands apart, in *The Dynasts,* from its sequence of event.

Even Tolstoy, in *War and Peace,* has to make one episode symbolic of the rest, signifying all; and particularly so as the novel continues (its opening party has all the inconsequence of such a gathering in *The Dynasts),* for the death of Petya and the pilgrimage of Pierre with Karataev have a propriety to the great events of 1812, from the comparatively narrow standpoint of a Russian aristocrat, which is also bound to be the kind of prejudiced selection that suits it. This is as true of *War and Peace* as of *La Chartreuse de Parme*; but Hardy does not, as it were, belong to the world of history either as a historian does by research, or as a novelist does by dominating his material.

His presentation of history is allied with – almost a part of – his powers of creating and maintaining an illusion. We feel in the simple way that everything he writes has really happened, in novels and poems as much as in his recollections and accounts of history. The novel today repudiates illusion, as a responsibility for which it would rather not be held accountable; but to Hardy it is not an embarrassment but an inevitability, a natural consequence of his attitude towards his material. It is in him a fulfilment of fact, making *Desperate Remedies* or *The Dynasts* alike as 'true' as *Robinson Crusoe* – truer – because whatever may have been his purpose in *The Poor Man and The Lady,* he never afterwards gave any sign of creating by *intention* an appearance of sober authenticity. The illusion comes from all the effects of encounter and disjunction I have been examining, but still more, ultimately, from the nature of his own sense of his creations.

He is as much at home with what he makes up as with what he observes and records, his fancies existing in the open alongside fact. When a serial of Dickens was coming out, people stood on the pier at New York to ask after the fate of Little Nell; but that magic was only for the moment, however powerful and hypnotic it was, and the reason must be that Little Nell was strong magic for Dickens too, a compulsion shared with his audience below the surface of suspense, an indulgence removed from the bustle of his life and its tumult of daily inspiration. Hardy's fancies are not in the least like that: even his possessiveness about Tess is not. She exists for him – like the girl in the quarry, or Parson Thirdly under the gravestone, or the 'brush' of the huge composite ghost over the rocks and grass of Portland – as an external personality – his specification for what God must be, if he were to exist.

Such a permanence in place and time is what makes Hardy's illusion so compelling to us, if we respond to it at all. Even the Spirit of the Pities and the President of the Immortals are there in exactly the same sense as the 'tall soldier of Rome' who lies curled up four feet below the turf on Maiden Castle, to be discovered in *A Tryst at An Ancient Earthwork*.

When they come to Stonehenge, Tess says to Angel: 'Do you think we shall meet again after we are dead? I want to know'. He does not reply.

'O, Angel – I fear that means no'! said she, with a suppressed sob. 'And I wanted so to see you again – so much, so much! What, not even you and I, Angel, who love each other so well?'

Like a greater than himself, to the critical question at the critical time he did not answer; and they were again silent. In a minute or two her breathing became more regular, her clasp of his hand relaxed, and she fell asleep. The band of silver paleness along the east horizon made even the distant parts of the Great Plain appear dark and near; and the whole enormous landscape bore that impress of reserve, taciturnity and hesitation which is usual just before day.

The idea of a real meeting after death has mingled itself in a strangely moving manner with the idea of reality in the novel itself. Though we can see how few pages there are left, we too can hardly believe we shall not see Tess again. Clare's silence, compared with that of Christ in the Gospel, prefigures the silence beyond the novel. Clare, and Hardy, know that the parting is definitive: the one because of his beliefs, the other because his design is about to reach its climax. Just before day here is just before the end of the novel's world, when those factors implicit in Hardy's text – reserve, taciturnity, and hesitation – will be suspended by the ending of the illusion.

Tess's desire that Clare should marry his 'sister-law', Liza-Lu, is as hopeless as her desire to share him with her 'when we are spirits', for neither meeting nor marriage is possible within the world of the novel. 'The critical question at the critical time' – Christ's silence in response to Pilate's *Whence art thou?* – is the most muted and most effective of Hardy's appeals to classical and biblical precedent, on behalf of his text and characters. The novel, too, is about to be silent.

The formal in Hardy is also the literal – Tess's question seems addressed to her creator himself. And obviously the passage is so moving for a much simpler reason than analysis can indicate: Hardy too thinks Tess is real, he does not want to lose her. In his imagination she is as much at home as the day that brought the kiss 'in his foggy hand'; or as those 'cows and calves of bygone days' at the dairy, whose only memorial are the wooden posts rubbed to a glossy smoothness by their flanks, and who have now 'passed to an oblivion almost inconceivable in its profundity'. These are permanent comrades of his 'animula', as are all the commanders and statesmen and regiments and landscapes of *The Dynasts,* and even the President of the Immortals himself. Hardy is on terms as familiar with him – terms of 'grim friendliness' almost – as he is with all the others. Indeed he is more familiar than Aeschylus would have been, for his world is more animated by living gods and men, suppositions and stories, than that of the Greeks themselves.

This pantheon of his give him the lie when, in keeping with nineteenth-century notions, he disowns it and rebuffs the accusation that he really believed in malignant beings powerful in the universe: it gives him the lie in the same way that his 'intellectual being' does when he seeks to affirm the superiority of 'nescience'. The translation of the President from *Prometheus Bound,* which Hardy describes as literal, justly in a sense, in fact reminds us of the Dynasts' world, and of heads of tribunals, in revolutionary France or reactionary England, or at any time in the long repressions of history – awarding preferment or punishment, enforcing superstition or enlightenment. As a dynastic figure, the President is at home with all the rest of Hardy's anthropomorphic entourage, and is 'believed in' in the same sense as they; one factor among the many coincidences, meetings, non-meetings, partings, that he has conjured up – in fact or in fancy.

It is because Tess has a special place in his imagination that her death makes of the President more than such another familiar figment; for as Tess is the greatest feat of illusion in Hardy's world, so her death seems the most decisive in it, different in kind from the events that take place in that world. The deaths of John Loveday or Giles Winterborne are like the events in *The Dynasts,* and appear to have an authority in occurrence outside the mind of the author himself. The contrast with Tess here tells us a lot about the essential greatness of Hardy, and the kind of range he has. Like the 'some there be that have no memorial', Tess has hers purely in his imagination, and by vanishing as she does she defines the other reality of the permanent and the occasional in Hardy's world: the two are one and the same. What stands apart from them is Hardy's attempt, as he said, at 'trying to spread over art the latest illumination of the time'. What is occasional in his works has outlasted this illumination. At a time before his shorter poems were so widely admired as they are today, the critics used to say that they were too occasional for greatness, even though it was widely agreed that *The Dynasts* as an epic was his greatest achievement.*

But in fact *The Dynasts* is simply the most massive of all his occasional poems; it is their companion and continues with them in a logical sequence. If history is 'a version of events', then *The Dynasts* certainly does not remain with us as history, any more than the novels do as 'an illumination of the time'. Hardy always sought to 'give shape and coherence to a series of seemings', as he said in the Preface to *Jude,* yet he also knew that what remains is the seemings themselves, endowed with the immutable authority of fact, of things that were and are. Of all novelists, Hardy makes the things that he invents appear most like the things that have taken place throughout the time of man, and before it. Like Knight, on the 'cliff without a name', we confront with him the eye of the fossil embedded in the rock.

* See for example W. R. Rutland's well-documented and still invaluable survey, *Thomas Hardy: A Study of his Writings and their Background,* Oxford, 1938.

And this is – his own word – an 'unobtrusive' process. No other author appears to make his true greatness out of less than Hardy, nor does it without any of the creator's egocentric energy and will to power. His style is never taken in by its own pretension to epic size and philosophic weight. In his essay on 'The Profitable Reading of Fiction' he suggests that, where the novel is concerned, 'the unobtrusive quality may grow to have more charm for the reader than the palpable one'. He makes another point, too, of the same sort which he had once made about Barnes's poetry –

A sudden shifting of the mental perspective into a fictitious world, combined with rest, is well known to be often as efficacious for renovation as a corporeal journey afar.

Such chances of recruitment are not to be sneezed at. Our removal into Hardy's world is always 'combined with rest', the sense of repose which comes from our awareness of the author's vicinity during that corporeal journey.